Becoming a Computer Animator

Becoming a Computer Animator

Mike Morrison

SAMS PUBLISHING

201 W. 103rd St.
Indianapolis, IN 46290

To my love, Sandie, who, after nine years, still delights and inspires me.

Overview

Contents

x

Acknowledgments

First, I thank Richard Swadley, Jordan Gold, and Stacy Hiquet for their continued backing and support. Thanks to Dean Miller for his work in editing and coordinating another massive project and to Sandy Doell for her tireless editing efforts and continuing patience. I would also like to thank the other editors, Joe Williams and Denise Tyler.

Special thanks also goes to all the other people at Sams involved in the production and design of this book, and special thanks go to Wayne Blankenbeckler for completing the monstrous task of putting the CD-ROM together. I very much appreciate all the individuals who allowed me to interview them, as well as all the companies that allowed us to include their product demos on our CD-ROM. I deeply appreciate the great help and unceasing support from those at Caligari, especially Rick Denny and Roman Ormandy, both of whom were never too busy to offer suggestions or help me solve problems.

I also thank the many talented computer animators whose work graces these pages. All of us who love computer graphics really should appreciate the contribution that Alexander Schure has made to the industry. He's an individual who deserves a lot of credit but seldom receives it. Finally, I would like to thank my wife, Sandie Morrison, for her support and encouragement and for doing most of the work in transcribing the many interviews that appear throughout this book.

About the Author

Mike Morrison is a happy resident of San Diego, California, where he can be found during most of the summer enjoying the waves of the Pacific Ocean with his wife Sandie.

Mike has been active in computer graphics for the past eleven years. He writes for trade publications such as *Computer Graphics World, Digital Video World,* and *Computer Picture Magazine.*

Other Sams books written by Mike Morrison include:

On the Cutting Edge of Technology

This book covers 15 of the latest technology topics including artificial reality, 3-D animation with ray tracing, virtual reality, morphing, motion capture, nanotechnology, smart materials, and fractals.

The Magic of Image Processing

"A 300-page `monster tome' on basic image editing and 2-D morphing concepts. Besides covering various image editing concepts, it also discusses image scanning techniques, image compression technology, using PhotoCDs, basic graphics, and file formats."—Wallace M. Jackson, *3D Artist Magazine.*

The Magic of Interactive Entertainment

A close look at the hardware and software developments in all aspects of interactive entertainment. From the text-based adventures of a decade ago to today's CD games with real-time digital video, developers and industry insiders offer their views of the future. With the growing number of home and portable game systems and interactive entertainment's popularity, this book explains what's hot now and in the future with interactive television, multimedia, edutainment, and games on all systems.

Introduction

Becoming a computer animator is not easy.

There is something to be said for having the ability to create anything you can imagine; the ability to breathe life into it; the ability to produce, without any limits, your wildest imaginary creations for all the world to see. Despite the extremely hectic pace of looming deadlines, despite the agony of waiting hours to see the end result only to discover a flaw that means you must start again, despite the many frustrations of working in a 3-D universe through a 2-D interface, I haven't met one computer animator who would rather be doing something else.

Everyone who does it loves it.

In Chapters 1 and 2 of this book, you'll learn about the history and technology behind computer animation. A complete buyer's guide is offered in Chapter 3 for 3-D animation software covering Mac, Amiga, PC, and SOI platforms. The features and benefits of each package are discussed, and sample screen shots, as well as final renderings, are provided.

Demo versions of many programs discussed are provided on the CD-ROM. The CD-ROM also includes 3-D objects and surface textures that can be of great value to existing animators.

Hardware is explained, and recommendations are made for purchasing or building your own computer animation system.

Chapter 4, "Where the Jobs Are," offers information on finding work as a computer animator and such topics as education and keeping up with new technology. This chapter also offers a complete overview of the different fields where computer animation is used.

The book also includes interviews with such noted computer graphics personalities as Ed Catmull, president of Pixar, Richard Edlund, president of Boss Films, and

Mark Dippé, Visual Effects Supervisor for Industrial Light and Magic. The interviews cover various tips and tricks of computer animation as well as offer practical suggestions for starting or advancing a career in the business. Learn how these and other professionals got interested and began their careers in computer animation.

Many interviews are incorporated with tutorials for use with a special version of Caligari trueSpace for Windows, which is included on the CD-ROM. These tutorials are organized into five of the most common fields for computer animation: interactive entertainment, forensics, television, visualization, and motion pictures. They will give you a taste of what it's like to produce computer animation for each field. Finally, a reference section lists books, magazines, educational institutions, animation studios, online services, organizations, hardware and software providers, and sources for 3-D models.

Regardless of whether you know nothing about computer animation or have been working in the field for years, you will find this book a fascinating reference packed with useful and practical information.

Chapter

1

What is computer animation?

Liquid people dance to an African beat on an exotic beach. Dinosaurs growl and attack each other in a Jurassic theme park. In a bathroom, while a man shaves, the face reflected in the mirror smoothly transforms into another and another....

Computer animation has made the creation of such fantastic illusions almost commonplace.

Computer animation is a unique field, one in which you can express your artistic talent even if you lack the physical dexterity required by more traditional art forms. On the other hand, its apparent technical complexity can be intimidating.

Throughout history, artists have invested countless hours learning how to wield a brush, a pencil, or a musical instrument and then spent years practicing their art before producing something of value. Computer graphics helps shorten the time spent learning and lets artists start actually making art.

In the past, the various media that were available for expressing oneself artistically had limitations. Many artists were trapped in the two-dimensional world of flat canvases. Painting is a static medium; a painting is two-dimensional and represents a fixed moment in time. Even the colors are limited, since they are based on the reflective properties of paint. Computer-graphic imagery is limited by neither time nor space.

A sculptor can work in three-dimensional space, but sculpture also represents a fixed moment in time and suffers from the limitations of pigment-based colors. Theater allows more freedom and creativity, and it can incorporate motion and the passage of time. Performing on a fixed stage, however, still restricts artistic expression. Computer graphics can simulate motion or the passage of time and can do it without viewing restrictions.

Unlike computer graphics, the performing arts entail high overhead. Many people and resources may be needed to produce the end result. Videos and motion pictures allow considerable artistic freedom, but the cost is far too great for the average person to produce them. Today, with a very modest investment in a personal computer, practically anyone can create computer-graphic imagery and animation.

Computer graphics is very different from all other artistic media. It enables the artist to create entire worlds within the computer. Not only can you create three-dimensional models similar to sculpture, but you can also specify the color and position of lights, shadows, and even atmospheric effects like rain and snow.

With computer graphics, you can add motion. You can create the illusion of walking through the scene and move the light sources around, while the computer automatically updates the reflections and shadows within the artificial reality. The artificial worlds created within the computer can be explored from any vantage point.

ANIMATION

Before discussing how computers are used in animation, we should define our terms. Simply defined, *animation* is the illusion of movement. This illusion of movement can be achieved by quickly displaying a series of images that show slight incremental changes in one of the depicted objects. If you play back these images fast enough, the eye will perceive movement. This standard kind of animation is sometimes referred to as *stop-frame cinematography*.

Human visual acuity is low enough that only 12-15 different pictures (or frames) need to be displayed per second to produce the illusion of movement. However, these low speeds make the movements appear jerky, so television or video typically displays 30 frames per second (fps), while film uses about 24 fps. This means that when animation is created for television, 30 separate pictures are flashed before your eyes every second. Your mind perceives the sequence of individual still images as fluid, continuous movement.

Image courtesy of Animation Hash Inc.

This presents quite a challenge for the animator. Even a 15-minute cartoon on television requires over 27,000 frames, and a two-hour animated feature film requires about 216,000 frames! Imagine that an animator could create a single frame every 30 minutes. Working 40 hours a week, it would take him almost 52 years (2,700 weeks) to create an animated feature film. Because of this, animation studios have developed techniques, since the turn of the century, to increase productivity. Now, after nearly 100 years, these techniques have been honed to a fine art—so much so, that many of these techniques have been carried over into the field of computer animation.

TRADITIONAL ANIMATION

Traditionally, cartoons are created by a large team of artists. As a story idea develops, *roughs* are created. Roughs are early sketches illustrating how characters, costuming, and backgrounds will look. Story concepts are outlined with a technique called *storyboarding*. A storyboard is like a very detailed comic strip; it helps the producer visualize what the end product will look like.

In the case of cartoons, storyboards are refined and even filmed. The resulting storyboard film is called the *story reel*. This story reel is refined and adjusted so the producers can get the proper pace, timing, and story development of the car-

toon. Once the story is refined, the voice actors are cast, and sound effects and music are recorded. Layout artists start creating pencil drawings of the backgrounds and scenes for the cartoon. These go to the background artists, who create the finished background artwork.

Now the main animators/artists go to work, creating the key movements of the animated characters throughout the cartoon. Right away, the actors start recording the cartoon's dialogue. This allows the artists to closely analyze the sound track and then draw the characters to match the spoken words. To assist the animators, a *mouth chart* is used. This chart shows the length of vowels and consonant sounds, intervals between words, and breathing spaces.

Although several frames are needed for each second of movement, the principal artists usually only draw the frames that contain the "key" or main movements of the character. For example, the artists might only draw every 30th or 60th frame. If a character jumps, the artists may only draw the frame where the character begins the jump, then perhaps a frame about half-way through the jump, and finally, the ending frame where the character lands on the ground.

To fill in the missing frames, assistant artists called *in-betweeners* draw the in-between frames. The in-betweeners do their drawing work on a light table, using transparent sheets of paper. As they draw each frame, they overlay the next page on top of it and then vary the movement depicted in the new frame slightly, so when the sequence is played back at a high speed, the movement appears natural.

Note: As you might imagine, it is very time-consuming to draw a separate background scene for every frame when only the characters themselves are moving and the background is static. To solve this problem, John Bray, a pre-Disney animator, began printing copies of backgrounds on translucent paper in 1914. A year later, another pre-Disney animator, Earl Hurd, took the process one step further by painting the characters on celluloid sheets (*cels*) so they could

Image courtesy of Wavefront.

be overlaid on a single background. This greatly reduced the time required to create animation. *Cel animation* became a standard, and it is still in use today. Many cartoons still have fairly rich and detailed background scenes, while the foreground is often very simplistic.

Now the animation project moves into final production. The pencil drawings for each frame are cleaned up, drawn in ink, and painted. This step is known as *inking and painting*. One by one, the drawings are transferred to cells. The reverse sides of the cels are painted so the ink outlines remain clear.

The cels are eventually overlaid on their corresponding backgrounds, photographed, and stored on film. This is done with an automated camera suspended above an *animation stand,* which holds the cels while they are photographed. The layers of cels are held or locked in place with pegs. With the animation stand, animators can slowly move large background paintings to give the illusion of characters walking or moving through a complex back-

ground. Other cinematic effects, such as tracking and zooming, are also possible with the animation stand.

Today, many animation producers are using computers to enhance these traditional techniques. For example, you can scan early sketches into the computer, and the computer can play back these sketches as rough sample animations. *Scanning* is the process of converting a picture into a digital file that resides in the computer. To do this, the computer breaks the picture down into very small colored dots known as *pixels*, or picture elements. The smaller the pixels, the better the digital picture. If an animated cel is scanned for use on video, you need only 720 pixels horizontally by 486 pixels vertically. Motion-picture film has a much higher resolution and needs about 1280 pixels horizontally by 1024 pixels vertically.

The computer can also create some of the in-between frames, and in many cases it can do this automatically. All the artist has to do is tell the computer which

parts of the character are related for each keyframe. Then the computer can make as many in-between frames as needed by gradually moving pixels from their original position in the first frame to the new position in the second frame.

Because of the thickness of the acetate, traditional cel animation is limited in the number of cels that can be overlaid at one time. This limitation does not apply when the cels are scanned into a computer, because the cels are then a digital picture. Another great advance that computers have afforded artists is in inking and painting the individual cells. On the computer, this is an easy process using a fill tool.

The *fill tool* enables the artists to simply click on an area in the cell, which tells the computer to fill that area with the selected color. This is obviously much faster than painting each cel by hand. To make this even easier, the computer can display a small, fully-colored model frame in the corner of the screen. The artist can simply click on a color from the colored model frame and then click on a blank area of the uncolored frame. That area is then filled with the color from the model. So by clicking on the colored hair of the cartoon char-

acter in the color model frame, then clicking on the character's hair in the new frame, the computer artist gives the hair in the new frame the appropriate color.

Another advantage with computers is that you can alter the colors in the animation after the cels are painted. Changing the color once in a single frame changes it for every frame in the animation. The colors used in painting the cel also allow a transparency setting. This is useful for things like shadows, which may be a shade of gray, although you want the color of the object underneath the shadow to show through.

Thus computer graphics can be very useful in the traditional techniques of animators; but computers have also opened a new field of animation. This new *computer animation* uses the computer's processing power to create the in-between frames (a task that would be impossible even with computer-assisted traditional techniques), enabling a single artist to generate thousands of frames in a matter of hours.

2-D COMPUTER ANIMATION

Computer graphics animation can be divided into two main areas: 2-D and 3-D. Two-dimensional computer animation is commonly used for cartoons and special effects such as morphing. Because it is closely related to traditional animation techniques, 2-D animation uses much traditional terminology. As with traditional

animation media, an artist can hand paint each and every frame on a computer. The artist can also use the computer to manipulate the two-dimensional images.

Two-dimensional computer animation can be divided into four main categories: animated cels, optical effects, tweening or morphing, and color cycling. Consider the example of a *walk cycle,* which is a series of frames showing a character walking; the series can be looped to run continuously. Once an artist has created a walk cycle on the computer, it can be treated as an animated cel. Animated cels can be positioned or moved anywhere on the screen. Thus a sequence depicting a person walking can be slowly moved from the left side of the screen to the right side. This is an example of how an animated cel can be used.

Optical effects can take animated cels a step further. For instance, the story line may require our walking character to start walking up a hill. Using optical effects, you can slowly rotate the animated cel as the character starts walking up an incline. Another example would be the character walking away into the distance. Using optical effects, the computer can scale the character down slowly over a period of time.

7

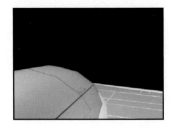

Tweening and morphing effects are very similar. Tweening takes two different objects (on different frames) and creates the in-between frames needed to make a smooth transition between them. Morphing simply means that as the first object starts to transform itself into the shape of the second object, the computer slowly fades the

8

first object out of the sequence. At the same time, the computer is fading in the second object. The result is that the first object smoothly transforms into the second object.

Tweening may seem to be the solution to the problem of creating in-between frames, but the computer is not smart enough to make realistic movements from 2-D images. Take for instance an animation of a man swinging his arms from his side to above his head. All the computer knows is that the pattern of black and white dots in frame 1 must be moved to match the pattern of black and white dots in frame 10. This can result in the person's shoulders stretching up into new arms in frame 10 while the original arms at his side melt into his torso.

It helps a little to give the computer more information about the 2-D image, to tell it which pixels make up the arms and that we only want those pixels moved between frames 1 and 10. Still, the computer does not understand how human joints bend and how the human skeleton works. So the result might be the person's arms taking the shortest path between point A and point B by squeezing

up through the man's shoulders. Although better than the computer's first effort, this too is unacceptable. So while tweening and morphing are good solutions to some problems, they are not a cure-all for animation.

Finally, we come to the last form of 2-D computer animation: color cycling. *Color cycling* is a method of animation wherein you only use one frame or picture, while the computer cycles, or shifts, the colors in a predetermined pattern. This is commonly used for simple animation effects, such as running water. Long strips of light bulbs, such as those found outside Las Vegas hotels, use a similar technique to create the effect of moving light. By alternating the light bulbs between on and off, and by slightly offsetting each bulb from its neighbor, they create the illusion that the light is moving in a specific direction. This is exactly what the computer does, but since each pixel in the computer can have hundreds (or thousands) of possible color values, the effect is much more interesting than the simple on/off lights of Vegas.

REAL TIME VERSUS SIMULATED TIME

Regardless of how the frames of animation are created on the computer, they still need to be played back in quick succession to give the illusion of movement. This high-speed playback can be accomplished in one of two ways: real time or simulated time.

T-Rex: Reconstructed © HD/CG New York.

Real time means that the computer can display the frames at a speed of about 15 fps or faster. Each frame is either generated at that high speed or pulled from memory and displayed on the computer's screen at that speed. In the case of real-time animation, you can basically hook up a video recorder to the computer and record the animation as it plays.

Most commercial animation, however, requires a high resolution (number of pixels) for each frame. This increases the amount of data in the frame. Without special equipment, present-day personal computers are incapable of playing back high-resolution frames at speeds of 30 fps, which is the rate needed for broadcast-quality animation. To solve this problem, the individual frames are stored in the computer's memory and called up one-by-one. As each frame is displayed on the computer screen, it is recorded by either a high-quality video recorder (capable of accurately recording one frame at a time) or by a film recorder (like those used for motion pictures). This method is commonly called frame-by-frame animation. *Frame-by-frame animation* results in the highest possible quality, since each picture can have a very high level of detail and can be recorded at a very high frame rate.

A new breed of personal computer add-on equipment promises to bridge the gap between real time and simulated time by compressing the individual frames so that they don't consume as much memory. Once compressed, the frames can be played back at speeds and resolutions that are acceptable for some video applications. As this new technology is popularized, we can expect the quality to increase to the point where you could create broadcast-quality animation on your personal computer without the hassles of frame-by-frame animation.

3-D COMPUTER ANIMATION

3-D animation involves creating three-dimensional worlds within the computer. You must specify the objects (in three dimensions), the placement of the light sources, and the viewpoint of the camera.

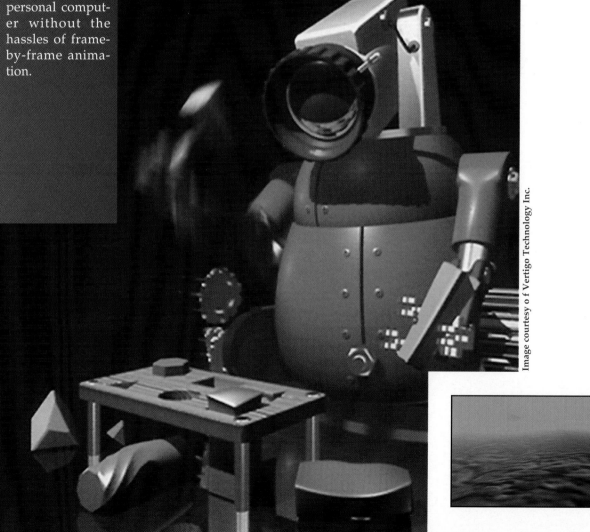

Image courtesy of Vertigo Technology Inc.

9

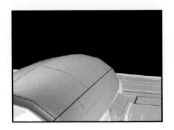

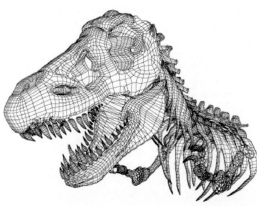

Once this information is specified, the computer can use mathematical formulas to create a simulated 3-D scene.

In one sense, 3-D computer graphics is similar to photography. You need a subject to photograph (the 3-D objects) and some light to illuminate the scene (the light sources). Then you look through your camera's viewfinder, line up the subjects, and click the shutter (which is analogous to setting the camera viewpoint and telling the computer to create the image).

The computer artist has complete control over all of these elements. The artist can create 3-D objects in any shape, size, or color; can specify the color and location of lights; and can position a virtual camera. Depending on the location of the camera, the computer then generates an image that represents the 3-D scene as it appears from the camera's viewfinder.

Once the 3-D scene looks correct to the artist, it is ready to be animated. The artist can specify a path for the camera to follow. Then the computer can be instructed to take several pictures as the camera moves along its path. Likewise, the artist can make any objects or lights travel along a path. When the finished images are played back from videotape or film, the result is computerized animation. In this respect, the computer artist is part painter, part sculptor, part photographer, and part director.

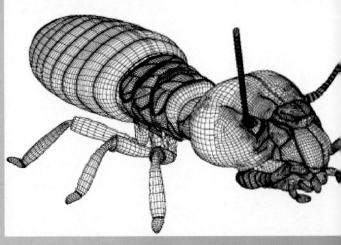

MODELING

3-D objects are created with a process called, appropriately enough, *modeling*. During modeling, you can create objects by instructing the computer to make simple geometric shapes, such as a sphere, cube, or cylinder. These *geometric primitives* are fairly easy for the computer to

10

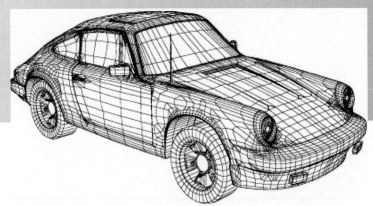

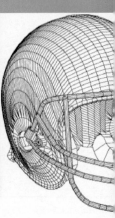

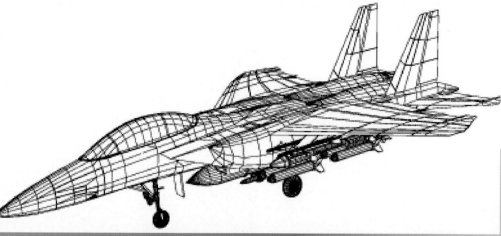

model since they are easily defined with mathematical formulas.

Many times, you can create complex shapes by combining these geometric primitives. At other times you may

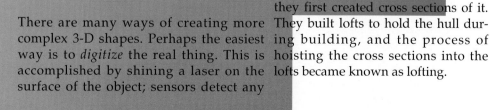

need to create a complex 3-D object that requires advanced modeling techniques.

There are many ways of creating more complex 3-D shapes. Perhaps the easiest way is to *digitize* the real thing. This is accomplished by shining a laser on the surface of the object; sensors detect any

variations as the laser pans across the surface. This method is commonly used to create models of actors when a computer-generated version of the actor needs to appear for special effects, such as those seen in the movie *Terminator 2*.

Companies such as Viewpoint Engineering of Orem, Utah, have made a business of providing high quality 3-D scanned objects. They currently have over 1,000 3-D data sets including everything from dinosaurs to F-15 fighter jets to termites.

Other ways of modeling complex surfaces involve fairly commonplace techniques. One such technique is called *lofting* or *extruding*. The term itself comes from ancient ship builders. To build a complex hull, they first created cross sections of it. They built lofts to hold the hull during building, and the process of hoisting the cross sections into the lofts became known as lofting.

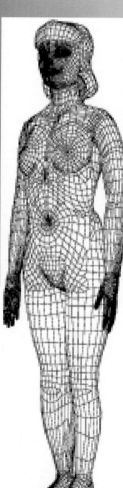

Say, for instance, that you want to create a 3-D cube by lofting it instead of simply using a geometric primitive. You start by drawing a square on the computer screen. Then you tell the computer to loft that flat 2-D square into 3-D space. The computer then stretches the flat square into a 3-D cube.

Another modeling technique is the *lathe*, sometimes called the *surface of revolution*. This is similar to the standard loft, except that instead of stretching the 2-D shape in one direction, it revolves the shape around itself. You can use this technique to quickly create a wine glass by simply drawing a cross section of the glass. Then you use the lathe technique to revolve that cross section around 360 degrees.

11

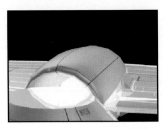

Some 3-D computer graphics programs enable you to draw top, front, and side views of a 3-D object. The computer uses these views to create a 3-D object for you. There are also other methods of creating objects in which the computer uses mathematics and procedurally creates the 3-D models or scenes. One example is *fractal geometry*, which can create natural, organic-looking geometry. Fractal formulas enable the computer to generate randomly varied, natural-looking objects, such as mountain ranges, rocks, planets, plants, and trees.

A second, common way of simulating natural phenomena is with particle systems. *Particle systems* are not real geometric shapes; they are collections of very tiny particles that move in any direction you specify. Particle systems can simulate natural phenomena such as splashing water, snowfall, sun flares, and volcanic eruptions.

Another new technology, developed in 1982, enables computer animators to create very lifelike, organic-looking models. The technology is called metaballs. *Metaballs* are similar to drops of liquid that the artist can enlarge, stretch, and fuse with other metaballs to form naturally curving surfaces. This technique is increasingly popular in video and film.

Note: Included on the CD-ROM that accompanies this book is a metaballs editor called BLBGUI10.EXE. With it you can create metaball models and load them into trueSpace, included on the CD, for rendering.

Regardless of how you create your 3-D objects, the next step is to position them in 3-D space. At first, the computer simulates a vast, dark void in which you can position your 3-D models. To illuminate this dark void, you need to set up some lights. There are four basic kinds of light you can use in a 3-D scene: ambient, omni, spot, and distant.

Ambient light refers to the background light in the room. *Omni lights* are similar to light bulbs; they cast

Image courtesy of Softdesk.

12

light in all directions for a limited distance. *Spotlights* consist of a source (where the light is located), target locations (where the light is pointing), and the width of the cone of light. Spotlights are similar to invisible flashlights that you can position and point in any direction. Finally, *distant lights* point in a specific direction, like spotlights, except that all the rays of a distant light are parallel, simulating the effect of a distant light-source such as the sun.

The camera, like the spotlight, has a source (where the camera is located) and a target (where the camera is pointed.) Most programs allow you to adjust the depth of field and the lens focal length for creating dramatic effects. The final step is *rendering*, wherein the computer creates an image that represents the scene from the camera's point of view.

RENDERING

Rendering can be the most time-consuming step in 3-D computer animation. The computer must perform mathematical somersaults to create a full perspective of the 3-D scene. Rendering involves a number of complex steps. The computer must determine the location of the lights, the shape of the objects, the properties of the camera (field of view, focal length, etc.), and many other details about the scene.

Image courtesy of Ray Dream.

The computer sets up a virtual screen and then projects the 3-D scene onto that screen. This final projection (also known as the rendering) is the result.

RENDERING BASICS

Let's discuss for a moment how the computer simulates solid 3-D objects. As I mentioned earlier, the computer artist creates the basic 3-D object, usually in *wireframe* mode. Wireframes are much like the framework of a house or the steel work of a large office building. There are no solid walls, just a framework that specifies where the walls will be when the building is complete. Likewise, the wireframe of a 3-D computer object specifies where the solid surfaces will appear when the object is rendered.

Once the wireframe is built, the computer can render the object as if the wireframe were a solid object. The object's color will vary from light to

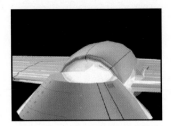

dark, based on the surface location and the brightness of the lights in the 3-D scene.

To further enhance the appearance of 3-D objects, you can render them with *texture maps*. Texture maps are simply flat 2-D images that the computer wraps around the 3-D object. This is similar to applying wallpaper. To make a sphere look as if it's made of brick, you would take a picture of a brick wall and apply it as a texture map to your 3-D objects.

Another technology that is used to enhance realism is *bump maps*. Bump maps take texture maps one step further by using an image to make an object look bumpy. It does this by using light and dark highlights on the texture map to simulate

14

dents and bulges, respectively.

Finally we come to reflective surfaces. There are three ways to simulate a reflective surface with a computer: reflection maps, environment maps, and ray tracing.

Reflection maps reflect a single image off

the surface of the object. If the camera moves around the object, the reflection shifts realistically. For some applications this looks okay, but reflection maps do not reflect other objects in the scene and thus lack some realism.

Environment maps are similar to reflection

Image courtesy of SDSU Super Computing Center.

maps except that the reflected image is created at the time the computer renders the object. The computer renders a view of an object's surroundings from inside the object. It uses this rendering as the reflection for that object. The result can be very convincing, since the object reflects its surroundings. There are limitations, however; if an object intersects the reflective object, it may not appear on the other object's reflection as it should.

To solve this problem, you must go one step further, to the technique of ray tracing. Ray tracing simulates real-world optics by tracing every ray of light in a 3-D scene, from the viewpoint of the camera, through the scene, to the origin of the ray of light. This is the opposite of what happens with the human eye, where every ray of light starts from its origin and bounces off objects and into the human eye.

Since every ray of light is traced, the results of ray tracing can be spectacular. There are many added benefits to ray tracing, such as refraction and radiosity.

Refraction is the effect of light shining through a solid object or a liquid. For example, looking through a fish bowl full of water causes the background to distort. Ray tracing can simulate refraction effects.

Radiosity is a technique that simulates the way light bounces and reflects off of objects. Formulas similar to those that calculate heat dispersion are used to determine the amount of light a given object reflects. Radiosity can create beautiful images where scenes are illuminated with reflected light.

Note: Included on the CD-ROM is a radiosity renderer called RAD386.EXE. With it you can render scenes with radiosity.

ANIMATING THE 3-D SCENE

Once the models, lights, and cameras are created, the last step is animating the 3-D scene. As we mentioned in the beginning of this chapter, the artist can create paths that the objects, lights, or camera will follow. This is done by specifying *keyframes*.

Say the animation has 100 frames, and the artist wants object 'A' to move to the right during those 100 frames. Instead of telling the computer exactly how much to move object A for each frame, the artist only needs to tell the computer where he wants object A to be in frame 100. The computer calculates exactly how much to move the object each frame, so that by frame 100, it is exactly where the artist wants it to be.

In this instance, frames 0 and 100 are keyframes. If the artist tells the computer to rotate the object 360 degrees between frames 0 and 100, the object moves to the right and rotates as it travels along its path.

In some cases, such as animating objects that are falling to the ground, the artist may not want to deal with moving the objects manually. In those cases, computer artists can use *inverse kinematics*. Inverse kinematics enables the user simply to specify that the object should fall. The artist only needs to specify how much gravity the computer should simulate and where the floor is. The computer handles the rest of the animation, by causing the object to pick up speed as it falls, then bounce and tumble when it hits the ground. Although this is a useful and powerful technique, you have little control over how the object bounces or tumbles. Inverse kinematics is controlled by the laws of physics, and sometimes those laws aren't aesthetically pleasing.

15

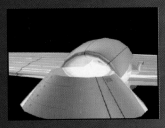

Tutorial: Getting Your Feet Wet

Now that you have some basic knowledge about how 3-D computer graphics work, let's create some animation. We will begin by creating two simple objects, a flat plane and a torus. We will then animate the torus and save the result as a Video for Windows .AVI file. You must first install the demo version of trueSpace for Windows from Caligari Corporation. Instructions for installing trueSpace can be found in Appendix C.

Note: A version of trueSpace is included on the CD-ROM that accompanies this book. It is a Windows-based 3-D rendering and animation program. This is a demo version, but you can use all aspects of the program and render images or animation to disk. However, it only offers limited saving capabilities.

To start trueSpace, load Microsoft Windows and double-click on the "Caligari" icon. The first time you load trueSpace, it presents you with an empty workspace. The first thing you will notice is that, unlike most other Windows-based software, trueSpace has its menu bar at the bottom of the screen. (See Tutorial Figure 1.1.) Although at first this may seem awkward, you will soon see that it is very practical for the way trueSpace deals with the 3-D environment. If you decide you just can't deal with the menu bar being on the bottom of the screen, you can adjust it with the Settings dialog box.

3-D modeling and animation programs are by nature fairly complex. The process of creating objects in 3-D space by using 2-D input devices (the mouse) and 2-D displays (the monitor) is, understandably, not very easy. Many programs use long and complex menus, or they divide the processes into different programs designed to handle individual aspects of 3-D modeling and animation. trueSpace performs all the needed 3-D functions in one workspace. In order to do this and still keep the user interface simple, it uses icon-based *tool strips*. These tool strips contain buttons (tools) that enable you to access different functions in the program. For example, to create a 3-D geometric primitive like a sphere, cube, or torus, you simply click on the Primitives button (tool) in the Model strip. This makes the program very intuitive, because all the functions are accessed by graphical pictures as opposed to text-based menus. There are eight different tool strips in trueSpace.

16

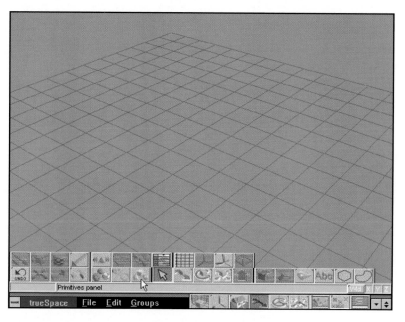

Tutorial Figure 1.1. *The trueSpace workspace.*

Tutorial Figure 1.2. *Here the cursor is over the "Up One Level" icon, so the gray help bar shows the shortcut key on the left and the function of the icon on the right.*

Across the bottom of the workspace is a gray *help bar*. (See Tutorial Figure 1.2.) This help bar displays context-sensitive help when you are using any of the tools in trueSpace. Move the cursor over any of the tools, and descriptions of that tool will appear on the help bar. The help bar also displays the shortcut key (if one is available) for the current command. Once a specific tool is activated, the help bar displays instructions on using that tool.

For our first tutorial, we will create a 3-D torus and animate it to spin while flying toward you, then reverse direction and move back to its original location. Whenever a tutorial requires you to select an icon to perform a function, the icon appears next to the tutorial step. This should assist you in finding the correct commands.

In the first part of our tutorial we will create a 3-D scene and apply surface textures to the objects. This is always the first step in any 3-D animation. Then we will set up a simple animation and render it to disk.

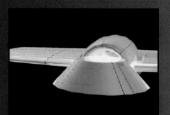

1. Start Microsoft Windows and load trueSpace.

2. Click on the *Primitives Panel* icon.

3. When the Primitives control panel appears. (See Tutorial Figure 1.3), click on the *Add Torus* icon. As soon as you click on the Add Torus icon, a 3-D torus will appear in the work-space.

4. To create a floor, click once on the *Regular Polygon* icon. The Polygon Modes panel appears. (See Tutorial Figure 1.4.) This allows you to specify how many sides you want your polygon to have.

5. If the number of sides specified in the polygon Modes panel is not 4, click on the arrow to the right of the number. By dragging the mouse left or right you can increase or decrease the number of sides for your new polygon. Set it at 4 to create a perfect square.

6. Now move the cursor to just above the center of the new

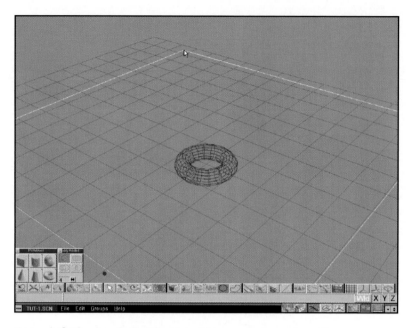

Tutorial Figure 1.3. *The Primitives control panel enables you to create any geometric primitive.*

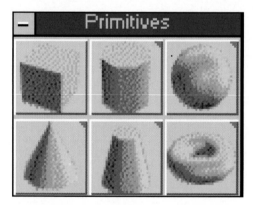

Tutorial Figure 1.4. *The Polygon Modes panel enables you to specify the number of sides for a new polygon.*

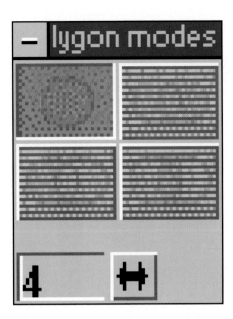

Tutorial Figure 1.5. *Click to set the center of the regular polygon just above the torus.*

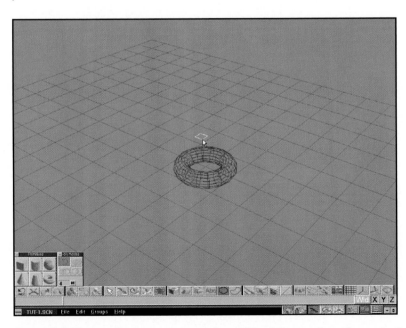

Tutorial Figure 1.6. *Drag to set the width of the regular polygon to the width of the screen.*

torus. Click and drag a new square polygon to cover most of the screen. (See Tutorial Figures 1.5 and 1.6.)

7. Now let's take a look at our first 3-D scene. Move the cursor to the *Render Object* icon. Click and hold the mouse button down for a moment until the render icons pop up. Now drag the cursor up to the second icon from the top. The help bar should read "Render Scene." Release the mouse button and you should see our scene being rendered by the computer.

8. The first thing you notice is that our two objects are rendered in a light pink material. This is the default material for newly created objects. Let's change the material by clicking on the *Show Material Library* icon.

9. The Material Library stores all of your materials for the current 3-D scene. (See Tutorial Figure

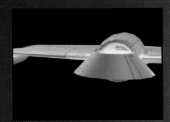

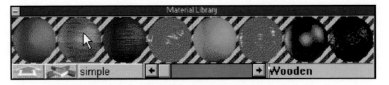

Tutorial Figure 1.7. *The Material Library is a graphical way to store and recall surface materials.*

1.7.) For now, choose the wood sphere by clicking on it. Notice the name of the current material in the lower-right corner of the Material Library changes to Wooden.

10. Click once on the torus to select it as the current object. The current object is always drawn in a white wireframe. Unselected objects are drawn in a dark blue wireframe.

11. Move the cursor to the *Paint Face* icon. Click and hold the mouse button down for a moment until the render icons pop up. Now drag the cursor to the top icon. The help bar should read "Paint Object." Release the mouse button and you should see the Wooden texture being rendered on the torus.

12. Now assign the blue and white checkered pattern to the square polygon by repeating steps 10 and 11. This time, use the Material Library scroll bar to locate the checkered material.

Tutorial Figure 1.8. *Here is our scene rendered with textures applied to the objects. Notice how the torus is sunken into the square floor.*

Click on the material, click on the regular polygon, and finally click on the Paint Face icon. Notice that the checkered polygon paints directly over the torus. This will not happen when you render the entire screen. When you are finished, click on the Render Scene icon to view the results. (See Tutorial Figure 1.8.)

13. Before starting our animation, we need to move our torus up so it isn't sunken into the middle of the floor. To do this, click on the torus to select it. Notice that the screen switches from the rendered view back to the wireframe view.

14. Now click on the *Move Object* icon. Holding down the left mouse button, try dragging the torus around the screen. Notice how you can move it on the X

21

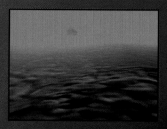

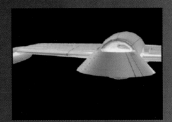

and Y axes (left and right, forward and backward). Now try holding down the right mouse button. This enables you to move an object on the Z axis (up and down). Move the object up about half an inch, and keep it near the middle of the screen. To verify that the torus is above the floor, click on the Render Scene icon.

Now our scene is finished and we are ready to animate the torus. In this tutorial, we will create a simple 30-frame animation of the torus flying up toward the viewer. At the same time, we will make it spin. When it reaches frame 30, the torus will have returned to its original position.

1. To create an animation in trueSpace, you must open the Animation Panel by clicking on the *Animation Panel* icon.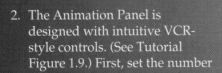

2. The Animation Panel is designed with intuitive VCR-style controls. (See Tutorial Figure 1.9.) First, set the number

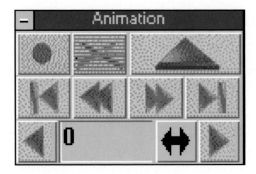

Tutorial Figure 1.9. *The Animation Panel enables you to record movement and play it back in a preview mode.*

of frames to 30 by either typing the number *30* in the active frame number box or clicking on the arrows to the right of the active frame number and dragging the mouse to the right until the active frame reaches the number 30.

3. Make sure the torus is the object currently selected and that the *Move Object* icon is depressed. Then click the *Set Key Frame* icon in the upper-left corner of the Animation Panel. This records the current movement of the torus at frame 30. Now click on the *Rotate Object* icon. Then click again on the *Set Key Frame* icon. This records the current rotation of the object at frame 30.

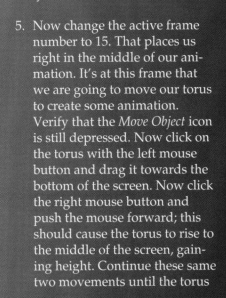

4. Since we did not move or rotate the torus before setting the keyframe at frame 30, the torus

doesn't move at all when we play back all 30 frames in quick succession. Try this by clicking on the *Play* icon in the upper-right corner of the Animation Panel. Notice that as the frames play, the torus remains perfectly still.

5. Now change the active frame number to 15. That places us right in the middle of our animation. It's at this frame that we are going to move our torus to create some animation. Verify that the *Move Object* icon is still depressed. Now click on the torus with the left mouse button and drag it towards the bottom of the screen. Now click the right mouse button and push the mouse forward; this should cause the torus to rise to the middle of the screen, gaining height. Continue these same two movements until the torus

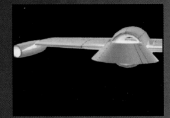

fills most of the screen. (See Tutorial Figure 1.10.)

6. To see the result, press the Play icon on the Animation Panel. You should see the torus moving from its starting point to its new location at frame 15 and then back to its original starting point at frame 30.

7. Now let's add some spin to the torus. Move back to frame number 15 with the Active Frame Number setting. Choose the *Rotate Object* icon and click on the torus. Click on the torus, drag the mouse, and rotate the torus about 90 degrees in any direction. (See Tutorial Figure 1.11.) Click the *Play* icon to see the animated preview.

Notice how the rotation and location of the torus return to the original values at frame 30. This is because we set a keyframe there before making any other movements. This is an important step if you want an animation to run continuously and you want the beginning to sync perfectly with the ending.

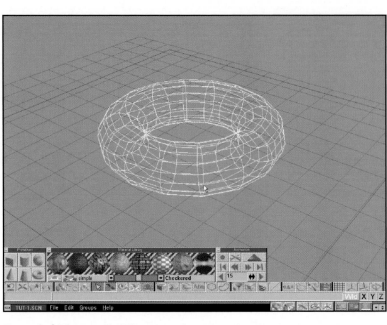

Tutorial Figure 1.10. *Move the object close to the current view so that it occupies most of the screen.*

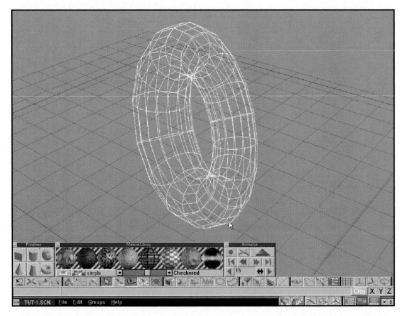

Tutorial Figure 1.11. *Here the torus has been rotated at frame 15.*

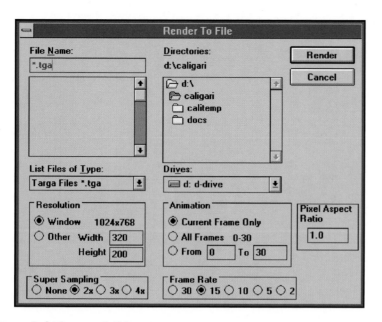

Tutorial Figure 1.12. *The Render to File dialog box.*

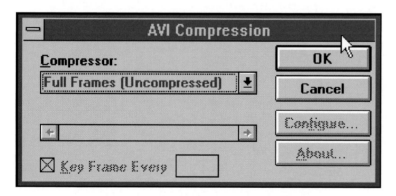

Tutorial Figure 1.13. *The AVI Compression dialog box.*

8. Now that our animation is complete, we are ready to render it to the disk. From the Render Strip of icons, select the *Render To File* icon This causes the Render to File dialog box to appear. (See Tutorial Figure 1.12.) Here you specify the filename and type of rendering or animation that you are going to create.

9. To keep it simple, choose "AVI Files .avi" from the file-type list. Next, enter the filename TUT-01. For resolution, choose Other, and for animation, choose All Frames 0-30. Click on the Render button when you are finished. This causes the AVI Compression dialog box to appear. When it does, make sure that Full Frames (Uncompressed) is the current method and click on OK. (See Tutorial Figure 1.13.)

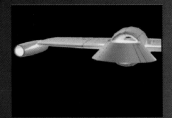

You have just created your first 3-D computer animation. Where is it? It resides as a Video for Windows .AVI file in your \CALIGARI directory. To view it, you must load the Microsoft Media Player. Once the Media Player is loaded, use the File menu and choose Open. Load the TUT-01.AVI file from the \CALIGARI directory. When it loads, you will see the first frame of your animation along with the Media Player control window. (See Tutorial Figure 1.14.)

Before playing any trueSpace animations, there are a few setting you must adjust in the Media Player. First, from the Edit menu choose Options. In this dialog box, make sure that Auto Repeat and Control Bar on Playback are both selected. (See Tutorial Figure 1.15.) Next, from the Device menu

26

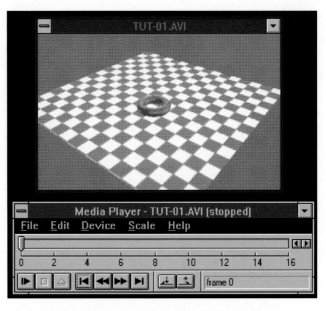

Tutorial Figure 1.14. *The Media Player plays back your AVI files.*

Tutorial Figure 1.15. *The settings for the Media Player Options.*

Tutorial Figure 1.16. *The settings for the Video Playback Options dialog box.*

choose the Configure option. You can experiment with these settings, but make sure that the option called Skip Video Frames If Behind is turned off. (See Tutorial Figure 1.16.)

This tutorial has been deliberately kept simple. It uses no special lighting effects, camera perspectives, or shadows. You should experiment with trueSpace by trying some of the following extra projects.

27

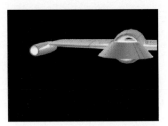

Image courtesy of
Macromedia.

Extra Projects

- Assign different textures to the objects.

- Create different objects with other geometric primitives.

- Move the objects in different directions and re-creating the animation.

- Use the Scale button to animate changes in the object's size.

- Animate multiple objects at the same time.

Chapter Summary

Now you should have a basic knowledge of how 3-D computer animation works, a sense of the terminology used, and some basic hands-on experience. Before moving on to specific fields in which computer animation is used, we will discuss the history of the art form. Learning about the development of computer graphics should help you understand why things are done the way they are today. You will also learn about milestones in the history of animation—in theoretical research, motion pictures, and television.

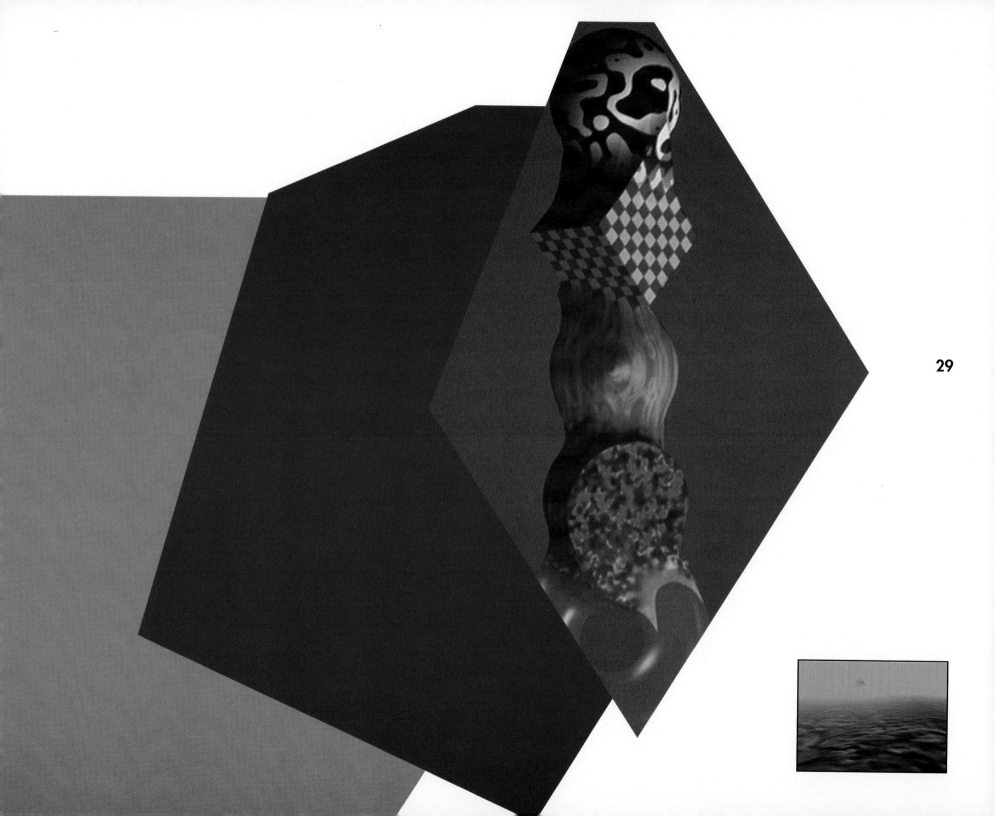

29

The HISTORY 2 of computer animation

chapter

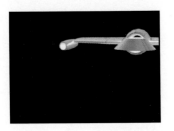

To gain a better understanding of the terminology and techniques of computer animation, it is important to learn its history. In this chapter we will review the history of computer animation, from the very first animation machines of the 1800s to the latest advances in computer-generated imagery.

Animation Before Computers

Animation was actually the precursor to film and motion pictures. In 1824, a scholar named Mark Roget published a paper called "The Persistence of Vision with Regard to Moving Objects," which stated that the human eye retains an image for a fraction of a second longer than the image is actually present. To demonstrate this principle, scientists invented many optical parlor toys in the early 1800s.

One such device was the *thaumatrope*, created in 1825. It used a round disk with different pictures on both sides and strings attached to opposite ends. When the disk was spun, the two pictures appeared as one.

In 1832, Simon Ritter von Stampfer in Vienna, Austria, and Joseph A. F. Plateau in Ghent, Belgium, invented the first animation devices. Plateau called his device the *phenakistiscope*, which consisted of two

disks; one had slits radiating from the center of the wheel, and the other had a sequence of hand-drawn pictures. The disks were attached to each other by means of a shaft, and the shaft was supported by a handle. When the user looked through the slits and spun the disks, the pictures appeared to move. The slits isolated each picture for a brief moment; thus the viewer did not see a blur of spinning pictures. Stampfer's device, the *stroboscope*, was similar, except that only one disk was used. The pictures were drawn on one side of the disk, and the viewer had to hold it up to a mirror when looking through the slits.

The next step in animation was the development of the *zoetrope* in 1834, a device that used a band of drawings mounted on the inside of a revolving drum. When the viewer looked through slits in the side of the drum as it was spun, the drawings appeared to move. Such optical toys were very popular in 19th-century homes.

The *magic lantern* was a device invented in the 17th century. It was used to project transparencies onto a screen, much like our modern-day slide projectors. Between 1845 and 1853, an Austrian military officer named Baron Franz von Uchatius combined the magic lantern with the revolving disk to create the first movie projector.

In 1869, the *kineograph* (commonly known as the flip book) was patented. A flip book has pages with sequential pictures on them. When the pages are flipped quickly,

the illusion of motion is created. (You may have noticed by now that on the margins of this book, we have included some computer animations that you can view by flipping the pages.)

Around the same time, some early advancements were being made in photography. In the mid-1800s, photographers attempted to capture

32

motion, but due to the slow exposure time of the wet-plate process then in use, they had to pose each movement and photograph it separately. These photos could then be used with the modified magic lantern to project fairly realistic moving pictures. By the late 1870s, photographic emulsions and camera shutters were improved to the point where photographers such as Eadweard Muybridge could photograph continuous motion.

Muybridge was hired by Leland Stanford, the railroad baron and former governor of California, to solve a bet he had made with a friend. Stanford maintained that the legs of a running horse are all off the ground simultaneously at one point during every stride. To settle the bet, Muybridge set up 12 cameras (and later used 24) on a race-track; as the horse ran past, it tripped strings to activate the shutters and expose the plates. Stanford won his bet, and Muybridge went on to invent the *zoopraxiscope*, a machine that projected motion photographs onto a screen.

In 1877, an inventor named Charles Emile Reynaud created the *praxinoscope*. A descendant of the zoetrope, the praxinoscope used a drum with a ring of mirrors to project the images from a strip of film onto a screen.

The next major step in animation came with the development of light-sensitive transparent film. In 1887, the Rev. Hannibal Goodwin, an amateur photographer in Newark, New Jersey, created a light-sensitive emulsion on celluloid film. Shortly after that, George Eastman developed a similar film that could be used with the Kodak camera he invented. This new celluloid film had many advantages, and ultimately it gave birth to modern-day film cameras and projectors.

Thomas A. Edison created the first celluloid-film motion pictures, and, working along with William K. L. Dickson, he developed the *kinetoscope* in 1891.

Operated in a cabinet, it allowed only one person to view the movie at a time. The kinetoscope used a sprocket-driven, 50-foot continuous loop of film. A few years later in Paris, Louis and Auguste Lumière invented the cinématographe, and they opened the first movie theater, in a French cafe, in 1896. Soon other such cinema theaters opened in Europe and the United States. Continuing his research and development, Edison created the *vitascope*, a cinema player capable of projecting a movie on a screen for larger audiences. A major advance in the vitascope was its use of intermittent projection. This is the process wherein each image is stopped for a brief moment instead of continuously streaming past the projector lens.

As cinema theaters sprouted around the United States, animated cartoons became more and more popular. The first in the United States was J. Stuart Blackton's *Humorous Phases of Funny Faces*, in 1906. *Gertie the Dinosaur* appeared in 1909, and the Felix the Cat series started in 1917. In France, Emile Cohl was creating cartoons around 1910.

During this early period, an entire drawing was required for each frame of animation. This problem was overcome by John Bray around 1913. Bray started using

translucent paper to print cartoon backgrounds. Earl Hurd also used celluloid sheets, but he painted the characters on them so the characters could easily be overlaid on complex backgrounds. This is where the term *cel animation* originated. In 1918, Winsor McCay created *The Sinking of the Lusitania*, although he didn't use the cel-animation technique.

A few years later, one of the most memorable cartoon characters made his debut: Mickey Mouse. In 1923, Walt Disney began creating cartoon children's stories, and in 1928 he created *Steamboat Willie*, the first short film starring Mickey Mouse. At this time, the popular trend in movies was to include a synchronized sound track. Steamboat Willie followed this trend and became the first animated cartoon with sound. In 1937, Disney released the first animated feature-length film, *Snow White and the Seven Dwarfs*. Following the financial and critical success of *Snow White*, Disney continued to create feature-length cartoons, including the landmark *Fantasia* in 1940. Today, Walt Disney Studios continues to put out the highest-quality feature-length cartoons.

Even though experiments with color motion pictures began back in 1906, it wasn't until 1933 that the process was perfected and made commercially viable. The movie *Becky Sharp* (1935), based on a novel by William Makepeace Thackeray, was the first to use this new Technicolor (three color) system. Color quickly grew in popularity, and by the 1950s very few films were produced in black- and-white. From the '50s until today, most movie-making techniques have not changed very much.

TELEVISION

In 1923, the Russian physicist Vladimir Kosma Zworykin invented the *iconoscope*, the first practical video camera. Previous attempts at creating a video camera were unsuccessful, but Zworykin's design worked. The lack of a good video camera had been the main restriction on the development of television. (As far back as the 1870s, cathode-ray tubes were being created and used in various scientific experiments.) Thus, with a working video camera and other electronic advances such as the vacuum tube, television became a reality in the 1920s.

It is important for our purposes to understand in a general sense how television works. A video camera converts light patterns into analog electrical signals. These signals are then encoded and can be transmitted through the air or via cable-TV wiring. When the television set receives these signals, they are decoded and sent to the picture tube. Using an electron gun, the picture tube shoots a stream of electrons at the back of a phosphor-coated screen. Starting at the upper left-hand corner of the screen, the gun shoots a stream of electrons of varying intensities horizontally across the screen in a single line that moves to the right. When the gun reaches the right side of the screen, it shuts off and returns to the left side of the screen (slightly lower than the previous position). This returning to the left side of the screen is called the *retrace*. From there, the gun turns on again and produces another row of illuminated phosphor across the screen. However, every time the gun draws a row, it skips a row. In other words, the gun only draws every other row on its way down the screen.

Image courtesy of XAOS.

Once the gun reaches the bottom of the screen, it turns off and resets itself to the upper left-hand corner. This step is called the *vertical retrace*. Once it is back at the upper left-hand corner, it repeats the same pattern; however, this time it fills in the missing rows from the first pass. Each pass happens so quickly (in about a 60th of a second), that your eye does not notice the missing rows.

The first television broadcasts were made in England in 1927 and then in the United States in 1930. By 1939, television broadcasts were made on a regular basis. In 1946, there were 12 television broadcasting stations in the United States; this jumped to 46 in 1948, with about 78 more stations under construction and more than 300 new applications submitted to the Federal Communications Commission (FCC). Television became a booming business, while the motion-picture industry faltered and thousands of movie theaters closed.

Concurrent with the popularizing of color motion pictures in the 1950s, there was a growing interest in color television. The technology was already in place, but the problem was how to implement the new color-television technology without making the existing black-and-white equipment obsolete. In 1953, the National Television System Committee (NTSC, a group of engineers who cooperated in the development of the engineering standards) proposed a "compatible color" standard to the FCC, and it was subsequently accepted. This standard came to be known as the

NTSC standard, and it is still used in television broadcasting today.

A color television camera splits the incoming light into the three primary colors of the visible-light spectrum: red, green, and blue (RGB). Each color is then scanned by its own camera tube. Thus the camera outputs the scene in three signals divided into the three primary colors. To reproduce the color scene, the television set requires a color picture tube. This is a tube that has three electron guns (one for each primary color). The inside of the picture tube contains tiny RGB phosphor dots, and each electron gun hits only its respective color dots. (The red gun hits the red dots, the blue gun hits the blue dots, etc.) The dots are placed close enough together that the human eye tends to blend the three primary colors into a single color. The color brightness is controlled by the intensity of the electron beams.

This, however, does not solve the problem of a compatible color signal to keep all the black-and-white equipment from going obsolete. To make the signal compatible, a black-and-white video image is created by adding the three RGB brightness values together. However, instead of broadcasting three color signals along with the black-and-white signal, the RGB signals are converted to *luminance* (brightness) and *chrominance* (hue). Doing this reduces the number of signals required from three (RGB) to two (LC). This new luminance/chrominance signal is piggybacked onto the existing black-and-white signal

and broadcast over the air. The result is that existing black-and-white television sets can still use the familiar black-and-white signal, while newer color sets receive all three signals and combine them to produce a color picture.

NTSC color technology does have its limitations. For instance, some colors (such as a pure red) are impossible to reproduce on an NTSC color television. Also, there is a wide variation in color reproduction from one set to another. This has earned the NTSC standard the nickname of "Never The Same Color."

European countries standardized on a different format, known as PAL. PAL stands for Phase Alternation by Line. It offers a slight improvement over the color distortion of NTSC. However, the format is not compatible with NTSC, so videotapes recorded in the PAL format will not work on NTSC televisions or video recorders.

In the 1950s, a new graphics tool began to take shape, a tool that would eventually become an essential element for every motion picture and television program produced. That tool was the computer.

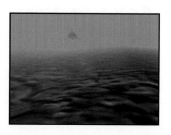

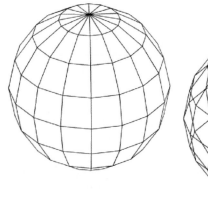
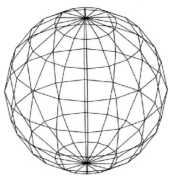

THE BIRTH OF COMPUTER GRAPHICS

In the mid-1940s, a young engineer at the Massachusetts Institute of Technology (MIT) named Jay Forrester was picked to head a research group. This group was responsible for designing equipment that could train new pilots and test the aerodynamics of new aircraft designs. It was decided that a digital computer would be the best tool for this project—even though none existed at the time.

The new digital computer came to be known as Whirlwind. After a few years, the project's focus shifted from a simulator/tester to a computerized radar defense system. Linked to radar sites, the Whirlwind would display a map of the area on its CRT screen and plot blips representing incoming aircraft. On April 20, 1951, it was given its first live demonstration and was a complete success. But more than being a very successful computer project, the Whirlwind represented the first practical use of computer graphics.

Around this time, an abstract filmmaker named John Whitney, Sr., was interested in composing both music and graphics at the same time. In 1958, he started experimenting with analog computers to create art. Whitney used an M-5 anti-aircraft gunsight computer and created visual animation by using the analog computer to control the movement of the artwork and camera.

Whitney used this system to created the title sequence for Alfred Hitchcock's *Vertigo*, and in 1961 he produced a film of his own called *Catalog*. *Catalog* showcased the various animation effects that were possible using Whitney's techniques, and it led to other feature-film projects. In 1966, Whitney and his brother John produced another graphics film, titled *Lapis*.

Digital Equipment Corporation (DEC) opened in August 1957 in Maynard, Massachusetts. With only three employees, the company had 8,500 square feet of production space in a converted woolen mill. Lawn chairs constituted most of its furniture. In November 1960, DEC introduced the PDP-1 (Programmed Data Processor), the world's first small, interactive computer. Thirty years later, Digital would post annual revenues of $12.9 billion and employ more than 124,000 people worldwide. Through the years, Digital has played an important role in the development of computer graphics.

In 1959, the first computer drawing system, DAC-1 (Design Augmented by Computers), was created by General Motors and IBM. It enabled the user to input a 3-D description of an automobile and then rotate it and view the image from different angles. It was unveiled at the Joint Computer Conference in Detroit in 1964.

COMPUTER GRAPHICS IN THE 1960s

The next big advance in computer graphics was to come from another MIT student, Ivan Sutherland. In 1961, Sutherland created a computer drawing program called Sketchpad. Sketchpad enabled the user to use a light pen to draw simple shapes on the computer screen, save them, and recall them later. The light pen itself had a small photoelectric cell in its tip. This cell emitted an electronic pulse whenever it was placed in front of a computer screen and the screen's electron gun fired directly at it. By simply timing the electronic pulse with the current location of the electron gun, the computer could pinpoint where the pen was touching the screen at any given moment. Once that was determined, the computer could place a cursor at that location.

Even today, many standard computer-graphics interfaces are derived from this early Sketchpad program. One example of this is drawing constraints. If you want to draw a square, for example, you don't have to worry about drawing four lines perfectly to form the edges of the box. You can simply specify that you want to draw a box,

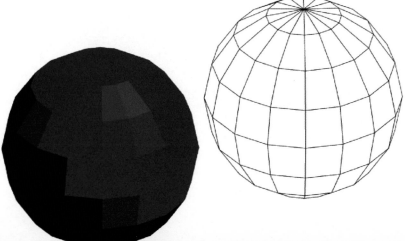

and then specify the location and size of the box. The software will then construct a perfect box for you, with the right dimensions and at the right location. Another important element of Sketchpad was that Sutherland's software modeled *objects*, not just *pictures* of objects. In other words, with a model of a car, you could change the size of the tires without affecting the rest of the car, or you could stretch the body of the car without deforming the tires.

These early computer graphics were *vector* graphics, comprising thin lines, whereas modern-day graphics are *raster* based, using pixels.

The difference between vector graphics and raster graphics can be illustrated with the example of a shipwrecked sailor. Imagine that he creates an SOS sign in the sand by arranging rocks in the shape of the letters "SOS". He also has some brightly colored r o p e , w i t h

which he makes a second SOS sign by arranging the rope in the shapes of the letters. The rock SOS sign is similar to raster graphics. Every pixel has to be individually accounted for. The rope SOS sign is equivalent to vector graphics. The computer simply sets the starting point and ending point for the line and perhaps bends it a little between the two end points. The disadvantage to vector files is that they cannot represent continuous tone images and they are limited in the number of colors available. Raster formats, on the other hand, work well for continuous tone images and can reproduce as many colors as needed. They are, however, quite memory-intensive.

In 1961, another student at MIT, Steve Russell, created the first video game, Spacewar. Written for the DEC PDP-1, Spacewar was an instant success, and copies started flowing to other PDP-1 owners. Eventually, even DEC got a copy. The engineers at DEC used it as a diagnostic program on every new PDP-1 before shipping. The sales force picked up on this, and when installing new units, they would run the world's first video game for their new customers.

E. E. Zajac, a scientist at Bell Telephone Laboratory (BTL), created a film called

37

Simulation of a Two-Gyro Gravity Attitude Control System in 1963. In this computer-generated film, Zajac showed how the attitude of a satellite could be altered as it orbits the Earth. He created the animation on an IBM 7090 mainframe computer. Also at BTL, Ken Knowlton, Frank Sindon, and Michael Noll started working in the computer graphics field. Sindon created a film called *Force, Mass and Motion* illustrating Newton's laws of motion in operation. Around the same time, other scientists were creating computer animations to illustrate their research. At Lawrence Radiation Laboratories, Nelson Max created the films, *Flow of a Viscous Fluid* and *Propagation of Shock Waves in a Solid Form.* Boeing Aircraft created a film called *Vibration of an Aircraft.*

It wasn't long before major corporations started taking an interest in computer graphics. TRW, Lockheed-Georgia, General Electric, and Sperry Rand were among the many companies getting started in computer graphics by the mid 1960s. IBM responded to this interest by releasing the IBM 2250 graphics terminal, the first commercially available graphics computer.

In 1963, Doug Englebart of the Stanford Research Institute invented the first *mouse.* Two types of mouse-devices exist today: optical and mechanical. The mechanical mouse has a rubber ball within its casing, along with two tracking rollers (one for vertical movement and one for horizontal movement). As the user moves the mouse, the ball rolls, and the direction of the movement is picked up by the encoders and converted to coordinates for the computer. The optical mouse emits a light onto a special pad that reflects the light back to the mouse and its optical sensors. These sensors can then detect the direction of the mouse movement by the movement of the reflected light.

Also in the mid-1960s, the *digitizing tablet* was developed. Digitizing tablets use a wire grid just beneath the surface of the tablet. Electrical pulses are sent through this wire grid and detected by a puck or stylus. By accurately timing the pulses, the tablet can determine where (horizontally and vertically) the stylus happens to be at any given moment. This information is converted to coordinates and sent to the computer. The computer can then use the coordinates to update the cursor on the screen.

Ralph Baer, a supervising engineer at Sanders Associates, created a home video game in 1966 that was later licensed to Magnavox and called the Odyssey. While it was very simplistic and required fairly inexpensive electronic parts, it enabled the player to move points of light around a screen. It was the first consumer computer-graphics product.

Also in 1966, Sutherland at MIT invented the first computer-controlled head-mounted display (HMD). Dubbed "The Sword of Damocles" because of the hardware required for support, it displayed two separate wire-frame images, one for each eye. This enabled the viewer to see the computer scene in stereoscopic 3-D. After receiving his Ph.D. from MIT, Sutherland became director of information processing at the Defense Department's Advanced Research Projects Agency, and later he became a professor at Harvard.

Dave Evans was director of engineering at Bendix Corporation's computer division from 1953 to 1962, then worked for the next five years as a visiting professor at Berkeley, where he continued his interest in computers and how they interfaced with people. In 1968, the University of Utah recruited Evans to form a computer-science program, and computer graphics

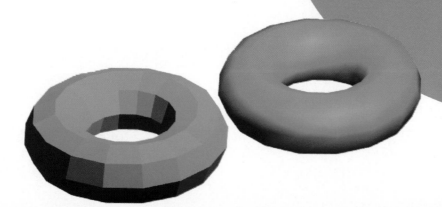

quickly became his primary interest. This new department would become the world's primary research center for computer graphics.

In 1967, Evans recruited Sutherland to join the computer science program at the University of Utah. There Sutherland refined his head-mounted display. (Twenty years later, NASA would rediscover his techniques while researching virtual reality.) At Utah, Sutherland and Evans were highly sought-after consultants for large companies.

A student named Ed Catmull started at the University of Utah in 1970 and signed up for Sutherland's computer graphics class. Catmull had just come from the Boeing Company and had just received his degree in physics. Growing up on Disney films, Catmull loved animation, but he discovered that he didn't have the talent for drawing. Now Catmull (along with many others) saw computers as the natural progression of animation, and he wanted to be part of the revolution. The first computer animation that Catmull saw was his

own—an animation of his hand opening and closing. It became one of his goals to produce a feature-length motion picture using computer animation. (In the same class, Fred Parkes created an animation of his wife's face.) Because of Evan's and Sutherland's presence, the University of Utah was quickly gaining a reputation as *the* place to be for computer graphics research.

The Utah computer-graphics laboratory was attracting people from all over, and John Warnock was one of those early pioneers. He would later found Adobe Systems and create a revolution in the publishing world with his PostScript page-description language. Tom Stockham lead the image-processing group at Utah, which worked closely with the computer-graphics lab. Jim Clark was also there. (Clark would later found Silicon Graphics, the maker of high-end graphics workstations.)

A major advance in 3-D computer graphics that came out of the Utah program was the *hidden-surface algorithm*. In order to draw a representation of a 3-D object on the screen, the computer must determine which surfaces are "behind" the object (from the viewer's perspective) and therefore should be "hidden" when the computer renders the image; the hidden-surface algorithm solved this problem.

Once the problem of removing hidden surfaces was solved, the next major ambition of computer-graphics researchers was to enhance realism. During the late 1960s, both Warnock and W. J. Bouknight did important work on shading 3-D objects with color. (This is when computer graphics started to switch from vector graphics to raster graphics.) One of the first methods used to create shaded objects was based on the work of a 16th century physicist and astronomer, Johann Lambert. The Lambert Cosine Law deals with the intensity of reflected light as it strikes an object. This law, when applied to 3-D computer graphics, enabled computer animators to create colored solid objects instead of wireframe models. This method was later improved and is commonly referred to today as *flat shading.* Flat shading colors every polygon in a 3-D object the same color; then that color is varied, based on its orientation to a light source. When the polygons or surfaces making up the 3-D object are small enough, flat shading can provide adequate realism.

In 1968 Evans and Sutherland left the University of Utah to form a company called Evans & Sutherland. Beating IBM at its own game, they created custom line-drawing routines and manufactured them

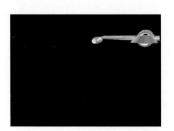

right into the circuitry. This was the beginning of hardware-accelerated graphics. Their first system, the LDS-1 (Line Drawing System), was more than 100 times faster than the IBM 2250. At this point, computer graphics equipment was very expensive, costing hundreds of thousands of dollars for a single terminal. However, with improvements in integrated circuit (IC) technology and the advent of the random access memory (RAM) ICs, these costs came down rapidly.

COMPUTER GRAPHICS IN THE 1970s

The 1970s saw the introduction of computer graphics to the world of television. Computer Image Corporation (CIC) developed complex hardware and software systems such as ANIMAC, SCANIMATE and CAESAR. All of these systems worked by scanning existing artwork, then manipulating it, making it squash, stretch, spin, fly around the screen, etc. The Bell telephone companies and CBS Sports were among the many firms that made use of the new computer graphics.

While flat shading can make an object look as if it's solid, the sharp edges of the polygons can detract from the realism of the image. Although you can create smaller polygons (which also means more polygons), this increases the complexity of the

scene, which in turn slows down the performance of the computer. To solve this, Henri Gouraud in 1971 presented a method for creating the appearance of a curved surface by interpolating the color across the polygons. This method of shading a 3-D object has since come to be known as *Gouraud shading*. One of the most impressive aspects of Gouraud shading is that it hardly takes any more computations than flat shading, yet it provides a dramatic increase in rendering quality. One thing that Gouraud shading can't fix is the visible edge of the object.

One of the most important advances in computer graphics came in 1971 with the invention of the microprocessor. Using integrated-circuit technology first developed in 1959, the electronics of a computer processor were miniaturized to a single chip (sometimes called a CPU or central processing unit). One of the first desktop microcomputers designed for personal use was the Altair 8800 from Micro Instrumentation Telemetry Systems (MITS). Sold through the mail in kit form, the Altair (named for a planet in the popular *Star Trek* TV series) retailed for around $400. Eventually, personal computers would advance to the point where film-quality computer animation could be created on them.

In that same year, Nolan Kay Bushnell started the Atari company. In 1972, Atari released an arcade video game called Pong that gave birth to an industry that

remains one of the principal outlets of computer-graphics technology.

In the 1970s, a number of animation houses were formed. (*Animation house* is a term used to describe an animation production facility.) In Culver City, California, Information International Incorporated (better known as Triple I) formed a motion picture computer-graphics department. In San Rafael, California, George Lucas formed Lucasfilm. In Los Angeles, Robert Abel & Associates and Digital Effects were formed. In Elmsford, N.Y., MAGI was formed. In London, Systems Simulation,

Ltd., was formed. Of all these companies, almost none of them were still in business ten years later. At Abel & Associates, Robert Abel hired Richard Edlund to help with computer motion control of cameras. Edlund was later recruited by Lucasfilm to work on *Star Wars,* and eventually he established Boss Film Studios, creating special effects for television and motion pictures and winning four Academy Awards.

In 1970, Gary Demos was a senior at Caltech when we saw the work of John Whitney Sr. He immediately developed an interest in computer graphics. This interest was further developed when he saw the work being done at Evans & Sutherland and the animation that was coming out of the University of Utah. In 1972, Demos went to work for E&S. At that time, the company used Digital PDP-11 computers, along with the custom-built hardware for which E&S was becoming famous. These systems included the Picture System, graphics tablet systems, and color frame buffers (originally designed at the University of Utah). It was at E&S that Demos met John Whitney Jr., the son of the original graphics pioneer.

E&S started to work on some joint projects with Triple I. Founded in 1962, Triple I was in the business of creating digital scanners and other image-processing equipment. Between E&S and Triple I, there was a Picture Design Group. After working on a few joint projects between

E&S and Triple I, Demos and Whitney left E&S to join Triple I and formed the Motion Picture Products group in late 1974. At Triple I, they used PDP-10s and a Foonley Machine (which was a custom PDP-10). They developed another frame buffer that used 1,000 lines. They also built custom film recorders and scanners, along with custom graphics processors, image accelerators, and the software to run them.

These developments led to the first use of computer graphics for motion pictures, in 1973, when Whitney and Demos worked on the film *Westworld*. They used a technique called *pixellization*, which achieves a computerized mosaic effect. This is done by dividing the picture into square areas and then averaging the colors within that area into one color.

In 1973, the Association of Computing Machinery's (ACM) Special Interest Group on Computer Graphics (SIGGRAPH) held its first conference. Solely devoted to computer graphics, the convention attracted about 1,200 people and was held in a small auditorium. Eventually, the SIGGRAPH conference and exposition would become the primary showcase of the computer-graphics industry.

Since the 1960s, the University of Utah had remained the focal point for research on 3-D computer graphics and algorithms. Over the years, Utah personnel used various 3-D models for their research, including a VW Beetle, a human face, and the most popular, a teapot. It was in 1975 that

M. Newell developed the Utah teapot, and throughout the history of 3-D computer animation, it has served as a benchmark. Today it is almost an icon for 3-D computer animation. The original teapot on which Newell based his computer model can be seen at the Boston Computer Museum displayed next to a computer rendering of it.

Ed Catmull received his Ph. D. in computer science in 1974; his thesis covered texture mapping, z-buffers and rendering curved surfaces. *Texture mapping* brought computer graphics to a new level of realism. Catmull had come up with the idea of texture mapping while sitting in his car in a parking lot at the University of Utah, talking to a student named Lance Williams about creating a 3-D castle. Most objects in real life have very rich and detailed surfaces, such as the stones of a castle wall, the material on a sofa, or the wood veneer on a kitchen table. Catmull realized that since there were patterns and textures on real-life objects, he could do the same for their computer counterparts. Texture mapping is a method of taking a 2-D representation of what an object's surface looks like and then applying that flat image to a 3-D, computer-generated object (much in the same way that you can hang wallpaper on a blank wall.)

The *z-buffer* aided the process of hidden-surface removal by recording the depth of any given point in an image. A *z* coordinate represents depth, just as *y* represents vertical position and *x* represents horizontal position. The z-buffer is thus an area of memory devoted to holding the depth data for every pixel in an image. Today, many high-performance graphics workstations have z-buffers built-in.

Photo-realism remained an elusive goal in the computer-graphics community. While Gouraud shading represented a great improvement over flat shading, it still had a few limitations. A Gouraud-shaded torus has slight variations in the shading that reveal the underlying polygons. These variations can also cause reflections to appear incorrectly or even disappear altogether in certain circumstances.

This was corrected, however, by Phong Bui-Toung, a programmer at the University of Utah (of course). Bui-Toung arrived at Utah in 1971, and in 1974 he developed a new shading method that came to be known as *Phong shading*. (After the University of Utah, Bui-Toung went on to Stanford as a professor. He died in 1975.) Phong's shading method accurately interpolates the colors over a polygonal surface, producing accurate reflective highlights and shading. The drawback is that

Phong shading can be up to 100 times slower than Gouraud shading. Because of this, animators who are creating small, flat 3-D objects that are not central to the animation still use Gouraud shading instead of Phong. Like Gouraud shading, Phong shading cannot smooth over the outer edges of 3-D objects.

A major breakthrough in simulating realism came in 1975 when a French mathematician, Dr. Benoit Mandelbrot, published a paper called *A Theory of Fractal Sets*. Mandelbrot's findings represented 20 years of research in what he called *fractal geometry*. To understand what a fractal is, consider that a straight line is a one-dimensional object, whereas a plane is a two-dimensional object. However, if the line curves around in such a way as to cover the entire surface of the plane, then it is no longer one-dimensional (yet not quite two-dimensional). Mandelbrot described it as a fractional dimension between one and two.

To understand how this helps computer graphics, imagine creating a random mountain terrain. You may start with a flat plane, then tell the computer to divide the plane into four equal parts. Next, the new center point is offset vertically by some random amount. Following that, one of the new smaller squares is chosen and then subdivided, with its center slightly offset at random. The process continues recursively until some limit is reached and all the squares are offset.

Mandelbrot followed up his paper with a book titled *The Fractal Geometry of Nature*. This showed how his fractal principles could be applied to computer imagery to create realistic simulations of natural phenomena such as mountains, coastlines, wood grain, etc.

After graduating in 1974 from the University of Utah, Ed Catmull worked for a company called Applicon. His tenure there didn't last very long, however, because in November of that same year he was given an offer he couldn't refuse. Alexander Schure, founder of New York Institute of Technology (NYIT), had gone to the Utah to see the computer graphics lab. Schure had a great interest in animation and had already established a traditional animation facility

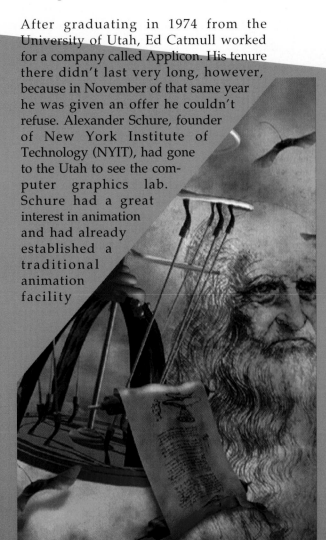

Image courtesy of Ray Dream.

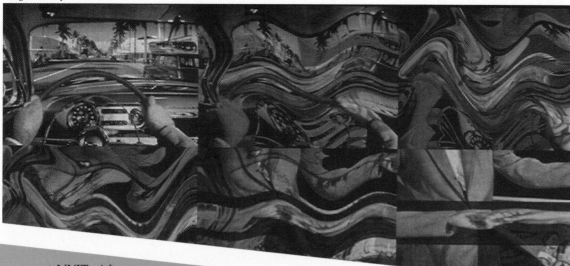

at NYIT. After see-
ing the setup at Utah, he asked Evans what
equipment he needed to create computer
graphics. He then told his people to "get
me one of everything they have." The timing happened to be just right, because the
program at Utah was running out of
money. Schure made Ed Catmull the director of NYIT's new Computer Graphics
Lab. Soon, other talented people in the
computer graphics field left the Utah cam-
pus and went to NYIT, including Malcolm
Blanchard, Garland Stern, and Lance
Williams. Thus the leading center for computer graphics research switched from
Utah to the New York Institute of
Technology.

One talented recruit to the NYIT program
was Alvy Ray Smith. As a young student
at New Mexico State University in 1964,
Smith had used a computer to create a picture of an equiangular spiral for a Nimbus
weather satellite. Yet despite his early success, Smith didn't take an immediate interest in computer graphics. He moved on to

Stanford University, got
his Ph.D., then promptly took his first
teaching job at New York University.
Smith recalls: "My chairman, Herb
Freeman, was very interested in computer
graphics. Some of his students had made
important advances in the field. He knew I
was an artist, and yet he couldn't spark
any interest on my part. I would tell him,
'If you ever get color, I'll get interested.'
Then one day I met Dr. Richard Shoup,
and he told me about Xerox PARC [Palo
Alto Research Center]. He was planning
on going to PARC to create a program that
emulated painting on a computer the way
an artist would naturally paint on a canvas."

Shoup had become interested in computer
graphics while he was at Carnegie Mellon
University. He then became a resident scientist at PARC and began working on a
program he called "SuperPaint." It used
one of the first color frame buffers ever

built. Around this same time, Ken
Knowlton at Bell Labs was also creating a
paint program.

Smith, on the other hand, wasn't thinking
much about paint programs. However, he
had broken his leg in a skiing accident and
had time to rethink the path his life was
taking. He decided to move back to
California, to teach at Berkeley, in 1973. "I
was basically a hippie, but one day I
decided to visit my old friend Shoup in
Palo Alto. He wanted to show me his
progress on the painting program, and I
told him that I only had about an hour,
and then I would need to get back to
Berkeley. I was only visiting him as a
friend, and yet when I saw what he had
done with his paint program, I wound up
staying for 12 hours! I knew from that
moment on that computer graphics is
what I wanted to do with my life." Smith
managed to get himself hired by Xerox in
1974, and he worked with Shoup in writing the software for SuperPaint.

In 1975, in nearby San Jose, Alan Baum
invited his Hewlett-Packard co-worker
Steve Wozniak to a meeting of the local
Homebrew Computer Club. Homebrew,
started by Fred Moore and Gordon
French, was a club of amateur computer
enthusiasts, and it soon became a hotbed

43

44

of ideas about home-built personal computers. From the Altair 8800 to TV typewriters, the club discussed and built virtually anything that resembled a computer. Through the Homebrew Club, Wozniak acquired a box full of electronic parts, and it wasn't long before he was showing off his own personal computer/toy at the Homebrew meetings. A close friend of Wozniak, Steve Jobs, who worked at Atari, helped Wozniak develop his computer into the very first Apple. They built the units in a garage and sold them for $666.66.

In that same year, 1975, 19-year-old William Gates III dropped out of Harvard and founded a

company called Microsoft with his friend Paul Allen. Together they wrote a version of the BASIC programming language for the Altair 8800 and put it on the market. Some five years later, when IBM was looking for an operating system to use with their new personal computer, they approached Microsoft. Gates remembered an operating system for Intel 8080 microprocessors written by Seattle Computer Products (SCP), an operating system called 86-DOS. Taking a gamble, Gates bought 86-DOS from SCP for $50,000, rewrote it, named it DOS, and licensed it (smartly retaining ownership) to IBM as the operating system for their first personal computer. Today, Microsoft dominates the personal-computer software industry, with gross annual sales of almost $4 billion, and now it has moved into the field of 3-D computer graphics.

Meanwhile, back at PARC, Xerox had decided to focus solely on black-and-white computer graphics, dropping everything that was in color. So Alvy Ray Smith called Ed Catmull at NYIT and went out east with a colleague named David DiFrancesco to meet

with Catmull. Everyone hit it off, so Smith made the move from Xerox over to NYIT (just two months after Catmull himself had gotten there). The first thing Smith did at NYIT was write a full color (24-bit) paint program, the first of its kind.

Later, other computer-graphics pioneers joined NYIT's program, including Tom Duff, Paul Heckbert, Pat Hanrahan, Dick Lundin, Ned Greene, Jim Blinn, Rebecca Allen, Bill Maher, Jim Clark, Thaddeus Beier, Malcom Blanchard, and many others. In all, the computer-graphics lab at NYIT would eventually be home to more than 60 people. Many of these individuals would continue to lead the field of computer animation for the next twenty years.

The first computer-graphics application that NYIT focused on was 2-D animation and creating tools to assist traditional animators. One of the tools that Catmull built was "Tween," a tool that interpolated in-between frames from one line drawing to another. NYIT researchers also developed a scan-and-paint system for pencil-drawn artwork. This would later evolve into Disney's CAPS (Computer Animation Production System).

Eventually the NYIT group branched into 3-D computer graphics. Lance Williams wrote a story for a movie called *The Works* and sold the idea to Schure; this movie became NYIT's major project for the next two years. A lot of time and resources were spent in creating 3-D models and rendering test animations.

Image courtesy of XAOS Tools.

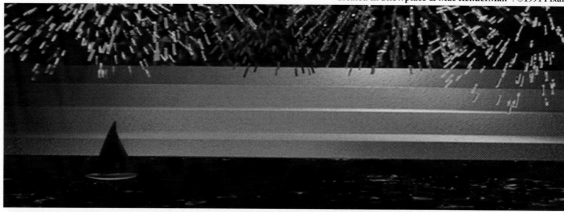

The atmosphere at the NYIT lab was exciting. "NYIT in itself was a significant event in the history of computer graphics," explains Alvy Ray Smith. "Here we had this wealthy man [Alex Schure] having plenty of money and getting us whatever we needed. We didn't have a budget; we had no goals; we just stretched the envelope. It was such an incredible opportunity. Every day someone was creating something new. None of us slept. It was common to work 22 hour days. Everything you saw was something new. We blasted computer graphics into the world. It was like exploring a new continent."

However, the problem was that none of the people in the Computer Graphics Lab understood the scope of making a motion picture. "We were just a bunch of engineers in a little converted stable on Long Island, and we didn't know the first thing about making movies," says Thaddeus Beier (now technical director for Pacific Data Images). Gradually, people became discouraged and left for other places.

Smith continues: "It just wasn't happening. We all thought we would take part in making a movie. But at the time it would have been impossible with the speed of the computers." Alex Schure made an animated movie called *Tubby the Tuba* using conventional animation techniques, and it turned out to be very disappointing. "We realized then that he really didn't have what it takes to make a movie." explains Smith. Catmull agrees: "It was awful, it was terrible. Half the audience feel asleep

at the screening. We walked out of the screening room thinking 'Thank God we didn't have anything to do with it and that computers were not used for *anything* in that movie!'" The time was ripe for the arrival of a computer-graphics aficionado with genuine film making credentials: George Lucas.

Lucas, with the success of *Star Wars* under his belt, was interested in using computer graphics in his next movie, *The Empire Strikes Back.* So he contacted Triple I, who in turn produced a sequence that showed five X-Wing fighters flying in formation. However, disagreements over money caused Lucas to drop his arrangement with Triple I and go back to handmade models.

The experience nonetheless showed that photo-realistic computer imagery was a possibility, so eventually Lucas decided to assemble his own computer-graphics department within his production company, Lucasfilm. Lucas sent out an emissary to find the brightest minds in the world of computer graphics. Initially he went to

Carnegie Mellon University and talked to a professor, who referred him to one of his students, Ralph Guggenheim, who in turn referred him to Catmull at NYIT. After a few discussions, Catmull flew out to the West Coast, met with Lucas, and accepted his offer.

Initially, five people from NYIT went with Catmull, including Alvy Ray Smith, David DiFrancesco, Tom Duff, and Ralph Guggenheim. Later, others would take up the opportunity. Slowly the NYIT computer graphics lab started to fall apart and ceased to be the center of computer-graphics research. The focus had shifted to Lucasfilm (as well as the new graphics department at Cornell University). Over the next 15 years, the Lucasfilm special-effects subsidiary, Industrial Light & Magic, would be nominated for 21 Academy Awards, winning 13 Oscars,

45

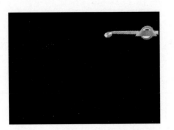

including six Academy Awards for Technical Achievement, and two Emmys.

Looking back at his years at NYIT, Catmull reflects: "Alex Schure funded five years of great research work, and he deserves credit for that. We published a lot of papers, and were very open about our research, allowing people to come on tours and see our work.

Catmull continues: "We really had a major group of talented people in the lab, dedicated to research and development for animation. We were actually quite stable for a long time, that first five years until I left. However, the primary issue was to make a feature film, and to do that you have to gather a lot of different kinds of skills: artistic, editorial, etc. Unfortunately, the manager of the school did not understand this. They appreciated the technical capabilities, so as a group we were well taken care of; but we all recognized that in order to produce a feature film, we had to have another kind of person there, movie people, and basically those people weren't brought into the school. We were doing the R&D, but we just could not achieve our goals there. So when Lucas came along and proved that he did have those kind of capabilities and said 'I want additional development in this area (of computer graphics),' we jumped at it."

Thus in 1979 George Lucas formed the new computer-graphics division of Lucasfilm to create computer imagery for motion pictures. Catmull became vice president, and during the next six years, this new group would assemble one of the most talented teams of artists and programmers in the computer-graphics industry. The advent of Lucasfilm's computer-graphics department is viewed by many as a major milestone in the history of computer graphics. Here the researchers had access to funds, but at the same time they were working under a serious moviemaker with real, definite, goals.

In 1976, the Association of Computer Machinery for the first time allowed exhibitors at the annual SIGGRAPH conference. Ten companies exhibited their products that year. By 1993, this would grow to 275 companies touting their wares to over 30,000 attendees.

In 1976, Systems Simulation, Ltd. (SSL), of London created an important computer-animation sequence for the movie *Alien*. The scene called for a computer-assisted landing sequence where the terrain was viewed as a 3-D wire-frame. Initially, a polystyrene landscape was going to be digitized in order to create the terrain. However, the terrain needed to be very rugged and complex and would have required a huge database if digitized. Alan Sutcliffe of SSL decided to write a program to generate the mountains at random. The result was a very convincing

mountain terrain displayed in wire-frame with the hidden lines removed. This was typical of early efforts at using computer-generated imagery (CGI) in motion pictures: using graphics to simulate futuristic computer read-outs.

In 1976, the Triple I team was busy working on the sequel to *Westworld*, a film called *Futureworld*. In this film, robot Samurai warriors were supposed to materialize into a vacuum chamber. To accomplish this, Triple I digitized still photographs of the warriors and then used image-processing techniques to manipulate the digitized images and make the warriors materialize over the background. Around this time, Triple I developed custom film scanners and recorders for working on films in high resolutions, up to 2,500 lines.

Also in that same year, at the University of Utah (before going to NYIT), James Blinn developed a new technique similar to texture mapping. However, instead of simply mapping the colors from a 2-D image onto a 3-D object, the colors were used to make the surface appear as if it had a dent or a bulge. To do this, a monochrome image is used where the white areas of the image will appear as bulges and the black areas of the image will

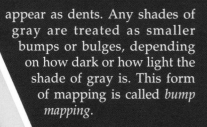

appear as dents. Any shades of gray are treated as smaller bumps or bulges, depending on how dark or how light the shade of gray is. This form of mapping is called *bump mapping*.

Bump maps can add a new level of realism to 3-D graphics by simulating a rough surface. When both a texture map and a bump map are applied at the same time, the result can be very convincing. Without bump maps, a 3-D object can look very flat and uninteresting.

According to Blinn, "Unfortunately, our frame buffer at Utah was broken so I paid a visit to my friends at NYIT over Christmas of 1976 to try out a crude version (of bump mapping) pictorially. Then in the spring of 1977, I figured out how to do it right and put it in my Ph.D. thesis. After I finished my thesis, I went to work at the Jet Propulsion Laboratory in Pasadena, California, where I worked from July of 1977 until 1988."

Blinn also developed a technique for rendering surfaces that reflect their surroundings. This is also accomplished by rendering six different views from the location of the object (top, bottom, front, back, left, and right). Those views are then applied to the outside of the object in a way that is similar to texture mapping, except that the computer uses the "environment map" to calculate reflected colors on the object. The result is that an object *appears* to reflect its surroundings.

Blinn continues, "Martin Newell and I actually came up with the environment mapping idea in 1975. Our environment mapping paper was accepted by SIGGRAPH for the 1976 conference, but instead of printing it in the proceedings, they submitted it to CACM where it appeared in October of 1976. Originally I didn't use six different views of the environment but rather just one view distorted into a latitude, longitude projection. Ned Greene came up with the idea to use 6 views several years later in a paper for IEEE, CG, & A. The concept of environment mapping also made it into my 1976 thesis along with several other techniques for lighting simulation and curved surface rendering."

In December of 1977, a new magazine called *Computer Graphics World* debuted. Back then, the major stories on computer graphics involved 2-D drafting, remote sensing, IC design, military simulation, medical imaging, and business graphics. Today, *CGW* continues to be the primary resource for computer-graphics news and reviews.

Computer-graphics hardware was still prohibitively expensive in the mid 70s. In 1977, the National Institutes of Health paid $65,000 for its first frame buffer. It had a resolution of 512×512 with 8 bits of color depth. Previously, NYIT had paid $80,000 for the same frame buffer. Today, a video adapter with the same capabilities can be purchased for under $100.

During the late 1970s, Don Greenberg at Cornell University started a computer-graphics lab that produced new methods of simulating realistic surfaces. His graduate student Rob Cook realized that the lighting model that everyone had been using best approximated plastic. Cook wanted to create a new lighting model that enabled computers to simulate objects such as polished metal. This new model addressed the energy of the light source rather than the light's intensity or brightness.

As the '70s drew to a close, the computer-graphics industry was showing tremendous growth. In 1979, IBM released its 3279 color terminal, and within 9 months, more than 10,000 orders had been placed for it. By 1980, the retail value of all the computer-graphics systems, hardware, and services sold worldwide exceeded $1 billion.

47

COMPUTER GRAPHICS IN THE 1980s

During the early 1980s, SIGGRAPH really took off. Catmull explains: "SIGGRAPH was a very good organization. It was fortuitous to have the right people doing the right things at the right time. It became one of the very best organizations, where there is a lot of sharing and a lot of openness. Over the years, it generated a tremendous amount of excitement, and it was a way of getting a whole group of people to work together and share information; and it is still that way today."

At the 1980 SIGGRAPH conference, a stunning film titled *Vol Libre* was shown. It was a computer-generated, high-speed flight through rugged fractal mountains. For this film, a programmer from Boeing named Loren Carpenter had studied the research of Benoit Mandelbrot and applied it to the simulation of realistic fractal mountains.

Carpenter had been working in the Boeing Computer Services department since 1966, when he was an undergraduate at the University of Washington. Beginning around 1972, he started using the University's engineering library to follow the tech-

nical papers being published on computer graphics. He eventually worked his way into a group at Boeing that was working on a computer-aided drawing system. This finally got him access to computer-graphics equipment. There he developed various rendering algorithms and published papers on them.

In the late '70s, Carpenter was creating 3-D rendered models of aircraft designs, and he wanted some scenery to go with his airplanes. He read Mandelbrot's book, but he was immediately disappointed when he found that the formulas were not practical for what he had in mind. Around this time, *Star Wars* had been released and, being a big fan of the sci-fi imagination, Carpenter had long dreamed of creating some type of alien landscape. The film compelled him to actually do it, and by 1979 he had a new idea how to create fractal terrain in animation.

In 1979, Carpenter learned that Ed Catmull had just been hired by George Lucas to set up a lab at Lucasfilm. Carpenter was immediately interested, but he didn't want to send in his resume yet, because he was still working on his fractal mountain movie. "At the time, they were getting enough resumes to kill a horse," explains Carpenter.

Carpenter continues: "I wanted to demonstrate that these (fractal) pictures would not only look good but would animate

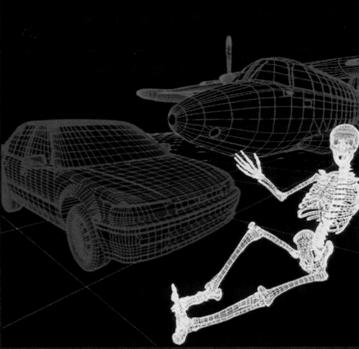

Image courtesy of Viewpoint.

well, too. After solving the technical difficulties, I made the movie, wrote a paper to describe it, and made a bunch of still images. I happened to be on the A/V crew of SIGGRAPH 1980, so one of my pictures ended up on an A/V T-shirt. I had this campaign to become as visible as possible, because I wanted to work at Lucasfilm, and when I showed my film, the people from Lucasfilm were there in the audience. Afterward they spoke to me and said, 'You're in—we want you.'" In 1981, Carpenter wrote the first renderer for Lucasfilm, called REYES (Renders Everything You Ever Saw). REYES would eventually turn into the Renderman rendering engine. Today, Carpenter is with Pixar, the computer-graphics spin-off of Lucasfilm.

Turner Whitted published a paper in 1980 about a new rendering technique for simulating highly reflective surfaces. Known today as *ray tracing*, it makes the computer trace every ray of light, starting from the viewer's perspective, that would strike the objects in the 3-D scene. If an object happens to be reflective, the computer follows the ray of light as it bounces off the object until it hits something else. This process continues until the ray of light hits an opaque, non-reflective surface or it goes shooting off away from the scene. As you can imagine, ray tracing is extremely computer-intensive. Indeed, some 3-D animation programmers (such as the Yost Group, which created 3D Studio) refuse to put ray tracing into their software. On the other hand, the realism that can be achieved with ray tracing is spectacular.

Around 1980, Steven Lisberger, a traditional animator, and Donald Kushner, a lawyer-turned-movie-distributor, decided to do a film about a fantasy world inside a video game. Lisberger and Kushner put together a presentation and sought backing from the major film companies around Los Angeles. To their surprise, Tom Wilhite, a new production chief at Disney, took them up on the idea. After some additional presentations to Disney executives, they were given the OK to proceed.

The movie, called *Tron*, was to be a fantasy about a man's journey inside a computer.

It called for nearly 30 minutes of film-quality computer graphics—a daunting task for computer-animation studios at the time. The solution was to split up the various sequences and farm them out to different production houses. The two major houses were Triple I and MAGI (Mathematical Applications Group Inc.). Also involved were Digital Effects of New York and Robert Abel & Associates.

The computer-generated imagery for *Tron* was very good. Unfortunately, the movie as a whole was very bad. Disney had sunk about $20 million into the picture, and it bombed at the box office. This had a strong negative impact on Hollywood's attitude toward computer graphics. Triple I had created computer animation for other movies (such as *Looker* in 1980), but after *Tron*, they sold off their computer-graphics operation. Demos and Whitney left to form a new computer-graphics company called Digital Productions in 1981.

Digital Productions had just gotten s t a r t e d when it

landed its first major film contract. It was to create the special effects for a sci-fi movie called *The Last Starfighter*. For *Starfighter*, everyone made sure that the story was passable before generating any computer animation. Digital Productions invested in a Cray X-MP supercomputer to help process the computer-graphics frames. The effects themselves were very impressive and photo-realistic; however, the movie cost $14 million to make and only grossed about $21 million, which was just enough to classify as a "B" grade movie by Hollywood standards, so it didn't make Hollywood sit up and take notice of computer graphics.

In 1980, a Stanford educated engineer named Carl Rosendahl launched a computer-animation studio in Sunnyvale, California, called Pacific Data Images (PDI). A year later, Richard Chuang, one of his partners, wrote some anti-aliasing rendering code that led to a significant increase in PDI's client base. While other computer-animation studios were focusing on film, PDI concentrated solely on television-network ID's, such as the openings for movie-of-the-week programs. This enabled them to establish a significant niche for themselves.

50

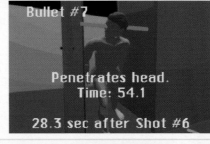

Bullet #7

Penetrates head.
Time: 54.1

28.3 sec after Shot #6

In 1981, Chris Woods set up a pioneering computer-graphics department at R/Greenberg Associates in New York.

In August of 1981, IBM introduced its first personal computer, the IBM PC. The IBM PC, while not the most technologically advanced personal computer, introduced PCs into the business community in a serious way. It used the Intel 16-bit 8088 microprocessor and offered 10 times the memory of other personal-computer systems. From that point on, personal computers became serious tools that business needed, and sales skyrocketed.

Another major milestone for computer graphics in the 1980s was the 1982 founding of Silicon Graphics, Inc. (SGI), by Jim Clark. SGI focused its resources on creating the highest performance graphics computers. These systems offered built-in 3-D graphics capabilities, high-speed RISC (reduced instruction set chip) processors and symmetrical (multiple processor) architectures. In 1983, SGI rolled out its first complete system, the IRIS 1000 graphics terminal.

In 1982, Lucasfilm signed up with Atari for a first-of-its-kind venture between a film studio and video-game company. They created a home-video game based on the Lucas/Spielberg hit movie *Raiders of the Lost Ark*. They also developed arcade games and computer software together. Some of Lucasfilm's games included PHM Pegasus, Koronis Rift, Labyrinth, Ballblazer, Rescue on Fractalus, and Strike Fleet. They also developed a networked game called Habitat that is still very popular in Japan. Today, the LucasArts division of Lucasfilm creates the video games and is one of the world's most high-profile users of 3-D computer animation.

In 1982, John Walker, Dan Drake, and eleven other programmers established Autodesk, Inc., a dominating presence in computer-aided design. That same year, they released AutoCAD version 1 for S-100 and Z-80 based computers at COMDEX (Computer Dealers Exposition). Autodesk shipped AutoCAD for the IBM PC and Victor 9000 personal computers the following year. The company's yearly sales would rise from $15,000 in 1983 to $353.2 million dollars in 1993.

At Lucasfilm, motion-picture special effects were handled by the Industrial Light and Magic (ILM) division; yet at first, they didn't want much to do with computer graphics. Catmull explains: "They considered what we where doing as too low of a resolution for film. They felt it didn't have the quality, and they weren't

52

Image courtesy of Softdesk.

really believers in it. There wasn't an antagonistic relationship between us—we got along well. It was just that they didn't see computer graphics as being up to their standards. However, as we developed the technology, we did do a couple pieces, such as the Death Star projection for *Return of the Jedi*. It was only a single special effect, yet it came out looking great." (For one scene in *Return of the Jedi* in 1983, Lucasfilm created a wire-frame "hologram" of the Death Star that was under construction and protected by a force field.)

The computer-graphics division of Lucasfilm was next offered a special-effects sequence for the movie *Star Trek II: The Wrath of Khan*. There was an effect that could have been done either traditionally or with computer-generated imagery. The screenplay called for the actors to go into a room containing a coffin-shaped case in which there was a lifeless rock. In the original story, the "Genesis" machine would then shoot this rock and make it look green and lifelike. ILM, however, didn't think this would be very impressive, so they went to the computer-graphics division and asked if they could generate the effect of the rock becoming lifelike. Alvy Ray Smith came back and said, "Instead of having this rock in front of this glass box, why don't we do what's meant to be a computer simulation and a program showing how it works for the whole planet?" ILM decided to go with Smith's idea, and they generated a minute-long sequence. It

was largely successful because within the story itself it was meant to be a computer-generated image, so it didn't need to have the final touches of realism added to it. The effect was rendered on Carpenter's new rendering engine, REYES. It turned out to be a very, very successful piece. As Smith would later say, "I call it 'the effect that never dies.' It appeared in three successive *Star Trek* movies, Reebok and other commercials, the Sci-Fi channel—you see it everywhere."

Following the "Genesis" effect, Lucasfilm used computer graphics for the movie *Young Sherlock Holmes*. In this movie, a stained-glass window comes to life to terrorize a priest.

At the 1982 SIGGRAPH conference, Tom Brigham, a programmer and animator at NYIT, astounded the audience. Tom Brigham had created a video sequence showing a woman distorted and transformed into the shape of a lynx. Thus was born a new technique called *morphing*. It was destined to become an important tool for anyone producing computer graphics or special effects in the film or television industries. However, despite the impressive response of viewers at the conference, no one else seemed to pay much attention the technique until 1987, when Lucasfilm used morphing in the movie *Willow* for a scene in which a sorceress is transformed through a series of animals into her final shape as a human.

Scott Fischer, Brenda Laurel, Jaron Lanier, and Thomas Zimmerman were some of the key people at the Atari Research Center (ARC) during the '80s. Jaron Lanier, while working as an Atari programmer, developed the DataGlove in 1983. The DataGlove is a device that fits over the user's hand to detect and transmit hand movements to the computer. The computer interprets the data and enables the user to manipulate objects in 3-D space within a computer simulation. Lanier left Atari later that year and teamed up with Jean Jacques Grimaud; together they founded a company in 1985 called VPL Research, which would develop and market some of the first commercial virtual-reality products. Thomas Zimmerman, an MIT graduate who had developed the "Air Guitar" software and a DataGlove that enabled the user to play a virtual guitar, also joined VPL Research.

AT&T formed the Electronic Photography and Imaging Center (EPIC) in 1984 to create PC-based videographic products. In the following year, the company released the TARGA video adapter for personal computers. This enabled PC users for the first time to display and manipulate 32-bit color images on the screen. EPIC also published the .TGA Targa file format for storing these true-color images.

Initially, computer-animation companies such as Triple-I, Digital Productions, Lucasfilm, etc., had to write their own software. However, this began to change in 1984 with the opening of a new company in Santa Barbara, California, called Wavefront. Wavefront produced the first commercially available 3-D animation system to run on off-the-shelf hardware. Wavefront started a revolution that would shape the future of all computer-animation studios. In that same year, Thomson Digital Image (TDI) was founded by three engineers working for Thomson CSF, a large defense contractor. TDI released its first 3-D animation software in 1986.

Up until this point, all of the available image-synthesis methods were based on *incidental light*, wherein a light source is depicted as shining directly on a surface. However, most of the light we see in the real world is *diffuse*, that is, light reflected from surfaces. In your home, you may have halogen lamps that shine incidental light on the ceiling, but then the ceiling reflects diffuse light onto the rest of the room. If you were going to create a 3-D computer version of the room, you might place a light source in the lamp, shining up on the ceiling. However, the rest of the room would appear dark if the software was based on direct, incidental light. To solve this problem, a new rendering method was needed, and in 1984, Cindy Goral, Don Greenberg, and others at Cornell University published a paper called "Modeling the Interaction of Light Between Diffuse Surfaces." The paper described a new method called *radiosity*, which uses the same formulas that simulate the way heat is dispersed throughout a room to determine how light reflects between surfaces. By determining the exchange of radiant energy between 3-D surfaces, very realistic results are possible.

In January 1984, Apple Computer released the first Macintosh computer. It was the first personal computer to use a graphical interface. The Mac was based on the Motorola microprocessor and used a single floppy drive, 128 KB of memory, a 9" high resolution screen, and a mouse. It would become the best-selling non–IBM-compatible personal-computer line ever introduced, and it remains a popular choice for graphics applications.

Around 1985, the concept of *multimedia computing* started to make its big entrance. The International Standards Organization (ISO) created the first standard for Compact Discs with Read-Only Memory (CD-ROM). This new standard was called High Sierra, after the area near Lake Tahoe where ISO created the standard. (This standard later changed into the ISO 9660 standard.) CD-ROM drives can store such memory-intensive data as digitized music and full-motion video much more easily than floppy disks. Today, with CD-ROM drives on nearly half of all new PCs sold, multimedia computing is a major application for 3-D animation. Also in 1985, Commodore launched the new Amiga personal computer line. The Amiga remains a favorite of many computer animators and video-production companies. It offers several advanced features, including hardware-level compatibility with the IBM personal computer line. The Amiga uses Motorola's 68000 microprocessor and has its own proprietary operating system. The base unit's retail price is $1,295.

In 1986 in Montreal, Daniel Langlois founded a company called Softimage to fulfill his vision of a commercial 3-D computer-animation program. The Softimage software was released at the 1988 SIGGRAPH show and it quickly became the animation standard in Europe, with over 1,000 installations worldwide by 1993.

In the late '80s, Jim Henson (of Muppets fame) approached Brad DeGraf at Digital Productions with the idea of creating a digital puppet. Henson brought with him a "Waldo" unit that he had previously used to remotely control one of his puppets. The device had gotten its name, Waldo, from NASA engineers years earlier. NASA had taken the name from a 1940s sci-fi book by Robert A. Heinlein about a disabled scientist who built a

robot to amplify his limited abilities. The scientist's name was Waldo.

The programmers at Digital Productions managed to hook up the Waldo and create animation with it, but the animation was never used for a commercial project. Nonetheless, the idea of using mechanical devices to capture motion, now known as *motion capture*, was born. Today, motion capture continues to be a major component in creating computer animation.

For Digital Productions, the mid-1980s were a growth period. The company had purchased a Cray X-MP supercomputer because it was the fastest computer that

money could buy. They were interfacing film recording and scanning equipment and had about 75 to 100 employees. They had just finished their first big movie project, *The Last Starfighter*, and they did some special effects for the movie *2010* (such as the swirling surface of Jupiter). They also worked on *Labyrinth* in 1986. Things were going very well for Digital Productions—perhaps too well.

In 1986, Digital and Robert Abel & Associates, the two largest computer animation houses in the United States, were bought out by Omnibus Computer Graphics, Inc., in hostile takeovers. Both companies had invested heavily in high-end super-computers

like the Cray X-MP (which cost about $13 million each). They had put their focus on buying the fastest number-crunchers money could buy and then creating their own custom software.

As soon as Omnibus took control of Digital Productions, the two co-founders of Digital, John Whitney and Gary Demos, sued the majority owner of Omnibus, Santa Clara-based Ramtek, for a portion of the sale proceeds. Omnibus subsequently locked both of them out of their offices at Digital Productions. In September 1986, Omnibus obtained a temporary restraining order against Whitney and Demos, alleging that the two had founded a competing firm, Whitney Demos Productions, and had hired at least three employees away from Omnibus and were using software and other information that rightly belonged to Omnibus. The restraining order required Whitney and Demos to temporarily return certain property to Omnibus.

Soon after acquiring Robert Abel & Associates in October 1986, Omnibus started defaulting on the $30 million it had borrowed from several major Canadian creditors. Most of the debts were the result of acquiring the Digital and Abel compa-

nies. In May 1987, Omnibus officially closed down and laid off all its employees.

According to Gary Demos, "Abel & Associates was sunk just the same as us. At the time, we were the two largest effects studios, and that crash fragmented the entire industry. It changed the whole character of the development of computer graphics." Talented people from both studios nonetheless found their way into other animation houses. Jim Rigel went to Boss Films. Art Durenski went to a studio in Japan. Some went to PDI, some went to Philips Interactive Media (then known as American Interactive Media), and others went to Rhythm & Hues, Metrolight, or Lucasfilm. Whitney and Demos created Demos Productions. Demos Productions lasted for two years; then they split up and formed their own companies in 1988. Whitney formed U.S. Animation Labs, while Demos formed DemoGraphics.

In the personal-computer field, animation software was booming. In 1986, Crystal Graphics introduced TOPAS, one of the first high-quality 3-D animation programs for personal computers. Over the years, Crystal Graphics would continue to be a major player in the PC-based 3-D animation field. The following year, Electric Image was founded and released a 3-D-animation package for both SGI machines and Apple Macintosh computers. In

Mountain View, California, a new 3-D software company was founded under the name Octree Software, Inc. The company later changed its name to Caligari Corporation and now offers 3-D animation programs for both the Amiga and PC platforms.

Also in 1986, computer graphics found a new venue: the courtroom. Known as *forensic animation*, these computer graphics are more geared to technical accuracy than to visual aesthetics. Forensic Technologies, Inc., started using computer graphics to help jurors visualize events that were pertinent to court cases. Today the company uses SGI workstations, from RS-4000s up through the high-end Crimson Reality Engines. For their 3-D software, they exclusively use Wavefront but have a few interfaces to CAD modeling packages. For 2-D animation, they use a program called Matador by Parallax.

In 1986, Disney animators made their first use of computer graphics, in the film *The Great Mouse Detective*. In this first Disney attempt at merging computer graphics and hand-drawn cel animation, they only used the computer for some of the mechanical devices depicted in the scenes, such as gears and clockworks. A Computer Generated Imagery (CGI) department was formed at Disney and eventually worked on such films as *Oliver and Company*, *The Little Mermaid*, *The Rescuers Down Under*, *Beauty and the Beast*, and *Aladdin*. With the highly successful results of *Aladdin* and *Beauty and the Beast*,

56

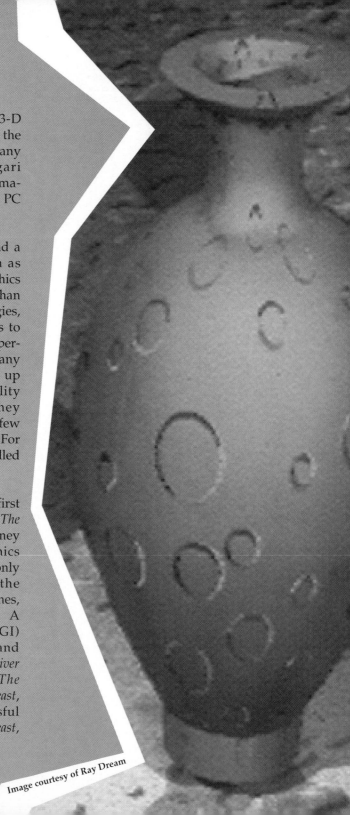

Image courtesy of Ray Dream

Disney has increased the number of animators in the CGI department from only 2 to 14.

About this time, things at Lucasfilm were getting a little complicated. The computer-graphics division wanted to do a feature-length computer-animated film, while ILM was mostly interested in the potential of computer-graphics effects within the confines of traditional film making. Catmull explains, "Lucas felt this company was getting a little too wide, and he wanted to narrow the focus into what he was doing as a filmmaker. Our goals weren't really quite consistent with his." So the computer-graphics division asked if they could spin off as a separate company, and Lucas agreed to do that.

The transition process took about a year. Catmull continues: "One of the last things I did was hire two people to come in and start a [new] CGI group for ILM, because they still wanted CGI special-effects capabilities. I went out to a number of people, but mainly focused on Doug Kay and George Joblove. They turned us down the first time. We talked to them and interviewed them, and they called up and said 'We decided not to come up, because we have our own company.' So I put down the phone and thought 'Damn, I have to keep on looking.' Then that night I called back again, and said 'Doug, you're crazy! This is the opportunity of a lifetime! Something went wrong in the interview. Come back up here and let's do this thing again.' He said OK, so I brought him up

again. We went through it all again, and this time they accepted."

The original computer-graphics division of ILM split off to become Pixar in 1986. Part of the deal was that Lucasfilm would get continued access to Pixar's rendering technology. It took about a year to separate Pixar from Lucasfilm, and in the process, Steve Jobs became a majority stockholder. Ed Catmull became president and Alvy Ray Smith became vice-president. Pixar continued to develop their renderer, eventually turning it into Renderman.

Created in 1988, Renderman is a standardized software specification for describing 3-D scenes. Pat Hanrahan of Pixar sorted out most of the technical details behind Renderman and gave it its name. (Since then, Hanrahan has moved to Princeton University, where he is currently an associate professor of computer science.)

The Renderman standard describes everything the computer needs to know before simulating a 3-D scene, such as the objects, light sources, cameras, atmospheric effects, and so on. Once a scene is converted to a Renderman file, it can be rendered on a variety of systems, from Macs to PCs to Silicon Graphics workstations. This new standard opened up many possibilities for 3-D computer-graphics software developers. Developers could simply bundle a Renderman rendering engine with their modeling packages and not worry about writing their own renderers. When the initial specification was announced, over 19

firms endorsed it, including Apollo, Autodesk, Sun Microsystems, NeXT, MIPS, Prime, and the Walt Disney Company.

An integral part of Renderman is the use of *shaders*—small pieces of programming code for describing surfaces, lighting effects, and atmospheric effects. Surface shaders are small programs that algorithmically generate textures based on mathematical formulas. These algorithmic textures are sometimes called *procedural* textures or *spatial* textures. Not only is the texture generated by the computer, but it is also generated in 3-D space. Whereas most texture-mapping techniques map the texture to the outside skin of the object, procedural textures run completely through the object in 3-D. Thus, if you were using a fractal-based procedural texture of wood grain on a cube, and then you cut out a section of the cube, you would see the wood grain running through the cube.

Interestingly, Kay and Joblove and their associates at the ILM CGI division became so efficient and the CGI group grew so fast that today the CGI group *is* ILM. One of the reasons the CGI group became so important is that it succeeded in what it intended to do. They set goals and budgets, and they met them.

Meanwhile, back at Pixar, Steve Jobs stepped down from his post as chairman in December 1988, and Ed Catmull took his place. Charles Kolstad, the company's VP of manufacturing and engineering, became the new president.

Paul Sidlo worked as creative director for Cranston/Csuri Productions from 1982 until 1987, when he left to form his own computer-graphics studio, ReZ.n8 (pronounced "resonate"). Since then, ReZ.n8 has been a leader in producing high-quality computer animation, attracting such clients as ABC, CBS, Fox, ESPN, NBC, and most of the major film studios.

Jeff Kleiser had been a computer animator at Omnibus, where he directed animation for the Disney feature film *Flight of the Navigator*. Before working at Omnibus, Kleiser had founded Digital Effects and worked on such projects as *Tron* and *Flash Gordon*. As things started to fall apart at Omnibus, he did some research into motion capture. When Omnibus closed, he joined up with Diana Walczak and formed a new company, Kleiser-Walczak Construction Company. Their new firm's specialty was human-figure animation. In 1988, they produced a 3-1/2 minute music video with a computer-generated character named Dozo. They used motion control to input all of Dozo's movements.

Brad DeGraf, also from Omnibus, joined forces with Michael Wahrman to form the DeGraf/Wahrman Production company. At the SIGGRAPH conference of 1988, they showed "Mike the Talking Head," which was an interactive, 3-D, computer-animated head. Using special controls, they were able to make it interact with the conference participants. Later DeGraf would leave Wahrman and go to work for Colossal Pictures in San Francisco.

The Pixar Animation Group made history on March 29, 1989, by winning an Academy Award for their animated short film, *Tin Toy*. The film was created completely with 3-D computer graphics using Pixar's Renderman. John Lasseter directed the film, with William Reeves providing technical direction.

At the 1989 SIGGRAPH in Boston, Autodesk unveiled a new PC- based animation package called Autodesk Animator. As a full-featured 2-D animation and painting package, Animator was Autodesk's first venture in the realm of multimedia tools. Its animation-playback capabilities were impressively fast, and the product soon became a standard for playing animation on PCs.

In 1989, James Cameron wrote and directed an underwater adventure movie called *The Abyss* that would have a tremendous impact on the field of CGI for motion pictures. Cameron came to the project with a specific idea for a special effect. He wanted a water creature, something like a fat snake, to emerge from a pool of water, extend itself, and interact with live characters. He felt that it couldn't be done with traditional special-effects tools, so he put the effect up for bid. Both Pixar and ILM bid on the project. ILM won the bid, although they used Pixar's software to create the effect.

Cameron viewed this effect as a test piece, and if it didn't work out, he could have done the movie without it. But it did work, and it worked so well and had so much of an impact, it convinced him that computer-generated imagery could create a major character in his next film: the influential *Terminator 2*.

COMPUTER GRAPHICS IN THE 1990S

In May 1990, Microsoft shipped Windows 3.0. It had a graphical user interface that was similar to that of the Macintosh, and it laid the foundation for future growth in PC multimedia. In 1990, only two of the nation's top 10 best-selling software programs ran under Windows; just one year later, this figure rose to nine out of 10.

In October 1990, Alias Research signed a $2.3 million contract with ILM. The deal called for Alias to supply 3-D, state-of-the-art computer-graphics systems to ILM for future video production. ILM, in turn, would test these new systems under real-world conditions and provide feedback.

Also in October 1990, the NewTek company released the Video Toaster. The Video Toaster is a video-production card for Amiga personal computers that retails for $1,595. The card comes with 3-D animation and 24-bit paint software, and it offers video capabilities such as a 24-bit frame buffer, switching, digital video effects, and character generation. The practical video-editing capabilities of the Video Toaster made it immediately popular, and today it is used for 3-D animation in such television shows as *Sea Quest* and *Babylon 5*.

In 1990, Autodesk shipped its first 3D computer-animation product, 3D Studio. Created for Autodesk by Gary Yost (of the Yost Group), 3D Studio is today the leader in PC-based 3-D computer-animation software.

Disney and Pixar announced an agreement in 1991 to create within two to three years the first computer-animated, full-length feature film. This project would fulfill the dreams of those early NYIT researchers. Pixar's animation group, with the success of their popular Listerine, Lifesavers, and Tropicana commercials, had the confidence that they could pull off the project on time and on budget. The film is on track and should be released in the fall of 1994.

James Cameron's landmark *Terminator 2* (a.k.a. *T2*) was released in 1991 and set a new standard for CGI special effects. The image of the evil T-1000 robot in *T2* alternated between the actor Robert Patrick and a 3-D computer-animated version of Patrick. Not only were the graphics photorealistic, but the effects were produced on time and under budget.

In that same year, another major film was released in which CGI played a large role: *Beauty and the Beast.* Having enjoyed success with computer-generated imagery in several earlier films, Disney pulled out all the stops and used computer animation throughout the movie. In terms of color and design, the Disney animators did things in this movie that they could not possibly have done without computers. Many scenes contained 3-D animated objects, yet they were flat-shaded with bright colors so as to blend in with the hand-drawn characters. The crowning achievement was a dance sequence in a photo-realistic ballroom, complete with a 3-D crystal chandelier and 158 individual light sources to simulate candles.

The effect that these two movies had on Hollywood was significant. Catmull

59

explains: "In 1991, *Beauty and the Beast* came out, *Terminator 2* came out, and Disney announced that they had entered into a relationship with us to do a feature-length computer-animated film for them. *Beauty* and *T2* where phenomenal financial successes, and all of the sudden, *everybody* noticed. That was the turning point—all the ground work that other people had been doing hadn't been noticed before. It all turned around in 1991. It was the year when the whole entertainment industry said 'Oh my God!' and it took them by storm. Then they all started forming groups and alliances."

Early in 1991, the hardware business failed for Pixar, "we were run over by the workstation companies" explains Ed Catmull "So we sold the hardware business and gave the axe to all hardware development at Pixar. We had underlying technology and applications, so Steve had a number of options available and one of them was to spin out the software, although he really didn't want to do that. So he gave the group a short period of time (30 days) to put together a reasonable deal. They went out and talked with venture capitalists and they weren't excited enough to do it. So there wasn't any reasonable interest within that 30-day period." About a year later, Alvy Ray Smith wrote an image editing tool and decided to spin off to form a new company called Altamira (with both Pixar

and Autodesk as partners). That product is now on the market under the name Composer.

Meanwhile, six developers from Walt Disney's Feature Animation department and three developers from Pixar received Technical Awards for their work on CAPS. CAPS is a 2-D animation system, owned by Disney, that simplifies and automates much of the complex post-production aspects of creating full-length cartoon animations.

In 1993, Wavefront acquired Thomson Digital Image (TDI), which significantly increased Wavefront's market share in the high-end computer-animation market. Wavefront immediately begin integrating products from TDI into its own line of computer-graphics software.

Early in 1993, IBM joined forces with James Cameron, special-effects expert Stan Winston, and ILM visual-effects executive Scott Ross to create a new visual-effects and digital-production studio called Digital Domain. Located in the Los Angeles area, Digital Domain hopes to give ILM a run for its money. Not to be outdone, ILM followed with an announcement that it was forming a joint "media lab" with Silicon Graphics, Inc., called JEDI (Joint Environment for Digital Imaging). Under this agreement, ILM would get the latest SGI hardware and SGI would get to use ILM as a testing facility.

PDI opened its Digital Opticals Group in Hollywood to create special effects for motion pictures such as *Terminator 2*, *Batman Returns*, and *The Babe*. PDI has become a one of the leaders in digital clean-up work, such as wire removal, for motion pictures. Often, wires are used for special effects such as people flying or jumping through the air, or sometimes scratches occur on irreplaceable film footage. For *Terminator 2*, PDI used image-processing technology to erase the wires that guided Arnold Schwarzenegger and

his motorcycle over a perilous jump. PDI uses software to automatically copy pixels from the background and paste them over the pixels that represent the wires.

Another edit for *T2* involved a semi truck crashing through a wall and down into a storm ditch. The original shot was made at an inappropriate angle. The director wanted the footage flipped left to right, to keep the continuity consistent with surrounding shots. Normally this would not be a problem, yet in this instance a street sign was in the picture, and the driver could be seen through the windshield of the truck. These

elements prevented the normal flip that any studio editing facility could have performed. To solve this, PDI first flipped the footage. Then they cut the sign from the unflipped footage and pasted it over the top of the flipped sign. Then they copied and pasted the driver from the left side of the truck to the right side. The finished sequence looked flawless.

PDI performed additional sleight-of-hand tricks for the movie *The Babe*, a bio-pic about baseball legend Babe Ruth. A number of challenges faced the producers, one of which was that the star of the movie, John Goodman, is righthanded, while Babe Ruth was lefthanded. As you can imagine, this really compromised the scenes where Goodman had to throw the ball. To resolve this problem, PDI used digital image processing.

To create the effect of a pitch, Goodman simply mimed the action without using a ball. Then the director filmed a lefthanded pitcher throwing the ball from the same position. The baseball from the second shot was then composited onto the first shot. However, the actor playing the catcher had to fake it along with Goodman, and the result was often that he didn't catch the ball at the same time it arrived. To solve this problem, the image was split down the middle and the catcher from the second shot was merged into the first shot. This resulted in a flawless left-handed fastball. "Clean-up" special effects such as this have become a mainstay for computer animation studios in the '80s and '90s.

Recently, Nintendo announced an agreement with Silicon Graphics, Inc. (the leader in computer graphics technology), to produce a 64-bit 3-D Nintendo platform for home use. The first product from "Project Reality" will be an arcade game to be released in 1994, while a home version will follow in late 1995. The home system's target price is $250.

In 1992, Steven Spielberg started working on a film version of the Michael Crichton bestseller *Jurassic Park*. Since the movie was basically about dinosaurs chasing (and eating) people, the special effects presented quite a challenge. Originally, Spielberg was going to take the traditional route, hiring Stan Winston to create full scale models and robots of the dinosaurs, and hiring Phil Tippett to create stop-motion animation of the dinosaurs running and any other movements where their legs would leave the ground.

Tippett is perhaps the foremost expert on stop-motion and is the inventor of go-motion photography. *Go-motion* is a method of adding motion blur to stop-motion characters by using a computer to move the characters slightly while they are being filmed. This new go-motion technique eliminates most of the jerkiness normally associated with stop-motion. For

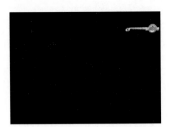

example, the original *King Kong* movie simply used stop-motion and the result was very jerky. *ET*, on the other hand, used Tippett's go-motion technique for the flying-bicycle scene, and the result was very smooth motion. Tippett went to work on *Jurassic Park* and created a test walk-cycle for a running dinosaur. It came out OK, but was not spectacular.

At the same time, animators at ILM began experimenting on other dinosaur simulations. There was a stampeding herd of gallimimus dinosaurs in a scene that Spielberg had decided to cut from the movie because it would have been impossible to create an entire herd of go-motion dinosaurs running at the same time. However, Eric Armstrong, an animator at ILM, experimented by creating the skeleton of the dinosaur and then animating a walk cycle for it. Then he copied that walk cycle and made 10 other dinosaurs running in the same scene. It looked so good that everyone at ILM was stunned. They showed it to Spielberg and he couldn't believe it. Immediately he put the scene back into the movie.

Next the ILM technicians tackled the animation of the Tyrannosaurus rex. Steve Williams created a walk-cycle and trans-

ferred the animation directly to film. The results were fantastic, and the full-motion dinosaur shots were switched from Tippett's studio to the computer graphics department at ILM.

The increasing quality of computer-generated imagery was a tremendous blow to the stop-motion animators. Tippett was later quoted in *ON production and post-production* magazine as saying, "We were reticent about the computer-graphic animators' ability to create believable creatures, but we thought it might work for long shots like the stampede sequence." However, as it progressed to the point where the CGI dinosaurs looked better than the go-motion dinosaurs, it was a different story. He continues: "When it was demonstrated that on a photographic and kinetic level this technology could work, I felt like my world had disintegrated. I am a practitioner of a traditional craft, and I take it very seriously. It looked like the end."

However, Tippett's skills were very much needed by the computer animators. In order to create realistic movement for the dinosaurs, Tippett and the ILM crew developed the Dinosaur Input Device (DID). The DID was an articulated dinosaur model with motion sensors attached to its limbs. As the traditional stop-motion animators moved the model, the movement was sent to the computer

and recorded. This animation was then touched up and refined by the ILM animators until it was perfect. Eventually, 15 shots were done with the DID, and 35 shots were done using standard computer-animation methods.

The animators at ILM worked closely with Stan Winston, using his dinosaur designs so the CGI dinosaurs would match the full-scale models Winston was creating. Alias Animator was used to model the dinosaurs, and the animation was created using Softimage software. The dinosaur skins were created using hand-painted texture maps along with custom Renderman surface shaders. The final dinosaur sequence in the movie, a showdown between the tyrannosaurus rex and the velociraptors, was added at the last minute by Spielberg because he could see that ILM's graphics would produce a realistic sequence. The results were spectacular and the movie earned ILM another special-effects Oscar in March 1994.

In February 1994, Microsoft Corporation acquired Softimage for $130 million. Microsoft's initial use of TDI technology will be internal, to enhance their multimedia CD-ROM products and interactive TV programs. Microsoft also plans to port the Softimage software to its Windows NT operating system. This may start a trend of shifting high-end graphics software from workstations to personal computers.

Image courtesy of Macromedia.

Chapter Summary

Animation has certainly come a long way from the zoetrope and the other parlor toys of the 19th century. Considering the quality and realism that we see in computer graphics today, it's hard to imagine that this field didn't exist just 30 years ago. Yet even today, exhibitors at the SIGGRAPH conference continue to excite and amaze the computer-graphics community with new techniques. And while companies have come and gone over the years, the key people have not. Most of the early pioneers are still active in the industry and just as enthusiastic about the technology as they were when they first started. Most of the pioneers discussed in this chapter can be reached on the Internet or by simply calling the companies they work for. As an educational opportunity, this is like being an apprentice artist and picking up the phone to call Monet, Michelangelo, Renoir, or Rembrandt.

3

Computer TOOLS

Chapter

Today there is no need to develop your own 3-D computer graphics software as many did just a decade ago. The market is flooded with software, ranging in price from $199 to $80,000. This software runs on a variety of machines, from personal computers costing under $1,000 to UNIX-based workstations costing over $100,000. In this chapter, we will discuss the hardware and software that are currently available for 3-D animation.

The hardware market can be divided into two main categories: high-end and low-end. Only three major hardware vendors, Silicon Graphics (SGI), Sun Microsystems, and IBM, offer high-end hardware. Three hardware platforms, IBM PC (and compatibles), Apple Macintosh, and Commodore Amiga, are available on the low end.

Software products abound, and often you can purchase the same software for different platforms. Will Vinton's Playmation, for example, is available for SGI, Mac, PC, and Amiga platforms.

Your choice of tools, both hardware and software, depends somewhat on the type of animation you want to create. If you are creating computer animation for motion pictures, you should use high-end equipment that is fast enough to render images at the high resolution needed for film. For all other applications of computer graphics, such as video, forensic, architectural, multimedia, and pre-visualization, you can use either high-end or low-end. Personal computers certainly have more than enough power to produce broadcast-quality graphic images. Indeed, they do so on a weekly basis for shows such as *Babylon 5* and Steven Spielberg's *SeaQuest DSV*.

The choice really comes down to how much money you can spend on computer graphics. Regardless of the type of application, people who can afford high-end workstations usually get them. Companies that can afford high-end equipment use it, even though they may simply create 3-D computer graphics for video games or multimedia products that run on personal computers. This also means that when the artwork is finished it must be translated to a format that will work on a personal computer.

First we will consider the low-end hardware platforms that are available and then discuss the software available for each platform.

LOW-END TOOLS

As mentioned, three low-end hardware platforms are on the market: PC, Mac, and Amiga. These three platforms have several things in common. They all need a monitor and a video card. The *monitor* is the display screen, and the *video card* is the circuit board that plugs into the computer and connects to the monitor with cables. Computer graphics are generated on the video card and then sent to the monitor. Although you usually purchase both these items when you buy your system, they come from different manufacturers.

MONITORS

Many companies, such as Sony, Mitsubishi, and NEC, specialize in creating video monitors. These monitors are compatible with most personal computers and even some workstations. Before purchasing a monitor, you should consider screen size, frequency, and dot pitch.

SCREEN SIZE

Monitors range in size from 10" (diagonal) to over 27". The most common sizes are 14", 17", 20", and 21". If you are just getting started in computer graphics, don't worry about spending a lot of money for a large screen. The size of the screen has no relation to the quality of the computer graphics that you produce. The only benefit is that, when you create images, you can view much more detail on a larger monitor than on a smaller one. You can still see details on a small monitor, but you must zoom in first. Also, because 14" monitors account for more than 76 percent of the market while 17" monitors only account for about 5 percent, you can certainly find a much wider selection and more competitive prices with 14" monitors.

Prices range between $200 and $800 for 14" monitors, between $700 and $1,600 for 17", and over $1,800 for 21". You should expect to pay more than $4,000 for anything larger. Cost will probably determine the size monitor you choose.

FREQUENCY

Frequency is the major concern when purchasing a monitor. The speed of the signal that passes between the video adapter card and the monitor is called its frequency. When a video card sends graphics from the computer to the monitor, it does so at a specific frequency. This frequency depends on the resolution of the image being displayed. As with televisions and other video display technologies, an electron gun runs horizontally down the screen drawing one line at a time. When it reaches the bottom of the screen, it does a vertical retrace (returns to the top of the screen). Naturally, the higher the resolution of video signal, the more lines the electron gun must draw. If the screen is at a resolution of 1280×1024, the gun must draw twice as many lines as at a resolution of 640×480. This, in turn, means that twice as much data needs to come from the video card at twice the speed.

Computers can use the same trick that televisions use: an interlaced signal. *Interlaced signal* means that the electron gun must draw every other line on the way down the screen instead of every line. It then makes a second pass and fills in the missing lines. The interlaced signal thus requires two full passes of the electron gun, so the screen is updated at about half the normal speed. Because of this slow speed, you can see a slight flicker of the screen when it is running in interlaced mode. The advantage, however, sometimes outweighs the disadvantage of seeing a flicker, because the data can come from the video card at half the normal speed. This means you can purchase a less expensive monitor and less expensive video card and still get a high resolution picture (if you can put up with the flicker). Display resolutions for both monitors and video cards are often classified under *interlaced* and *noninterlaced*. Again, the screen size of the monitor has nothing to do with display resolution. You can display a 1024×768 resolution image on a 14" monitor just fine. The only problem is that the pixels may be a little small.

The graphics card sends a horizontal and vertical sync signal to the monitor to control the electron gun. The number of frames (sometimes called frame rate, vertical scanning frequency, or vertical refresh rate) is determined by the frequency and whether or not the signal is interlaced. As you can imagine, the horizontal sync signal is much faster than the vertical sync signal because the electron gun must

67

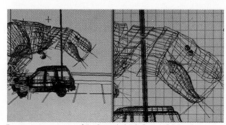

Images courtesy of Industrial Light and Magic.

move vertically only a little at the end of each line. Therefore the vertical frequency is described in hertz (Hz) and the horizontal frequency is expressed in kilohertz (kHz).

To identify the frequency of monitors, vendors usually use Hz (describing the vertical refresh rate). For a video resolution of 640×480, a vertical refresh rate of 60Hz is sufficient for a noninterlaced display. However, if you switch to a resolution of 1024×768 and stay at 60Hz, the display must switch to interlaced mode because the signal throughput isn't fast enough. For resolutions of 1024×768, we recommend that you have a vertical refresh rate of at least 72Hz to get a noninterlaced signal.

The two standard video resolutions are 640×480 and 1024×768. Some less expensive monitors are called *fixed frequency* because they only support these two resolutions. Thus even if your video card says it can work at 800×600 or 1280×1024 resolutions, a fixed-frequency monitor isn't capable of displaying it. For these in-between or extended resolutions, your monitor must be able to work at a variety of frequencies. Monitors with this capability are referred to as *multi-sync* (multiple horizontal and vertical sync signals). A multi-sync monitor adjusts itself to the frequency of the video card no matter what is thrown at it. Some monitors can reach very high refresh

rates. For instance, the Mitsubishi Diamond Scan monitor can go as high as 130Hz! The thing to remember is that the higher the vertical refresh rate (Hz), the better.

Dot Pitch

The *dot pitch* of a monitor is the measurement of how closely spaced the individual points of light are on the screen. Picture tubes use a *shadow mask,* which is a metal plate used to focus the electron beams onto red, green, and blue (RGB) phosphorous compounds. Holes in the shadow mask determine how close and sharp the combination of RGB dots appears on the screen. These "dots" are in groups of three (one for each of the colors: red, green, and blue). The holes are measured in millimeters. A dot pitch of .025mm is 25/100 of a millimeter vertically from the center of like-colored dots (say the green dot of one group to the green dot of its neighbor).

The Sony Trinitron picture tube is slightly different. Instead of round dots, it uses vertical strips, so the dot pitch is measured as the distance between the strips. Thus it is known as a *stripe mask* or *aperture mask* instead of a shadow mask. It is roughly comparable to a dot pitch.

Ideally, you want the smallest dot pitch available, but for a reasonable price, you can settle for anything up to a 0.28mm dot pitch. Don't go any larger than 0.28 because the screen appears fuzzy or out of focus. Again, remember that the monitor

has no relation whatsoever to the quality of your computer graphics. When you render your final images, they always go either to the computer's hard drive or to a video recorder of some sort. Remember, even if your screen is in low resolution and appears fuzzy, it in no way affects your graphic output.

In conclusion, your primary considerations in purchasing a monitor should be frequency, screen size, and dot pitch. Make sure you purchase a monitor that can run in noninterlaced mode for the resolution you will be working in most of the time. Get the largest screen size you can afford, and make sure the dot pitch does not exceed 0.28mm.

Image courtesy of Art Center College of Design and Jeff Hilbers.

VIDEO CARDS

Video cards win the prize for having the most names for a single product. They are referred to as video display cards, video adapter cards, display adapters, video adapters, graphics adapters, graphics cards, and video controllers. The most common of these seems to be *video card*, so that is the term we will use in this book.

The video card takes the digital information generated by the computer and converts it into an analog signal for the monitor. It also provides the appropriate connectors, so the analog signal can be sent from the computer to the monitor via a cable. The video card contains the frame

buffer, which is the large block of memory that stores, pixel by pixel, the contents of the current screen. The frame buffer contains the data that the video card converts to an analog signal for the monitor.

The three main considerations when evaluating video cards are resolution, color depth, and speed. Regardless of the personal computer platform you choose, you must decide the level of quality you need and can afford regarding these three aspects. The following sections provide information to help you in making these decisions.

RESOLUTION

Resolution refers to the dimensions (in pixels) of the screens the video-card is capable of displaying. Typically, video-card resolution is described at its highest capability. For example, a resolution of 1280×1024 often means that the card can run at all the common resolutions, from 320×200 to 1280×1024. Resolution has a direct relationship to the amount of memory in your video card. The more memory, the more pixels can be stored in its frame buffer. Likewise, the more memory, the more money the video card costs.

When purchasing a video card, don't be overly concerned with super-high resolutions. Although they provide a nice crisp look, you must have at least a 17" screen to make good use of resolutions that high. At such high resolutions very few video cards can run in noninterlaced mode. You will

probably only run the card in its highest noninterlaced resolution anyway, so don't waste your money.

COLOR DEPTH

When it comes to graphics, we use the terms *bit depth* and *color depth* to describe the number of colors a video card can produce. Since a bit can be in one of two states, "off" or "on" (0 or 1), it can store one of two possible colors in a pixel that has one bit assigned to it. Double that by assigning two bits per pixel and you raise the number of colors to four because two bits have four possible states between the two of them (00, 01, 10, 11). The following table shows the possible bit depths and the total number of colors for each.

Bit Depth	Number of Colors
1	2
2	4
4	16
8	256
16	64,000
24	16,700,000
32	16,700,000 + 256
64	16,700,000 + 256

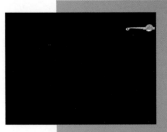

Notice that beyond a bit depth of 24 the number of colors remains the same at 16.7 million. This is because the human eye can't distinguish the difference between more than 16.7 million colors. The color is derived from three 8-bit *channels*, each containing 256 possible shades. The three channels represent red (256 possible shades), green (256 possible shades), and blue (256 possible shades). The total possible combinations of these 768 shades equals 16.7 million different colors.

There are some interesting tricks we can perform. For example, 32-bit graphics uses 24 bits to create the 16.7 million colors and has 8 bits (256 colors) left. The computer can use those extra 8 bits per pixel to specify how transparent that pixel is when it is overlaid on a different colored pixel. You can create a composite of separate images, even though the image you paste on top has some transparent item like a shadow or glass object. Using the extra transparency value, the computer can determine how much of the underlying image should show through for each pixel. This fourth channel is called the *alpha* channel.

The last color depth we mention, 64-bit, uses the extra data to help speed up animation and other graphics functions. While a few 64-bit cards are available for personal computers, they are most often found on workstations. Some workstations even

have 128-bit frame buffers, providing the ultimate in graphics performance.

For personal computer systems, 8-bit graphics has become the standard, but higher color depths are becoming more and more popular. It is reasonable to expect that 16.7 million colors will be standard on every desktop computer in the next couple of years. Of course, the greater the color depth, the more memory is required on the video card, and therefore the more expensive that video card is.

The combination of a resolution and a color depth such as 1024×768×256 is called a *video mode.* Most video cards support many different video modes. Some resolutions offer multiple color depths. If your video card can run at a resolution of 640×480 at a color depth of 8, 16, 24, or 32 bits and you are simply working with wireframe models and do not need a lot of color, you should use the video mode with the least amount of color. This speeds up the display since the less data the video card has to move, the faster it works. You can create 3-D computer graphics with an 8-bit (256 color) video card. It might be a good idea to start out with a less expensive card, but remember, every bit of color depth you can afford pays for itself. For serious animators, a 24-bit board should be the minimum.

SPEED

All of these aspects of video cards affect speed. High resolution means more pixels;

high color depth means more data. There are three methods to help the video card deal with this throughput issue: high-speed memory, a high-speed bus, and co-processors.

Memory

Some video cards now use *VRAM* (Video Random Access Memory) instead of normal *DRAM* (Dynamic Random Access Memory), which is used by the main computer. DRAM can do only one thing at a time, so when the video card is reading a DRAM frame buffer to send its contents to the monitor, the CPU cannot update the frame buffer at the same time. VRAM, on the other hand, can perform two functions at once. This allows the computer to write to the frame buffer at the same time the video card is reading the frame buffer and sending its contents to the monitor. This increases the overall performance, but naturally VRAM video cards are more expensive than DRAM video cards. If you are using a high color depth and high resolution video modes, you should consider video cards with VRAM.

Expansion Bus

Another way of speeding up video cards is to make sure they can communicate as quickly as possible with the computer's CPU. Video cards, like other computer peripherals, plug into a data bus. This data bus is the means of transmitting data between the CPU and the video card. While both Mac and Amiga platforms

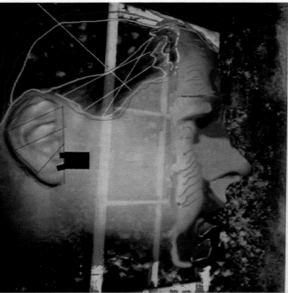

have their own proprietary bus, the PC platform has a variety of standards. As they say, "The nice thing about standards is that there are so many to choose from." Most personal computers come with a bus called ISA (Industry Standard Architecture), but it is very slow compared to the processing speeds of modern CPUs. A faster bus is the EISA (Enhanced Industry Standard Architecture), which allows faster throughput but is mainly geared toward hard disk controller cards and network interface cards.

Very few video cards work with the EISA bus. The next step is the Video Electronics Standards Association (VESA) local bus, and then the PCI (Peripheral Component Interconnect) bus. Both of these buses allow add-on cards to communicate directly with the CPU at its own speed. Local bus and PCI bus computers can dramatically increase the speed of your graphics and are well worth the extra expense.

Co-Processors

A fairly recent addition to the video card is some onboard intelligence. Many video cards now come with their own microprocessor, usually called a co-processor. This co-processor is used to compute graphics data, thereby relieving your personal computer's main CPU from that task. For example, to draw a solid square on the screen using a video card that does not have a co-processor, the personal computer's CPU must calculate the size and location of the square, then determine the exact row and column of every pixel with-

in that square. It must then instruct the video card to turn on every one of those pixels individually.

If the video card has a co-processor, the CPU need only pass to the video card the size and location of the square and then tell it to fill the square with a color. The video card then computes exactly which pixels need to be turned on. This frees the CPU to perform more important tasks. Video cards with co-processors have only two drawbacks: their cost and the constant improvement of CPU speeds. The CPU can often perform the graphics processing faster than the co-processor and still keep up with its other tasks. So be cautious about purchasing an older co-processing video card and putting it in a newer system with a high-speed CPU. The two may be mismatched.

LOW-END PLATFORMS

The term *platform* is a way of saying "computer type." For 3-D computer graphics, low-end platforms include the Commodore Amiga line, IBM PC compatibles, and the Apple Macintosh line. For power and capability, the low-end platforms are pretty much equivalent to each other. Each has its own strengths and weaknesses, but in the final analysis your choice of software will probably determine the platform you choose.

APPLE MACINTOSH

Apple's line of Macintosh computers is widely used for computer graphics applications. Recently Apple unveiled its new

71

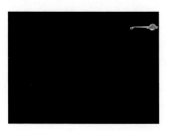

high-performance PowerPC system based on Motorola's RISC microprocessor called the PowerPC. These new RISC Macs are some of the fastest personal computers available and are perfect for 3-D computer graphics. The rest of the Mac line is based on Motorola 68030 and 68040 microprocessors. The 680x0 CPUs place the Macs in the class of Intel 80386- and 80486-based PCs.

For the person who wants ease of use, the Mac is a good choice. It comes with a built-in graphical user interface (GUI), and every aspect of the operating system, known as System 7.5, is based on point-and-click operation. The Macs have a high-speed expansion bus called NuBus, and they support standard SCSI devices such as hard disk drives and scanners.

A variety of Macs are available, ranging in price from less than $1,000 to more than $4,000, so you can find one that best suits your budget. Be prepared, however, for more expensive software. The average price for Mac 3-D animation software is about 30 percent more expensive than PC 3-D animation software. That's not to say that the software isn't worth it. Some packages, such as ElectricImage Animation System, really stretch the boundary of low-end computer animation.

While most Macs come with a standard color monitor, you can purchase third-party monitors from companies such as Sony and RasterOps. The resolution of the video cards varies, but you can get approximately the same graphics performance across all the low-end platforms.

Plans are already being made by three developers of 3-D animation software to port their software to the new PowerPC chip. This means that the Mac will probably have the fastest 3-D software by the end of 1995. This will no doubt beat PC developers at porting their software to the Intel Pentium microprocessor. If you are concerned with rendering speed and can afford it, Macs make a good choice.

COMMODORE AMIGA

The Amiga line of personal computers from Commodore Business Machines, Inc. is an engineering work of art. Three models of the Amiga are currently available: the Amiga 1200, 4000, and 4000T.

All Amiga models are based on the Motorola 680×0 class of microprocessors, as is the Apple Macintosh line. The Amiga 1200 uses the Motorola 68020 microprocessor and is geared toward the home and education markets, so it doesn't have much power in terms of speed and capacity for computer graphics. The 4000 and 4000T models, on the other hand, use the Motorola 68040 microprocessor and are graphics power hitters. Even though faster microprocessors exist, such as the PowerPC and the Pentium, the Amiga can still hold its own because it uses a number of co-processors for dealing with input/output, audio, graphics, etc. These co-processors can even multitask, allowing the computer to run more than one program or task at the same time. Multitasking with co-processors is much faster than multitasking with just one microprocessor as PCs and Macs do.

The most outstanding feature of the Amiga is that it has very high-quality video signal generation in the computer itself, without using a special video card. Right out of the box, the system is capable of generating an NTSC-compatible (15.5 kHz) composite signal that you can record straight to your VCR. For higher-quality output, enhanced video cards can be purchased.

All of the Amigas have two kinds of expansion slots: proprietary Amiga slots, called *Zorro slots*, and PC-compatible ISA slots. Amigas also offer a special video slot that allows graphics cards to use the broadcast-quality video signals coming directly from the Amiga. The newly released 4000T features two video slots. Amigas can be configured with industry standard IDE (Integrated Drive Electronics) or SCSI (Small Computer Systems Interface, pronounced "Scuzzy") hard disk drives.

The Amiga can display 256,000 colors simultaneously while using only 8 bits per pixel. This is accomplished by a custom graphics co-processor chip set called Advanced Graphics Architecture (AGA),

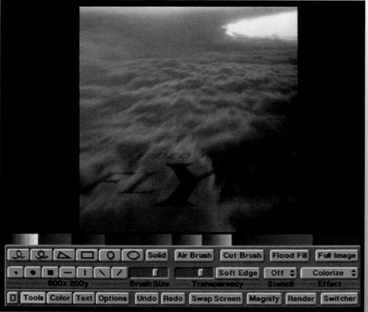

which can also work with resolutions from 320×200 to 1,500×480.

Amiga computers use an operating system called AmigaDOS, which allows multitasking. The operating system includes a program called CrossDOS for transferring files between the AmigaDOS and MS-DOS formats.

In 1985 when Commodore released the Amiga personal computer line, there were many skeptics. Despite gloomy predictions, the Amiga has held on, and today it has a very strong foothold in the world of desktop video, thanks to a company called NewTek.

NewTek developed the Video Toaster, a video production card for the Amiga. You can use it to create broadcast-quality 3-D animation along with digital video effects. The Video Toaster has a suggested retail price of $2,395, which is a little more than

that of the entire Amiga computer. The advantage, however, is that the Video Toaster card comes with a very high-performance 3-D animation software package, called Lightwave, along with other 2-D animation, painting, and titling software. It offers video capabilities, such as a 24-bit frame buffer, switching, digital video effects, and character generation. The practical video-editing uses of the Video Toaster have made it very popular, and today it is used for 3-D computer animation on broadcast television shows such as *SeaQuest DSV* and *Babylon 5*.

When all is said and done, the Amiga is certainly the least expensive way to get into 3-D computer graphics if you want to output your graphics to a video recorder. The software available for Amigas is on the cutting edge of technology, as we will see in the Amiga reviews later in this chapter.

IBM PC COMPATIBLES

For IBM PC compatibles, you have a wide variety of hardware from which to choose. Unlike the Amiga and the Mac, PC microprocessors are produced by a number of companies such as Intel, Cyrix, and AMD. This provides more competition in the market and more diversity as manufacturers try to distance themselves from others by creating unique products. Three main PC CPUs are in use today that work well for 3-D computer animation: the 386, 486, and Pentium. The first two are produced by all three manufacturers, while the Pentium is currently available only from Intel.

Operating systems for PCs are just as plentiful as CPU manufacturers. You can run Sun Solaris, MS-DOS, IBM's OS/2, Microsoft Windows NT, NeXT Step, and others. While almost all of the operating systems are more advanced than DOS, there is practically no 3-D animation software for any of them. Currently, the best choice of an operating system for 3-D animation is DOS.

When purchasing a PC, you should spec out exactly what you want, from the video card to the amount of memory to the type of hard disk drive you want. As with the other platforms, PCs use an expansion bus. Currently, the bus comes in three flavors: ISA (slowest), EISA (faster but not supported by many video cards), VESA Local Bus (VLB, a good medium between price and performance), and Peripheral Component Interconnect (PCI, the fastest expansion bus).

73

With the total number of installed PCs reaching some 70 million in the United States alone, there's little wonder that so much software is available for the PC. Most of the traditional Mac software has been ported to the PC's version of a GUI, Microsoft Windows. Developers are capitalizing on the large installed base of PCs, and this trend is bound to continue until everything that is on the Macintosh and Amiga is also available on the PC. Another strength in the PC is its price. PCs are less expensive than any of the other platforms.

A downside to PCs is that they require a lot of tweaking. Unlike the Mac, where you simply hit the "on" button and everything works, PCs can sometimes require a little attention. If you are a "hands-on" person, you will have no trouble using PCs for 3-D computer animation.

3-D GRAPHICS SOFTWARE

Now we will discuss the various 3-D graphics programs available for low-end platforms. In the following sections, the software is grouped alphabetically by developer according to the platform on which it runs. At the start of each section is a table listing all the 3-D graphics software available for that platform. The tables includes the developer's company name, the program's name, and a brief description. Following the table are reviews of the most popular packages for that platform. If a program runs on more that one platform, it will be reviewed with the first platform that uses it. (The platforms are listed alphabetically according to manufacturer.) In some cases, however, the software varies greatly from one platform to another. In those instances, a review is provided under both platforms' sections.

APPLE MACINTOSH SOFTWARE

A nice variety of 3-D animation programs are available for the Macintosh. They range in price from below $300 to around $7,500. It is common on the Macintosh platform to use separate modeling, rendering, and animation programs. So, while there are a few programs that perform all of those tasks, you might find the best solution lies in modeling in one program and using another for rendering and animation.

If you are looking for one package that performs all three functions (modeling, rendering, and animation), good choices are Infini-D and StrataVision 3-D. For modeling and rendering, some of the best software is Alias Sketch and Ray Dream Designer. For animation, the best software is ElectricImage Animation System.

The following table lists the 3-D computer graphics products currently available for the Apple Macintosh. For contact information, see Appendix A, "Resources."

Image courtesy of Demografx/Gary Demos/Digital Productions.

3-D Computer Graphics Programs Available for the Macintosh

Company	Product	Description
Anjon and Associates	Playmation 1.48.4	Modeling, Rendering, Animation
	Render24	Rendering
Autodessys Inc.	form*Z 2.1.5	Modeling
Byte by Byte Corp.	Sculpt 3D 3.0	Modeling, Rendering
	Sculpt 4D	Modeling, Rendering, Animation
	Sculptor	Modeling
Crystal Graphics Inc.	Crystal TOPAS 1.2	Modeling, Rendering, Animation
Dynaware USA Inc.	DynaPerspective 2.33	Modeling
Electric Image	Animation System	Rendering, Animation
Graphisoft U.S., Inc./ASYM	Zoom 3.0	Modeling, Rendering
Macromedia Inc.	Macromedia Three-D 1.2	Rendering, Animation
	Swivel-3D Pro 2.0.4	Modeling, Rendering, Animation
	SwivelMan	Modeling, Rendering, Animation
	MacroModel 1.5	Modeling
Pixar	MacRenderMan 1.1	Rendering, Animation
	ShowPlace 1.1.1	Rendering, Animation
Ray Dream Inc.	Ray Dream Designer 2.06	Modeling, Rendering
Sketchtek, Inc.	Sketch! 1.5	Modeling, Rendering
	UpFront 1.02a	Modeling, Rendering, Animation
Specular International Ltd.	Infini-D 2.5	Modeling, Rendering, Animation
Strata Corp.	StrataVision 3D 2.6	Modeling, Rendering, Animation
	StudioPro 1.0	Modeling, Rendering, Animation
SystemSoft America Inc.	Shade II 1.4.2	Modeling, Rendering, Animation
View by View Inc.	Turbo 3D 5.0.3	Modeling, Rendering, Animation
Virtus Corp.	Virtus WalkThrough 1.1.3	Modeling, Rendering, Animation
	Virtus WalkThrough Pro	Modeling, Rendering, Animation
VIDI	Presenter Professional 1.5	Modeling, Rendering, Animation
	ModelerPro 1.5	Modeling

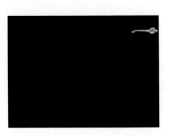

Following are brief reviews of some of the more popular Mac-based 3-D graphics software. For contact information, see Appendix A, "Resources."

Sketchtek, Inc.

Sketch!

Sketch! is considered one of the best modeling programs for the Mac platform. As a modeling/rendering program, Sketch! does not offer any animation capabilities, but what it lacks in animation it makes up in modeling capabilities. It is one of the few low-end programs that offer NURBS (Non-Uniform Rational B-Spline) modeling. Splines are mathematical descriptions of curves. They are sometimes used to model polygonal surfaces. Other times, spline surfaces are rendered directly. NURBS is an advanced way to model curved surfaces. You can easily manipulate your models with vertex editing and other advanced modeling tools.

All drawing and rendering is done within a single window. This is done in the traditional manner of creating a 2-D object and then lofting or revolving into a 3-D object. Sketch! can import Adobe Illustrator and Aldus FreeHand drawings as 2-D objects. Once an object is created, you can group or ungroup it with other objects. Objects can also be stored in a library that even provides preview images.

Sketch! has a match-backdrop tool that allows you to reverse-engineer the camera perspective of an existing photograph, so that your 3-D model can be overlaid in a scene after matching its perspective. To help you learn some of these more complex tools, Sketch! comes with a one-hour video tutorial and printed tutorials.

You can render realistic surfaces in Sketch! using texture maps, environment mapping, and ray tracing. Surfaces are created in a materials editor where you can set the colors, texture maps, bumpiness, transparency, and other attributes. For its price range, Sketch! is a very good renderer for Macs.

To help position texture maps, Sketch! uses an interactive mapping tool. Most of the standard lights are supported, including point, spot, and distant lights. Sketch! has a retail price of $995 and can output RenderMan RIB, DXF, and IGES files.

UpFront

UpFront is another product from Sketchtek, Inc., and it has a very different approach to the idea of 3-D modeling. UpFront is available for both Macs and PCs running Microsoft Windows. It offers a simple intuitive access into the 3-D modeling world for artists, designers, architects, or any professional who works with space. The price paid for simplicity, however, is just that, simplicity; the package offers very limited rendering and animation capabilities. It is geared to the idea of giving users a quick, intuitive method of creating 3-D concepts and even testing them with shadows from a light source.

UpFront gives you the ability to create objects "on" other objects by simply clicking on any part of the base object's surface. This alleviates the difficulty of creating an object floating in space and then trying to move it to the desired location on another surface. All of the geometric primitives (spheres, cubes, cylinders, etc.) are available, as well as complex 2-D shapes that can be revolved or lofted into 3-D objects. One unique feature is the ability to do 2-D freehand sketches right on top of your 3-D world. The new sketches appear on your current view. This can sometimes be a useful feature, allowing you to rough in trees, landscapes, and other "hard to model" things. Solid objects can be used to cut other objects using Boolean operations. Window and door frames can be created and saved as library objects, and later these can be cut into solid walls without having to draw the wall around the opening.

As with Sketch!, UpFront has the ability to load scanned images and use special reverse-engineering tools to determine camera location, lens size, and sun location of the original photograph. This allows you to duplicate existing shadows and perspective, thus giving you an optically correct rendering of your model in the existing image.

Enter the correct longitude, latitude, date, and time, and UpFront will calculate accurate shadows with your model. The sun's path also can be displayed with markers at half-hour intervals. This will tell you exactly where and when the sun will be blocked by trees or buildings for any day of the year.

UpFront can export models in the DXF and CSV (Comma Separated) formats, but it can't import DXF files. It currently lists for a retail price of $895, which seems a little steep when you have such limited functionality.

Anjon & Associates

Playmation

Playmation is currently available on practically every platform: the IBM PC, Apple Macintosh, Commodore Amiga, and Silicon Graphics. Retailing at $566, Playmation is certainly one of the least expensive 3-D animation and rendering packages available, especially for the Mac.

The most interesting thing about Playmation is that it is based completely on 3-D patch surfaces. Instead of creating objects with polygons, you create them with 3-D spline-based patches. Patch based modeling can create very organic looking shapes that bend and buckle realistically during animation. With spline models, the renderer is rendering mathematically defined curved surfaces, so they stay perfectly smooth no matter how close you get to them during your rendering. The challenging part of spline-based patches is modeling. Creating new splines in Playmation is very intuitive and straightforward, but editing existing splines can turn into a nightmare.

On all platforms, Playmation offers multitasking, which allows you to model in one window and set up your animation in another window while the rendering takes place in yet a third window in the background. Multitasking does slow down rendering, so a 24-bit renderer is also available for some platforms. It focuses the computer's attention on rendering in order to achieve the highest possible speed.

There are five main programs in Playmation: Sculpture, Character, Action, Direction, and Render. You start by creating objects in Sculpture. Character allows you to combine multiple objects into one, as well as assign surface attributes to the finished object. The Action module is where you set up the movement for each object. Direction is where you combine all of the elements on one stage and set up

lights and cameras for the final animation. Render renders the entire choreographed scene to an animation file.

An excellent feature of Playmation is its motion libraries. When it comes to animating your model, there are three different methods: skeletal, spine, and muscle. Skeletal allows you to animate segments of a model in a typical hierarchical fashion. Spine animation is where you can assign a single 3-D spline to act as a backbone for any type of model. That way you can bend the model and deform it freely regardless of its complexity. Muscle animation allows you to move and adjust individual control points in your 3-D patches.

Once you define the motion, you can save it independently of the model. This allows you to create the motion of a person walking, then apply it to the model of a heavy adult or a small child. Then all you need is a little adjustment to make the adult's walk a little more lumbering and the child's walk a little bouncier.

Playmation does ray tracing for accurate reflections and shadows. For increased speed you can switch the full ray tracing to a single-pass mode. This cuts rendering time in half, but at the expense of shadows

and reflections. The speed of Playmation is difficult to quantify because it is a patch-based renderer; it doesn't directly compare to other 3-D programs that are polygon based.

For character animation, there is nothing like it on the low-end platforms. By using organic, flexible 3-D patches, you can easily animate a character's emotions. The motion libraries give evidence of a program designed for 20-minute, 3-D cartoon programs instead of 30-second flying logo animations.

Byte by Byte

Sculptor

Sculptor is another spline-based modeling program that allows vertex and 3-D Boolean-based editing. It offers wireframe rendering through Phong shading with anti-aliasing. You can create images with 32-bit color depth (alpha channel). The modeling tools include a library of object primitives, splines, and the ability to reflect, rotate, and scale objects. With a retail price of $1,995, Sculptor is one of the high-end Mac-based modeling programs.

Sculpt 3-D

Sculpt 3-D adds to Sculptor's capabilities and offers advanced rendering such as ray tracing. A materials editor is also available for creating realistic materials. Sculpt 3-D is one of the fastest rendering engines on the Mac market. To help you learn the product, it ships with three tutorial video tapes. A special RISC-based accelerator board and software are available to speed up Sculpt 3-D. Of course, this power comes with a hefty price tag at $2,995 or $3,995 for the RISC version (software only).

Sculpt 4D

Sculpt 4D adds animation and VTR controls to Sculpt 3-D. Sculpt 4D can render scenes with motion blur to smooth out the final animation. It also features real-time wireframe playback. A scripting language is available to set up batch rendering for unattended operation. As with Sculpt 3-D, you can purchase a RISC-based accelerator board to speed up rendering. Video tutorials come with both versions. The retail price of Sculpt 4D is $3,995, or $4,995 for the RISC version (software only).

Electric Image Incorporated

ElectricImage Animation System

The very top of the top-end Mac 3-D animation programs is ElectricImage Animation System Version 2.0 (EIAS) by Electric Image Inc. Available on both Mac and SGI platforms, EIAS allows Mac users to render their animation on networked high-end workstations if they are available. EIAS does not offer any modeling capabilities; it simply does rendering and animation.

EIAS supports polygon models and can do all major types of surface mapping. It cannot do ray tracing; for that you must rely on the creative use of environment maps. Most of the animation and rendering work is done in a perspective view.

EIAS not only creates beautiful 3-D graphics and animation, but it allows you to sync sound to your animation. You can import soundtracks at frequencies from 5 to 64 kHz, then preview your animation in real-time by saving the graphics and sound together as a QuickTime movie.

With EIAS you can use special-effects filters on the finished images after rendering them. This is accomplished by the use of "plug-in" modules. 3-D plug-ins are also available for simulating particle systems. For instance, a module called Mr. Nitro can be used to explode any 3-D object in your animation. You can control the wind direction, amount of gravity, and other factors. Mr. Nitro was used for the scene in the movie *Terminator 2: Judgment Day* where the city of Los Angeles is destroyed by a nuclear bomb.

With a list price of $7,495, it is by far the most expensive product for the low-end platforms. Perhaps the price is justified because EIAS uses a rendering engine called Electric Engine that is also available for high-end workstations, such as the SGI computers, Iris and Indigo. The SGI version of Electric Engine costs $2,995. If you can afford an SGI, you are probably better off getting 3-D animation software for it and forgetting about the Mac. Overall, EIAS produces some of the best-looking pictures on the low-end platforms.

Crystal Graphics

Crystal Topas for the Macintosh

Crystal Topas for the Macintosh, Version 1.2, is a modeling, rendering, and animation program. It provides tools for creating geometric primitives, polygons, and spline-based objects. Objects, faces, and vertices can be edited with functions such as bend, twist, and taper. 3-D objects can be morphed into other 3-D objects.

Image courtesy of Art Center College of Design and Aaron Dorr.

You can view your animations in a time-line format or in a timegraph view that allows you to adjust your playback timing graphically. Various transitions are available, such as page turn and page roll. VTR control is available for Videomedia Inc. (San Jose, California) and DiaQuest, Inc. (Berkeley, California) hardware VTR controllers. You can create full-color, 32-bit images for transparency support. Crystal Topas for the Mac has a retail price of $1,995.

Specular International

Infini-D

Infini-D Version 2.5.1 from Specular International is a modeling, rendering, and animation program. While Infini-D doesn't support NURBS or spline-based modeling, it does support the standard lathe and extrude methods. Objects can be morphed in 3-D into other objects. 3-D TrueType and PostScript fonts can be imported. Using fractals, you can create realistic terrains.

On the rendering side, Infini-D supports ray tracing, procedural textures, and bump mapping. QuickTime movies can be applied to 3-D surfaces and to the background as well. Surface textures can be organized into libraries for quick access. It supports flat, Gouraud, and Phong shading; reflections; transparency; glow effects; and refractions. Multiple light sources and views can be created for each scene. Infini-D provides multiple 3-D cameras;

adjustable lenses; and zoom, pan, and roll controls. The final images can be rendered in 32-bit color.

Objects can be animated with spline-based motion paths or linear paths. For animation you can use Infini-D in conjunction with BackBurner (described below) to divide rendering tasks across a network of Macs. Infini-D's suggested retail price is $895.

BackBurner

BackBurner Version 1.0 is an add-on product for Infini-D that does network rendering. This allows you to speed rendering time dramatically by using multiple Macs to render the same animation. A Mac called the "Master" coordinates rendering with the other Macs on the network, called "Slaves." A batch processing mode allows multiple jobs to be rendered unassisted.

BackBurner has some very advanced crash recovery capabilities. If the master system crashes, it can be restarted and rendering continues uninterrupted. BackBurner makes efficient use of the network by transmitting only what is absolutely necessary for the slave stations to accomplish their renderings. For example, it will only transmit texture maps when the slave station needs them.

The suggested retail price for the first two nodes is $395. Each additional node is $295, and a three-node pack is $695. Speed combined with excellent on-line status information makes this an excellent product.

Macromedia

Macromedia Three-D

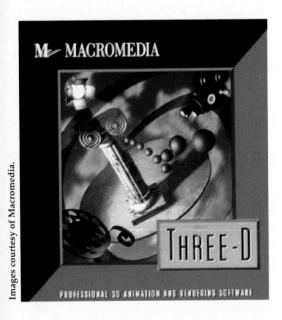

Images courtesy of Macromedia.

Macromedia Three-D is a rending and animation program. After importing geometry or TrueType fonts, you can render using Phong shading and texture maps. Macromedia Three-D doesn't support more advanced rendering features like bump mapping, opacity mapping, or ray tracing, but it can still produce some very nice images.

The program is divided into three sections: 3-DWorks, FireWorks, and RenderWorks. 3-DWorks is used to set up 3-D scenes with models and lights. Animation is also set up in 3-DWorks. FireWorks is a module for compositing and anti-aliasing images. RenderWorks is the module that actually renders the scene or animation. It supports MacRenderMan from Pixar. Macromedia Three-D features an easy-to-use interface. Both rendering quality and speed are very good. Shadows and 32-bit images are supported. Animation can be controlled by splines. The suggested retail price is $1,495.

Swivel 3-D Professional

Swivel 3-D Professional Version 2.04 is a modeling program that can be used in connection with Macromedia Three-D. It offers some limited animation and rendering capabilities, but it is primarily a modeler. With it you can quickly create any type of solid 3-D object. It doesn't support spline modeling or editing tools, but you can link objects with real life relationships, such as hinges, joints, wheels, and sliders. The suggested retail price is $695.

SwivelMan

SwivelMan Version 1.0.1 further enhances Swivel 3-D Pro by adding to it MacRenderMan from Pixar. This allows

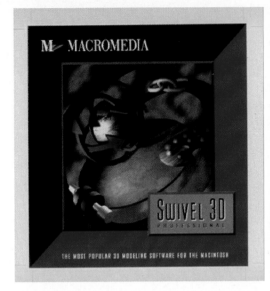

you to render photo-realistic scenes from SwivelMan models. MacRenderMan documentation and tutorials are also supported. As does Swivel 3-D Pro, SwivelMan supports hierarchical object links and motion axes. The suggested retail price is $895.

It comes with a variety of modules including RenderMonitor, RenderApp, PhotoRealistic RenderMan, ShaderApp, and a sample library of RIB files, shaders, and texture maps. RenderMonitor allows the user to render images in the background. RenderApp allows the user to view images and convert them into standard Macintosh file formats. PhotoRealistic RenderMan renders pictures from RIB files, and ShaderApp allows you to create new shaders.

MacroModel

MacroModel Version 1.5 is a modeler similar to Swivel 3-D. However, MacroModel supports more advanced modeling capabilities such as spline-based modeling and deformation tools. It also features cross-platform compatibility with a Microsoft Windows version of Macromodel. With the deformation tools, you can twist, taper, and bend entire objects without editing individual vertices. All of this is packaged in a very easy-to-use interface.

You can import and export 3-D objects with other modelers such as Swivel 3-D. The suggested retail price is $1,495. It is also available for the Windows platform for $1,795.

Images courtesy of Macromedia.

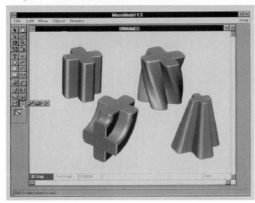

ModelShop II

ModelShop II Version 1.2 is a modeling package geared toward technical users. It supports unlimited drawing layers, Bézier curves, text, and precise measurements. It offers some limited rendering with multiple light sources but no texture mapping or other advanced features. The interface is

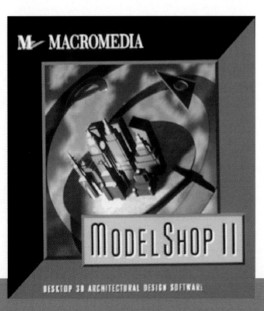

simple and straightforward. You can walk through any 3-D scene by using the mouse. The suggested retail price is $895.

Pixar

MacRenderMan

MacRenderMan Version 1.1 is the Macintosh version of the RenderMan rendering engine. Available from Pixar, it creates photo-realistic color images from files in RIB (RenderMan Interface Bytestream) format. RenderMan RIB files are text-based descriptions of 3-D scenes. MacRenderMan is bundled with a number of modeling and animation programs and supports almost all 3-D graphics software.

RenderMan is available on practically every platform. It works by copying the RIB file into a folder and then rendering in the background. It supports 32-bit color, transparency, surface textures, multiple light sources, natural or artificial light, reflected light, shadows, and motion blur. MacRenderMan comes bundled with ShowPlace. (See next subheading.) The only downside to MacRenderMan, and indeed all the RenderMan rendering engines, is speed. RenderMan, although able to produce some of the most beautiful

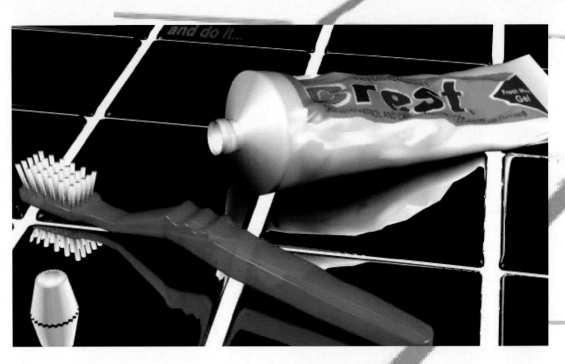

images, is admittedly one of, if not THE, slowest renderers on the market. NetRenderMan (see NetRenderMan subheading) has helped this issue a little, but it is still a major stumbling block for RenderMan as a whole.

ShowPlace

ShowPlace Version 2.0 is a 3-D scene composition program for creating RIB files. It doesn't perform any modeling or animation functions; it simply sets up static 3-D scenes for RenderMan to render. You can import objects in a variety of formats including DXF. Bundled with ShowPlace is a program called Glimpse that allows you to edit surfaces by using simple scroll bars and popup menus.

ShowPlace can create some very photo-realistic images by assigning surface shaders and lighting to 3-D objects. Since it uses MacRenderMan, rendering speeds are a little slow. However, it does come with NetRenderMan to speed rendering times. (See next section.) Another way to speed rendering is to adjust the shadow quality. ShowPlace comes with a tutorial videotape to help get new users up to speed quickly.

The suggested retail price is $695, and a CD-ROM version is available for $495 that does not include printed documentation. It includes an application that lets users edit

Looks, surface appearances that can be applied to 3-D images. ShowPlace comes with five megabytes of 3-D objects such as furniture, musical instruments, and industrial equipment. Special plug-ins allow you to generate some geometry such as stairways and venetian blinds.

NetRenderMan

NetRenderMan Version 1.1 is identical to MacRenderMan except that it can render RIB files across a network of Macs or UNIX computers. By running the same rendering job on multiple computers, you can achieve dramatic decreases in rendering time. The Master Mac sets up the rendering and distributes the needed data across the network. The rendered pixels are then sent back to the Master Mac to be saved as a PICT file. You can render multiple jobs and even set priorities for those

jobs. NetRenderMan has a suggested retail price between $250 and $1,500, depending on the platform on which you will use it.

Ray Dream Incorporated

Ray Dream Designer

Ray Dream Designer Version 3.0 is a modeling and rendering package. You can model objects with geometric primitives and spline and Bezier curves. A collection of 3-D objects that ships with the product can be added to your scene via a simple drag-and-drop interface. You can also import DXF objects. Ray Dream Designer supports ray tracing and can render images in the background. It supports 32-bit images and offers a preview mode for quickly checking your 3-D rendering. An advanced 3-D paint function allows you to paint directly on your 3-D objects. The

ANDREY ZMIEVSKIY

computer bends the painted texture around the 3-D surfaces automatically as you paint them. Ray Dream Designer has a suggested retail price of $399.

DreamNet

DreamNet Version 1.02 allows Ray Dream Designer files to be rendered across a Mac network. Similar to NetRenderMan and BackBurner, DreamNet is set up with a Master Mac and multiple slave clients to do the rendering. DreamNet's interface shows the slaves available and allows you to point-and-shoot jobs to be rendered on them. Macs can be grouped together, and the groups can be saved to facilitate future rendering tasks. It has a suggested retail price of $50 per node, making it the cheapest of the Mac-based network renderers.

Strata Corporation

Stratavision 3-D

Stratavision 2.5 is a modeling, rendering, and animation program. Objects can be rendered in wireframe, Gouraud, Phong, or ray tracing. It is one of the few low-end programs that support true radiosity. You can model objects with spline-based curves, geometric primitives, or lathing/extruding, or you can simply select from a variety of 3-D library objects that ship with the product. DXF files can also be imported into the modeler.

You can create unlimited light sources, and even use them as image projectors. A

background renderer allows you to keep working while the computer is rendering. It supports plug-ins for doing image processing. The suggested retail price is $995.

StudioPro

StudioPro Version 1.0 offers modeling, rendering, and animation like Stratavision, but adds to it some advanced features. One new feature is a sculpting tool that allows you to push and pull on individual vertices of a model much like working with clay. A training videotape and CD-ROM of sample images are included with the software.

Animation is controlled by an event-driven interface where you draw motion paths for objects. Users can apply special effects such as auto banking, shatter, explode, and atomize. StudioPro can import and export DXF files. It can even render surfaces with textures like chalk, drybrush, and watercolor. Strata StudioPro has a suggested retail price of $1,495.

RenderPro

RenderPro Version 1.01 is a network renderer for Strata's 3-D products. It can render in the background on both master and slave systems. You can adjust the level of access for each slave, which limits the master's access to that slave. A weekly rendering calendar can be set so each slave can have a predetermined time in which it can render scenes from the master. RenderPro has a suggested retail price of $299. A

three-node pack is $695, and a ten-node pack is $1,495.

Virtus Corporation

WalkThrough

Virtus WalkThrough Version 1.1 is a modeling program that also lets you move through a flat, shaded version of the world. While you can model some simplistic forms, Virtus Walkthrough is more geared to virtual reality than computer graphics. Walkthrough can import and export common CAD file formats. A Windows version is also available.

WalkThrough Pro

WalkThrough Pro gives you all the functionality of WalkThrough plus the benefit of being able to add texture maps to your objects and still move through the environment in real time. A variety of textures comes with WalkThrough Pro. QuickTime movies can be applied to any surface as a texture.

VIDI

Presenter Professional

Presenter Professional Version 1.5.2 falls on the high end of PC-based 3-D graphics software. It performs all the modeling, rendering, and animation functions. The software is divided into three components: the modeler, the presenter, and the projector. You can model objects in the modeler by using splines, and then modify them at a vertex level using the Digital Clay feature. The presenter module allows you to assign surface attributes to objects and set up animated sequences. The projector is where the scenes are rendered.

Presenter Professional even calculates the volume and surface volume for any 3-D object. This technical accuracy makes Presenter Professional very practical for mechanical engineering and product design applications. You can output RenderMan RIB files from your 3-D scenes. You can render scenes in flat or Phong shading, or with ray tracing. Despite its complexity, Presenter Professional is still easy to use. It has a suggested retail price of $2,995. VIDI Express, a hardware accelerator is available for $4,495.

ModelerPro

ModelerPro Version 1.5 is the same as Presenter Professional without the rendering and animation capabilities. You can import and export DXF, StrataVision 3-D, Electric Image, and Wavefront files. Its suggested retail price is $1,995.

Presenter

Presenter is the rendering and animation side of Presenter Professional without the rendering and animation capabilities. You can import and export DXF, StrataVision 3-D, Electric Image, and Wavefront files. Its suggested retail price is $1,995.

COMMODORE AMIGA SOFTWARE

The Commodore Amiga personal computer has been a favorite for computer animation since its inception. The following table lists the 3-D computer graphics products currently available for the Commodore Amiga. By far, the most popular is Lightwave 3-D by NewTek. For contact information see Appendix A.

Company	Product	Description
Adspec Programming	Aladdin 4D	Modeling, Rendering, Animation
Caligari Corporation	Caligari24	Modeling, Rendering, Animation
Impulse	Imagine	Modeling, Rendering, Animation
NewTek	Lightwave 3D	Modeling, Rendering, Animation

Next are brief reviews of some of these Amiga-based, 3-D graphics applications.

Adspec Programming

Aladdin 4D

Aladdin 4D allows you to model, render, and animate 4D objects. Modeling is accomplished by traditional methods such as geometric primitives, lathing, and extruding. Once objects are created, they can be edited easily. One editing tool, called the Magnet, allows you to pull or tug on a vertice and have the rest of the vertices follow the same pattern.

Both texture images and real-world are supplied with Topas. The procedural textures are very flexible and offer a wide variety of realistic surfaces. All of this power comes with the price of a fairly complex user interface that may take some time getting used to.

Caligari Corporation

Caligari24

Caligari24 for the Commodore Amiga is a modeling, rendering, and animation program. It offers a very friendly user interface and can perform such advanced feats as ray tracing. It has been very successful on the Amiga platform and is now available for Microsoft Windows.

An interesting aspect of Caligari24 is that all the modeling takes place in a single perspective view. 3-D movement is in real time and is controlled by means of axis constraints that you can turn on at any time to constrain movement to a given axis. Caligari24 is also available for Microsoft Windows under the name trueSpace. However, unlike trueSpace, Caligari24 cannot ray trace scenes. Caligari24's suggested retail price is $399.

Impulse

Imagine

Imagine Version 2.0 is a modeling, rendering, and animation program for both PCs and Amiga personal computers. Imagine is divided into six different modules. The first is the Project Editor, which allows rendering and animation of your current 3-D scene. Second is the Detail Editor where you perform the actual modeling by creating geometric primitives, extrusions, or Boolean operations.

The Cycle Editor allows you to create animated walk cycles or other repeating movements in your 3-D scene. The Forms Editor is another modeler optimized for creating smooth organic-looking shapes. The Stage Editor allows you to set up keyframe or path-based motion. The Action Editor lets you fine-tune your animation via a timeline. The suggested retail price for Imagine is $495.

NewTek, Inc.

Lightwave 3D

Lightwave 3D is perhaps the most popular of the Amiga 3-D graphics programs. It is the software of choice for the

special-effects artists who create the CGI for *Babylon 5* and *SeaQuest DSV*. The latest version, 3.1, offers ray traced refractions, 3-D morphable objects, skeletal animation, and more.

To run Lightwave, you must have some specific hardware on your Amiga: the Video Toaster or LightRave from Warm & Fuzzy Logic. The Video Toaster retails for $2,395 and comes bundled with Lightwave 3-D. With Lightwave, you have access to advanced modeling functions like wrapping an object around a sphere, PostScript import support, and Boolean functions. For special effects, you can create motion blur, lens flares, and depth of field.

To speed up Lightwave's rendering time, an add-on board called the Video Screamer is available. It uses 4 RISC microprocessors and has a retail cost of about $9,000. NewTek claims that the Lightwave animation system can be rendered twice as fast as on a Cray I supercomputer.

Realsoft International

Real 3-D 2

Real 3-D Version 2.0 from Realsoft International is a modeling, rendering, and animation program. A unique feature about it is its built-in inverse kinematic capabilities. This allows you to animate physical characteristics such as gravity and friction. Also, particle animation can be created to simulate sparks, fire, snow, etc.

To facilitate character animation, a skeletal control mode is available. As with Lightwave, Real 3-D offers advanced rendering effects like motion blur, field rendering, depth of field, sun glow, and soft shadows. The downside is the steep learning curve of Real 3-D. Its suggested retail price is $699.

PC Software

The following table lists the 3-D computer graphics products currently available for IBM PC compatibles. If you want to create 3-D animation under Microsoft Windows, trueSpace is the best choice. For character animation, Playmation is an excellent choice, and for overall performance and capability, 3D Studio and Crystal TOPAS are both good choices.

Image courtesy of Lightwave 3D.

3-D Computer Graphics Programs Available for IBM PC Compatibles.

Company	Product	Description
Alias Research Inc.	UpFront	Modeling, Rendering
Anjon and Associates	Playmation 1.48.4	Modeling, Rendering, Animation
	Render24	Rendering
Autodesk Inc.	3D Studio	Modeling, Rendering, Animation
Byte by Byte Corp.	Envisage 3D	Modeling, Rendering, Animation
Caligari Corp.	trueSpace	Modeling, Rendering, Animation
Crystal Graphics Inc.	Crystal 3D Designer	Modeling, Rendering, Animation
	Crystal Desktop Animator	Modeling, Rendering, Animation
	Crystal TOPAS Pro 5.0	Modeling, Rendering, Animation
Dynaware USA Inc.	DynaPerspective	Modeling
Impulse Inc.	Imagine 3.0	Modeling, Rendering, Animation
Looking Glass Software	Cheetah 3D	Modeling, Rendering, Animation
Lunar Graphics	Realize Rendering Tool	Rendering, Animation
Macromedia Inc.	MacroModel 1.5	Modeling, Rendering
Pacific Motion	3D Workshop	Modeling, Rendering, Animation
Pixar	RenderMan	Rendering, Animation
Realsoft International	Real 3D 2	Modeling, Rendering, Animation
Strata Corp.	StrataVision 3D	Modeling, Rendering, Animation
Virtus Corp.	Virtus WalkThrough 1.1.3	Modeling, Rendering, Animation
Visual Software	Renderize Live	Rendering, Animation
	Visual Reality	Modeling, Rendering, Animation

We will now offer brief reviews of some of the more popular PC-based, 3-D, graphics software. For contact information, see Appendix A.

Autodesk, Inc.

3D Studio—$2,995

3D Studio Version 3 is a modeling, rendering, and animation program geared toward the high-end of PC-based, 3-D graphics. It is divided into five components: 2-D Shaper, 3-D Lofter, 3-D Editor, Keyframer, and Materials Editor. The 2-D Shaper allows you to trace scanned images, or simply draw two-dimensional shapes. The 3-D Lofter converts those 2-D shapes into 3-D objects. The 3-D Lofter can deform any 2-D objects during the lofting process. You can scale, twist, teeter, bevel, and perform a special deformation called "fit." The fit deformation allows you to specify a 2-D top view and a 2-D side view of an object, and then carve out a resulting 3-D object from the two views. This can speed up the process of modeling unusual shapes like a telephone handset.

The 3-D Editor is where you create 3-D shapes from geometric primitives, create lights, place cameras, and assign surface materials to objects. You can also render a still image from the 3-D Editor. The Keyframer allows you to set up animated sequences that can be rendered to a Animator Flick (FLI) file or a series of Targa (TGA) files. The Materials Editor lets you create new materials and preview them rendered on a 3-D object.

The Keyframer is perhaps the most complex module of the whole system. Every object in your scene, such as meshes, lights, cameras, and camera targets, can be animated. 3-D objects can be scaled, squashed, even morphed into other objects (with the same number of vertices). Any objects, including lights and cameras, can be hierarchically linked with other objects. 3-D objects can be instanced to simplify the editing process. All *key frames* (where some type of movement takes place) can be viewed on the Track Info dialog box, where keys can easily be copied, moved to other frames, deleted, or added. Each key frame in turn has its own Key Info dialog box; this allows you to fine-tune the movement of the object being keyed. You can adjust the speed (for instance, slowing an object before it lands on a surface) or even adjust the tension, continuity, and bias setting of the spline controlling the movement. A Video Post feature allows you to coordinate the compositing of multiple images or animations using their alpha channels.

It does not support the RenderMan RIB file format, nor does it perform any ray tracing. The current retail price for 3D Studio Version 3 is $2,995. Network rendering capabilities are built into the renderer and can be used on up to 9,999 stations at no extra cost. The latest version (3) now renders images in a 64-bit color space and then optimizes those colors to standard 32-bit images. This provides better color reproduction than most other PC-based rendering packages. 3D Studio is also available for the SGI platform.

Another outstanding feature of 3D Studio is the IPAS routines. IPAS routines are plug-in modules available commercially for 3D Studio. You can also program your own routines for custom effects. They can generate particle systems, algorithmic geometry, algorithmic animation, and image-processing techniques. 3D Studio is also one of the few programs that accurately simulate metal surfaces.

Byte by Byte

Envisage 3-D

Envisage 3-D Version 1.1 is a modeling, rendering, and animation program that supports spline and polygon models. You can import PostScript fonts, build 3-D models using built-in procedural formulas or by using extrudes, lofts, and geometric primitives. Rendering is performed with Phong shading and 32-bit color output. Rendering engines are available for UNIX-based machines for high-speed rendering.

Envisage 3-D supports procedural textures, reflection mapping, and bump

Image courtesy of National Video Center, National CaveArt, and Christopher Cave.

Caligari Corporation

trueSpace

Caligari trueSpace is the port of Caligari24 over the PC platform. As a Windows-based program, it features an easy-to-use interface. trueSpace allows you to model in a perspective view and create surface materials on sample 3-D objects. The user interface is icon-driven, with a context-sensitive help status bar.

trueSpace also supports ray tracing for creating photo-realistic images involving reflective surfaces. Animations can be rendered to a sequence of files or to animator flic (FLI) format or Microsoft Video for Windows (AVI) format. The suggested retail price of trueSpace is $795.

Crystal Graphics Inc.

Crystal 3-D Designer

Crystal 3-D Designer Version 2.0 is an easy-to-use modeling and rendering package for creating still images. You can model objects with splines or with any of the other traditional methods. You can render 3-D scenes with photo-realistic textures, ray traced refractions, and shininess mapping.

Even though Crystal 3-D Designer is the entry-level 3-D product from Crystal Graphics, it still offers all the advanced modeling and rendering features of Crystal Topas Professional. For example,

mapping. Animation can be rendered to sequential files or to animator flic (FLI) files. For animation you can use advanced skeletal methods and automated special effects such as springs, shaking, and squeeze. Envisage 3-D has a suggested retail price of $399.

you can use the Match Perspective tool to make a 3-D object align with the perspective of an existing picture.

Here the Match Perspective tool is being used to line up the computer version of the railway to the street photograph. A CD-ROM filled with reflection maps, background pictures, models, and movies is also included in the package. 3-D Designer has a suggested retail price of $495.

Crystal TOPAS

Crystal TOPAS Version 5.0 offers the same features as Crystal 3-D and adds to them animation. However, the animation capabilities are not broadcast quality. Instead they are geared toward multimedia and PC-based presentations. The output for animation is through animator flics and FLI and FLC files. Animation is handled both through keyframes and path-based motion.

Crystal TOPAS comes with built-in custom effects such as page turn and roll effects. All components of 3-D objects can be animated. This includes shape, color, texture, shininess, roughness, and transparency; everything is fully *animatable*.

The suggested retail price of Crystal TOPAS is $995.

Crystal TOPAS Professional

Crystal TOPAS Professional 5.0 is the flagship product, including all of the previously described features, but adding to it broadcast-quality output. You can also rotoscope video and perform PAL/NTSC color correction, and it comes with a VTR controller for single frame output to professional VTRs.

Crystal TOPAS Professional also comes with network rendering capability. This is bundled with the product and can be used on an unlimited number of slave stations. The suggested retail price for Crystal TOPAS Professional is $2,495.

Looking Glass Software, Inc.

Cheetah 3-D

Cheetah 3-D Version 1.5 is a Windows-based modeling, rendering, and animation program. It can render scenes with flat, Gouraud, and Phong shading along with reflection maps, bump maps, and even ray tracing. Cheetah 3-D does not support spline-based modeling. Images can be rendered at 24-bit color even though you may be running Windows in an 8-bit color mode.

You can load True Type fonts and extrude them into 3-D characters. There is also a scripting language that allows you to write mathematical descriptions of object motions, and communicate via Windows OLE 2.0. Rendering and script execution can take place in the background. You can save animation in the Video for Windows AVI format. Cheetah 3-D has a suggested retail price of $349.95.

Pacific Motion

3-D Workshop

3-D Workshop Version 2 is a DOS-based modeling, rendering, and animation program. At a list price of only $299.95, it is one of the least expensive 3-D animation programs. It can import DXF files, to which you can assign surface materials, and create a very good looking rendering.

You can render objects with reflection mapping and bump mapping as well as the standard Phong and Gouraud shading. 3-D Workshop interface can be a little cumbersome at times.

Strata Corporation

StrataVision 3-D PC

StrataVision 3-D PC is not really a port of the Macintosh version to the PC platform. Instead, it is an entirely different product. StrataVision 3-D PC is a modeling, rendering, and animation package and was previously called AIM-3D. Prior to becoming StrataVision 3-D PC, it won "Analyst's Choice" in the July 29, 1989, issue of *PC Week*, over such packages as TOPAS, DGS, and 3D Studio.

StrataVision 3-D PC has some very unique features commonly found in other 3-D graphics software. For instance, scientific formulas can be directly entered to model the resulting grids in 3-D. 3-D bar graphs can be generated from data entered manually or from an existing spreadsheet. The ability to autotrace 2-D images can be used to quickly create 3-D models from existing 2-D logos.

StrataVision 3-D PC provides direct VTR control. It supports networked rendering without a network; all you need between the PCs is an RS-232 serial port and a cable. This allows one or more PCs to be dedicated to modeling and pass off the rendering to other attached PCs.

The 3-D editing side of the system is very flexible and easy to understand. Any 2-D drawing can be "revolved" or "swept" into the 3-D world. The sweeper method allows you to create a 2-D outline of your object, say some text. Next you draw the outline of a cutaway view of the object. This outline will be swept all the way along the previous outline to create a resulting 3-D object. To simulate something complex, such as a neon sign, you simply use the text as the outline and a small circle for the sweeper. The resulting 3-D text looks as if it were made out of round tubing. You can give the model the appropriate attributes to make it look like neon. This is a different approach to the usual extrusion methods other modelers use, but it gives you more control.

The rendering engine is very fast and can even perform tricks like casting colored shadows when a light shines through a semi-transparent object that is tinted a particular color. Another impressive feature of StrataVision 3-D PC is that is has a module called SuperSculpting that uses spline patches to create a contour of your sculpted model. The suggested retail price of StrataVision 3-D PC is $995.

Visual Software

Visual Reality

Visual Reality version 1.0 is a combination of four different programs: Renderize Live, Visual Model, Visual Image, and Visual Font. This package also includes 500 3-D clip art models and over 100 textures. Renderize Live (available separately for a suggested retail price of $395) is a rendering and animation program. By importing models from CAD software or other modelers, you can apply textures, set up lights, and render images.

A central feature to Renderize Live is ease of use. An icon system called EYES allows users to quickly manipulate objects, lights, and cameras to create a scene that can be rendered with a high level of realism. The concept is to offer a complex task (photorealistic rendering) without creating a

complex application. In this, Renderize has succeeded. Usually the downfall to simplicity is a lack of advanced features. This is not the case with Renderize, for many options and controls are available to the user through intuitive icons. Most of these options can be set with graphical "dials" that are easy to turn.

Renderize Live includes a number of advanced features such as a "Flipped" button to automatically mirror nonregular texture maps, such as granite or stucco, across an object's surface. A blurriness factor can be assigned at the object level without affecting the entire scene. Advanced transparency control is also available, such as edge and highlight opacity. With edge opacity you can simulate a sheet of glass where the edges are less transparent than the flat surfaces. Highlight opacity allows you to define how transparent an object is based on its shininess.

Visual Model, included with Visual Reality, is not available separately. However, it is a Windows-based, full-featured 3-D modeler. Visual Image is a 2-D image editor for Windows (available separately for $395). It supports 24-bit color images as well as the additional 8-bit alpha channel. Visual Font is a Windows utility that takes any TrueType font and creates a beveled 3-D DXF file from it. These 3-D characters can then be imported into Renderize Live for rendering. All of the programs are currently available on a number of operating systems including Windows, Windows NT, and UNIX. The

3-D clip art and textures are provided on two CD-ROMs.

HIGH-END TOOLS

On the high end of 3-D computer animation there are three major vendors of graphics workstations: Silicon Graphics, Sun Microsystems, and IBM. All of these systems run on the UNIX operating system. Of the three, Silicon Graphics has positioned itself in the lead with high-performance graphics architecture. Graphics workstations start in the price range of just below $10,000 and can go as high as hundreds of thousands of dollars. On the software side of graphics workstations, there are a number of 3-D graphics products available. The two main competitors are Alias Research and Wavefront Technologies. The following table lists the high-end 3-D computer graphics products currently available.

3-D Computer Graphics Programs Available for High-End Workstations

Company	Product	Description
Alias Research Inc.	Power Animator 5.0	Modeling, Rendering, Animation
ElectroGIG	3-DGO	Modeling, Rendering, Animation
Engineering Animation Inc.	VisLab	Modeling, Rendering, Animation
SoftImage	Creative Environment 2.65	Modeling, Rendering, Animation
Triple I	ARK Geometry & Hypermation	Modeling, Rendering, Animation
Vertigo	Vertigo version 9.5	Modeling, Rendering, Animation
Wavefront Technologies Inc.	Advanced Visualizer	Modeling, Rendering, Animation
	Explore Professional	Modeling, Rendering, Animation

Image courtesy of HD/CG. Dino Tours © MICO.

Following are reviews of these high-end 3-D graphics software programs. For contact information, see Appendix A.

SOFTWARE

ALIAS RESEARCH INC.
PowerAnimator

Alias PowerAnimator Version 5.0 is perhaps the most popular high-end modeling package. The program itself is divided into three primary components: Model, Render, and Anim. Each component handles its own aspect of the 3-D graphics process. Other secondary components combine to make up the complete system. PowerAnimator can create both NURBS and polygon-based 3-D models. This is done through existing geometric primitives or a variety of other construction methods. For example, you can use the skinning function to put a surface around existing objects and create a new object.

Materials are simulated through the Render module. You can adjust the appearance, color, shininess, and bumpiness of shaders. The Anim module allows you to set up your animations by using keyframes, motion paths, inverse kinematics, and several other possibilities.

PowerAnimator's most recent enhancement has been the addition of *Alias*

Cinematics. Cinematics simulates various cinematic effects, such as outer space explosions, headlights shining through the fog, or sunlight in a smoky room. PowerAnimator starts at about $7,000 and can go as high as $45,000 dollars.

ElectroGIG USA
3-DGO

3-DGO Version 2.4 is a modeling, rendering, and animation program. It uses solids as opposed to polygonal surfaces. This allows you to model 3-D objects by building and combining solid objects. This is referred to as *Constructive Solid Geometry* (CSG). ElectroGIG claims that such solid models render better and look more realistic than surface models.

3-DGO can also ray trace images for high-quality reflections. They even claim that their ray tracing renderer is faster than most scanline renderers. A variety of add-on products is available for 3-DGO, such as a particle system generator and a NURBS modeler. The program also includes context-sensitive help. 3-DGO has a suggested retail price of $4,995.

ENGINEERING ANIMATION, INC.
VisLab

VisLab is a modeling, rendering, and animation program that renders images using the graphics hardware available in Silicon Graphics computers. This allows the software to render complex 3-D scenes with 500,000 polygons in a few seconds. You can import geometry from other programs or simply model it yourself using the VisLab modeler.

Another great feature in this software is the smooth integration of inverse kinematics. For example, you can specify the type of connection between two objects, and when you animate those objects later on, their movement is constrained based on their connection type. Connections such as hinges, ball joints, bolts, and others can be simulated. Additional modules are available for rendering scenes using RenderMan software. ParticleLab is an add-on module for simulating natural phenomena such as fire, smoke, and fluid flow. The suggested retail price for VisLab is $9,500.

93

SoftImage
The SoftImage Creative Environment

Softimage Creative Environment Version 2.65 is considered the best program for animation on the market. You can animate objects using standard keyframe animation and go way beyond that with inverse kinematics using wind and flock animation (where objects move with respect to their surrounding objects). You can even animate using collision detection where objects will bounce off of each other.

The program is divided up into six modules: Model, Motion, Actor, Character, Matter, and Tools. Model is where you create your 3-D objects by using primitives, metaballs, splines, or standard polygon modeling techniques.

The Motion, Actor, and Character modules let you set up animation using forward and inverse kinematics, keyframing, dynamics, and skeletal animation. Again all of this adds up to make SoftImage the most powerful animation system on the market. The SoftImage Creative Environment has a suggested retail price of $6,000 to $55,000 depending on the platform you purchase it for.

Triple-I
ARK Geometry

ARKGeometry is a modeling and rendering program created by Triple-I, one of the pioneers in the computer graphics business. ARKGeometry supports geometric primitives, splines, and advanced edge-detection software that allows you to load an image, convert it to an outline, and then extrude that outline into a 3-D object.

Animation is handled by a program called Hypermation! that offers inverse kinematics. You can introduce variables, such as wind and gravity, which cause the 3-D objects to bounce and wobble as they would in the real world.

Vertigo
Vertigo 9.5

Vertigo Version 9.5 is a modeling, rendering, and animation program with the most comprehensive ties to Pixar's RenderMan interface of any commercial product. The software provides access to all parameters stored in RenderMan shaders and displays them so the user can make adjustments. When updates are made to these parameters, the screen is immediately updated.

Modeling can be done with Bi-cubic patches, B-splines, polygons, and metaballs. Scenes can be rendered with any shading method, including ray tracing.

Overall, the software consists of 15 modules and 8 utilities. All 3-D components, from objects to the lights and even the surface textures and bumps, can be animated. Vertigo has a suggested retail price ranging from $6,800 to $16,960.

Wavefront Technologies
Explore Professional

Explore Professional is a modeling, rendering, and animation program that allows you to interactively adjust surface material attributes directly, right in your 3-D scene. NURBS and metaballs are supported in the modeler. All of the modules are separate programs in Explore Professional, which makes transferring between them a little more cumbersome than need be. For example, to see a scene rendered you must save it, exit from the modeler, and then load the renderer and render it.

Its animation capabilities include forward and inverse kinematics, hierarchical animation, metaball animation, and keyframe animation. Particle systems can be created, and scenes are rendered in a 48-bit color space for high-quality color reproduction. The suggested retail price for Explore Professional is $38,000.

Wavefront Advanced Visualizer

Wavefront Advanced Visualizer Version 3.01 is a modeling, rendering, and animation program. It can render using Gouraud and Phong shading, reflection mapping, ray tracing, glass simulation, refraction, shadows, anti-aliasing, and fog effects. You can import objects or build them from scratch using any type of surface modeling technique from NURBS to metaballs.

Animation in Advanced Visualizer can be created with keyframes. A special module called Dynamation allows you to simulate physically based systems like water, fire, and smoke. Some animators find complaint in the fact that Advanced Visualizer's interface is not consistent throughout all of the modules. Advanced Visualizer has a suggested retail price of $15,000 to $80,000.

CHAPTER SUMMARY

You should now have a good feel for the tools that are on the market today. As with most things, "you get what you pay for." If you can afford high-end systems and software, then that's the ideal choice. If you don't want to spend that much, consider

the result of your animation; that will help you determine which hardware and software to choose. Chapter 4, "Where the Jobs Are," contains the first of our application tutorials, which continue through the rest of the book.

Chapter 4

Where the Jobs Are

There are many job opportunities for computer animators, everything from motion-picture special effects to medical visualizations. In this chapter, we will discuss just a few of these career fields and the type of animation that is used in them. The different fields can be divided into two major categories: science/engineering and entertainment.

In the category of science and engineering, there are architecture, forensics, and visualization. The most important criteria for animation in this category is a high level of technical accuracy. The scale and dimensions of the models that the animator creates must match their real-world counterparts exactly. Architectural animation involves modeling buildings and other structures, and then creating "flybys" of those structures. Forensic animation is the visual recreation of accidents or other complex events, making them easy for a jury to understand. Visualization is similar to forensic animation in that you model objects, complex data, or processes so they can be easily understood.

The entertainment category encompasses interactive entertainment, television, and motion pictures. Unlike the category of science and engineering, entertainment animation does not usually require a great deal of technical accuracy. In entertainment, the *look* is the most important aspect. If the image looks real or exciting, then it's accurate enough. Interactive entertainment includes

video-game and personal-computer products, and the animation typically does not use a lot of color (only 8-bit or 16-bit color depths). Television animation uses full color, but it is usually the lowest resolution animation among all the different fields. Motion-picture animation is currently the biggest money-making application for computer graphics. It requires high-resolution images, which almost necessitates that it be created on high-performance graphics workstations.

Let's take a look at these categories and applications individually and examine the type of animation that is required for each. Afterward, we include an interview with Richard Edlund, founder of Boss Film Studios. Edlund explains what he looks for in a computer animator.

Science and Engineering Animation

Architecture

Architectural animation can be very demanding, since it not only requires technical accuracy but also photo-realistic rendering. To ensure the technical accuracy, models are often ported from CAD software (where the structure was designed) into the animation software. Depending on the software you are using, you might be able to simply apply surface attributes to the imported models and render away. However, most of the time, these models will not render well and they require a lot of touch-up work. Sometimes these original models are even unworkable and can only serve as visual guides in creating new models.

Architectural animation does not require a formal education in architecture. All of the architectural work will be done prior to your getting the project. As an animator your main job will be to make a smooth sequence that gives good visual coverage of the structure. The most difficult challenge you'll face will be learning to read blueprints.

Architectural animation is most commonly produced for videotape. These tapes are then used to promote the project or get final approval from the developers. Sometimes animation is not required. When only still images are needed, you can use animation software to render the image at a very high resolution for a quality hardcopy.

FORENSIC

Notwithstanding its great dependence on technical accuracy, forensic animation is probably the easiest to create. This is because *looks* are not the primary concern in a court case. The jurors simply want the facts, and often you can effectively convey them with simple flat-shaded models. The most difficult aspect will be ensuring technical accuracy. All the 3-D objects must be to perfect scale, and most importantly, the objects must move with the exact speed and in the exact direction as in the original event.

Videotape is the most common output for forensic animation, so the resolution does not need to be exceedingly high. This means you can readily produce the animation on inexpensive personal computers. The tapes are then played back in court to the jurors. As with architectural animation, a single image may be required instead of an animation. This makes the whole process easier, since

you only have to worry about a single view of the object. This also alleviates the need for expensive video equipment and the large hard disk drives needed to create animated sequences.

VISUALIZATION

Visualization can involve anything from simulating the way an engine works to the way a human heart works. Typically, visualization is used to illustrate objects and events that are difficult or impossible to film with traditional methods. You might even think of a visualization as a *simulation* of the real thing. Animations or still images are often created to help sell products to prospective investors or buyers. While it may seem very technical, this type of animation does not always require a high level of accuracy. Many times, it is up to the animator to create a sequence that simply looks good. For example, you

Dino tours ©MICO

might need to create a scene of blood cells flowing through an artery. The actual dimensions and shapes of the blood cells are open to the artistic interpretation of the animator.

The output for visualization animation runs the gamut from motion-picture film to multimedia programs to still images. It all depends on the visualization itself and the specific job it is created for.

100

ENTERTAINMENT ANIMATION

INTERACTIVE ENTERTAINMENT

Interactive entertainment is a relatively new application for computer-generated graphics. One of the major reasons for its sudden popularity is the availability of personal computer-based 3-D animation software. With low-cost animation software, most multimedia companies are now taking advantage of the technology and doing so with outstanding results. Animation for interactive entertainment runs the gamut from crude flat shading to photo-realistic rendering and allows for a wide variety of artistic expression.

Animation for interactive entertainment does not have to be rendered at a very high resolution, and expensive video equipment is not needed since the end result will be used in some digital form, such as a CD-ROM or diskette. Also, no formal education is needed for this type of work, although some developers might prefer a degree in art or design.

TELEVISION

Television-broadcast animation requires high quality in both the design and output of the animation. The most common types of animation you see on television are photo-realistic—science-fiction special effects, station identifications, music videos, and commercials. Animation for television does not require the same high level of technical accuracy as forensic and architectural animation. If you can create exciting, highly visual animation, you can find a market for your work without investing in a lot of education.

While you can generate animation for television on relatively inexpensive personal computers, getting the animation out to tape in "broadcast quality" requires some pricey videotape recorders (VTR) along with other hardware to control them. There are some new digital animation recorders on the market that offer real-time digital storage and playback of animation, but these have yet to prove themselves in creating broadcast-quality animation. Thus, high costs can deter small-time animators from producing broadcast-quality animation on their own.

Motion-Picture Animation

Motion pictures are pretty much the Holy Grail for computer animators. Animation fo movies requires very high resolutions and therefore the fastest computers and most advanced software. There are few animation houses with the necessary equipment to produce this level of animation. Photo-realism takes on a new meaning with motion pictures because the high resolution can make visible even the slightest flaws.

Motion-picture film scanners and recorders are mandatory equipment for film animators, and the high cost of this equipment effectively prevents smaller animation houses from getting into the market. Theme-park attractions and other special-venue entertainment are also becoming big users of computer animation. This type of animation is rendered to film and thus suffers from the same drawbacks as motion pictures. When special format films are used, theme-park animation can require the highest resolution and fastest frame rate of any animation category.

Learning the Trade

How do you get started in computer animation? Fortunately, you don't have to go back to college and earn a degree. Computer animation is one of the few fields where you can simply teach yourself the skills and then get a job based on your talent. Of course, a formal education will help you develop your talents, but it's not

102

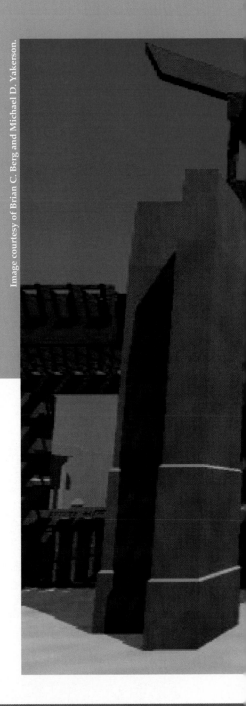

a requirement in this field. There are basically four ways to learn the trade of animation: you can teach yourself; get an internship at an animation house; attend a local trade school; or get a formal education and obtain a degree in design or computer science.

Be forewarned that regardless of the method you choose, you are about to embark on a process that takes a tremendous amount of time to master and one that has a never-ending learning curve. The technology is continually being improved, and it will be up to you to keep up with it, to learn and use the latest advances. Failure to do this will cause the quality of your work to fall behind that of your competitors in this fast-moving business. Before embarking on any of the following educational paths, contact your local animation houses and talk with them about getting started in the business. They should be able to provide information about the software that is currently being used, what companies accept interns, and which local trade schools,

103

colleges, and universities offer computer animation courses. One key thing that all animators agree on is that it's not the technical knowledge that makes a good animator—it's the creative and artistic ability. The best artists make the best animators, so if you pursue an education, stay focused on art and design.

Self Teaching

Teaching yourself is a very common practice in this field. Since computer animation is a relatively new art, many of the professionals in the workforce are self-taught. Another factor that encourages self teaching is that once you start producing animation, you will find that the software is updated or changed on a regular basis. When this happens, you will be on your own to learn the new changes.

You can teach yourself by purchasing some inexpensive animation software and then simply learning to use it. Whichever package you choose, learn it well. Perform all the tutorials included with your software's manual. Read the reference manuals from cover to cover to thoroughly acquaint yourself with the program's every function and capability. Then take the software to its limits in your own animation. Try to push it beyond what it is capable of doing. This will give you practical training for when you start receiving those impossible animation projects and deadlines. Also, contact users' groups and related professional organizations, and get involved with online services where animators gather to share tips and tricks.

Internships

A quick method of getting your feet wet in this field is to obtain an internship at an animation house. You may start out simply answering the phone, but it will get you into a production environment and you will learn very fast. A study taken at Northwestern University found that 58% of all internships result in a paying position at the same company. If you decide to go this route, decide exactly what it is you want out of your internship and ask for it before you start work. This type of training can be even more valuable than a formal education and may assure you a position at the company once your internship is finished.

Local Trade-School Offerings

Another possibility is to attend a local trade school in your area. Often these schools offer short, concentrated curricula that last from six months to two years. Most of them even offer job-placement assistance. Your challenge will be to find a trade school that offers a course in computer animation. You can look for related courses, such as computer-aided drafting (CAD) or computer art, and then check with the instructors about the emphasis of each course. You may be able to find one that can teach you a lot about computer graphics.

Image courtesy of Michael D. Yakerson.

105

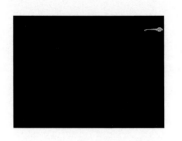

DEGREES IN COMPUTER ANIMATION

Because computer animation has become so popular in the last decade, you can now find a number of colleges and universities that offer courses in computer animation. Be forewarned, however, that obtaining a college degree will probably mean picking up a lot of excess knowledge about computer science and computer programming. Try to focus your training on art and design rather than hard computer science.

KEEPING UP WITH THE TECHNOLOGY

As I mentioned earlier, the field of computer animation moves very quickly. To keep up with the technology, there are three things you should do regularly: watch television and go to movies; subscribe to the trade magazines and read every issue cover-to-cover; and attend the trade shows.

BE A CONSUMER

To keep abreast of the latest developments in the field of computer animation, it is important that you be a consumer of computer graphics. This means watching television and going to the movies. This can be one of the easiest (and most enjoyable) ways of keeping up with the cutting-edge in computer-animation technology. Motion pictures will have the most advanced animation first; then you will see it later on television. With a little close observation and study, you'll start to recognize some of the styles of animation that different companies specialize in.

TRADE MAGAZINES

Subscribe to the computer graphics trade magazines and read every issue cover-to-cover. Magazines like *Computer Graphics World* will keep you up-to-date with the latest advances in research, behind-the-scenes looks at animation projects, and product reviews. For a listing of computer graphics-related magazines, see the Resources appendix.

TRADE SHOWS

Attend all the computer graphics-related trade shows that you can afford. Sit through every exhibitor demonstration that you can find, no matter how boring it may seem at first. Trade shows such as SIGGRAPH provide educational conferences and expositions that feature the latest hardware and software. For a listing of computer graphics-related trade shows, see the Resources appendix.

A DISCUSSION WITH RICHARD EDLUND, PRESIDENT OF BOSS FILMS

Richard Edlund has seen the special effects industry grow from his early work on the original *Star Trek* television series to his most recent work on *Cliffhanger* and *Batman Returns*. He's won four Academy Awards over the years and worked on such projects as *Star Wars*, *Battlestar Galactica*, *Raiders of the Lost Ark*, *Ghostbusters*, *2010*, *Die Hard*, *Alien 3*, and *Last Action Hero*. Edlund founded Boss Films in 1983, and today Boss Films is Hollywood's largest visual effects studio.

THE CURRENT MARKET

Edlund talks about some of the projects where computer graphics were used: "*Batman Returns* was a big computer graphics film for us, but the first digital compositing was in *Alien 3*. We also have been using digital techniques in thrill rides and commercials for a while, prior to using them in feature films. The reason was a resolution lag that existed for awhile. In other words, you could do digital effects, but the input, scanning, and recording capabilities were problematic for a period of time. *Alien 3* was the last movie we did that was, essentially, completely done photo-chemically. We had always used the so called *analog photo-chemical technique*, which is unreal because you really have to beat that technology

into submission or approach it as you would a sumo wrestler. To get the desired effect, you had to use everything from brute force to very subtle techniques.

"On *Batman Returns*, we were able to solve a fairly significant production problem by creating penguins with 3-D animation. We didn't create all of the penguins with computer graphics, just the ones in the shots where we needed massive numbers of penguins doing what you wanted them to do when the camera was rolling. They were not able to get that many penguins to do what they wanted them to do on the set, so we wound up modeling a penguin and multiplying it and using some fairly fancy software techniques to get them to march in formation," continues Edlund.

Boss Films has also been very busy using computer animation in theme parks. "The major project that we did for Expo '93 was a thrill ride that was about 75 percent

computer-generated and done for a large format process. We also did a lot of computer graphics work for *Cliffhanger*, melding traditional techniques with new computer-generated techniques. Mundane things, such as creating helicopter blades and getting wires and ropes that would do exactly what you wanted them to do."

How To Get Started

Edlund felt it was difficult to say the best way for someone to get started in this business. "The interesting thing about this business is that people come from all different walks of life and all kinds of disciplines. I've used everything from people who had nuclear physics backgrounds to no educational background at all, just a unique talent. Somebody who knows how to paint well, for instance, might become a great matte painter. In the computer graphics area, some people have a strong art background and later pick up the operation of the computer and the idiosyncrasies of computer graphics through an internship.

"I think that from the standpoint of computer graphics, you have two broad types that people fall in: those who enter it from the artistic end and those who enter it

from the technological end. So you have those people who are not daunted by the complex kind of brute force programming and who understand all the different kinds of computer languages. They may be stronger at coming up with technological ways of solving problems. Then you have those who have the artistic background, who are more into the visual nuances. I think you need both approaches in the business, and there are all sorts of gradients between those two extremes, the spectrum of talent."

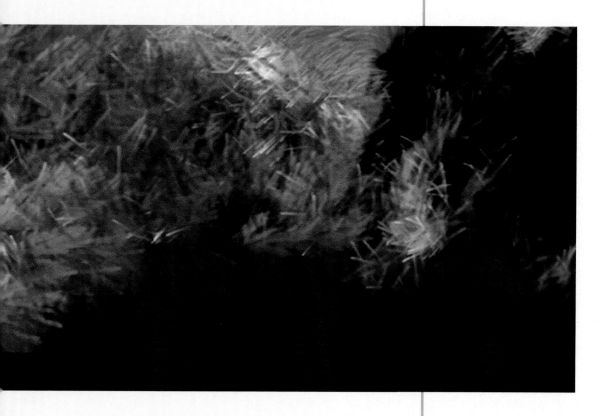

enhanced by computer graphics and computer animation."

Boss Films is a repository of special effects techniques. "It goes from matte paintings and miniatures to computer-generated imagery. Some of our miniaturization artists cross over because they are also computer literate and can go in and help the computer animators develop a model that looks right. Some people have all this visual sensitivity and experience in compositing so that they know a lot of tricks that are required to make a synthetic shot look like a real shot. So you have the visual mentors on the one hand and the young computer graphics whippersnappers who are loaded with talent and enthusiasm but don't have any experience. We're basically leaning on one another in a creative way."

At Boss Films, they are not necessarily concerned about a formal education "I think that it's not like you're looking for a professor who has *x* amount of education. What you are looking for is usually a person who is project-driven. If in a particular project we are dealing with generating a synthetic human being or generating some flashy new flying device, ship, or airplane, we would be looking for different talents."

"In the case of Boss Films, we're a visual think tank. The producer walks in, and you don't have any idea what's going to be on those white pages of script. On the scripts that are coming in right now, we're seeing an avalanche of creative, unrestricted imagination from the writers, because all of a sudden, they see you can do all these ridiculous things or magnificent things and it will look great. We have a couple of dinosaur scripts in here right now, and there are others where wild animals are doing very specific things that you could never train an animal to do. It's not like Francis the Talking Mule; we're talking about real nuance capable performances that could only be generated or

Edlund continues, "We look for talent; when you're dealing with computer animation you're losing old techniques like rotoscoping and cel animation. A lot of those old techniques are obsolete. We're now able to do those things on the

computer, but we still have to make it look real. So the fact that you can do all this stuff means that you must have talent at the workstation. In other words, if you want the Mona Lisa, you'll need Leonardo at the workstation. Today you need pretty heavy talent or a good collaboration of talent."

The Future of Computer-Generated Visual Effects

Edlund looks at the history of special effects to predict its future. "In *Star Wars* for instance, there was nobody who knew how to do motion control like the use of robotic cameras, or how to program an electronic camera system. If I was looking for an assistant, I basiucally had to train one because there was nobody who knew anything about this. So today we are in a sense at that same point with computer graphics. We don't know exactly where we're going, but we know we're in the elevator and we're going up. We just don't know how many floors the building has.

"My sense is that there has been a stigma attached to visual effects over the years because of the tremendous amount of labor required," continues Edlund. "In other words, if somebody wanted to do something in visual effects, there was a period where we just said `Look, it's about $50,000 a shot.' In the past, few would get involved in an effects show because of its complexity. It was sort of like building the pyramids. You had to quarry these huge rocks and get people to shove them up hills. It was complicated and it required many hands touching it. Likewise, with visual effects you had to have someone in the rotoscope department; you had to have a matte painter; somebody else was shooting an element on the stage; another person was making a garbage matte; and somebody was trying to be the maestro and organize these pieces so that the right cord played at the end.

"The process was painstaking, tedious, and time-consuming. Therefore, when directors came in to do some effects work, they would get very frustrated because it took so long to get the finished product. In the case of a complex show, you'd be working on numerous shots at the same time and shooting these elements five or six months before you would expect to see any kind of composite. The lack of instant creative gratification for the directors

made it unnerving for them. Just shooting and then having to wait one day until the lab processes the film is difficult. Of course, today video on the set has become very popular so directors can do playbacks and stuff like that.

"Computer graphics often provides instant gratification." There are many other advantages to computer graphics, as Edlund explains. "The director can see something happen much more quickly, and you're not dealing with seventeen people to do a shot; for the most part, you're dealing with just one person. Because one guy is going to be working on a shot using a workstation, you're cutting a lot of time, you're cutting a lot of complexity. Not that it isn't complex, but it doesn't *appear* so complex to the director who is working with someone in the shop. The cost comes down, the time involved comes down, and the confidence level rises because we have a real surgical way of playing with images. We now have control of every pixel on the image. We can break time down into 24 pictures per second and break each of those pictures down into pixels, each of which is addressable, giving us a fantastic amount of control."

This is something for which Edlund has been waiting for a long time. "What it's going to do in the long run is change the whole attitude of visual effects in movies. The movie that would never even consider having visual effects before will now. Maybe the director wants to do something like an extreme pullback on a shot or he wants to make the sun big and romantic in a particular scene, and the shot was done with a normal camera. As an afterthought, we can track the movie shot and put an oversize sun on the horizon, even make it reflect off the waves. Small things, such as removing billboards and television antennas for a Charles Dickens period movie. We can now remove those types of things easily. The visual barriers to getting an image the way you want it on film have become much more simplified. In the long run, visual effects will be producing more shots for more movies at less cost and will become a more familiar part of the grammar of film making. I believe that it is indeed a revolution and that we're looking at a white canvas out there again. You can paint anything on the canvas.

Image courtesy of Wavefront.

"I've been in the effects business for a long time. My big career opportunity was *Star Wars*, but I was in the effects business long before that. I worked on the original *Star Trek* TV show and have seen effects go from an extraordinarily complex and corroborative technique to this much more lively, quick, responsive and malleable technique that we have now with computer graphics.

"It was just two years ago that I was at the point where I was tiring of the inflexibility of the photographic process because we had pretty much pushed the envelope within the technology of photochemistry. We were starting to get bored with the tool kit that was available. I was frustrated because we couldn't effectively and convincingly do certain things that I wanted to do. The audience of course is no longer going to buy King Kong-style jerky motion; no audience is going to accept less than something that looks candidly real anymore.

"Houdini would be happy with the new set of magical implements we have now. We have

111

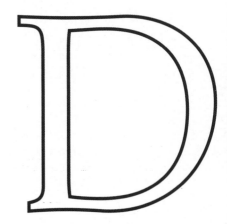

even talked with one producer about doing a full-length dinosaur movie using puppets for real-time motion capture animation of creatures. It's certainly possible to do things like this. It's a whole new field that's been opened up, and the median age of employees at Boss Film Studios has probably dropped a decade or two. We have a lot of young people here, and it's a wonderful thing. We are looking forward to the future and many new technological advances because the sky's the limit now."

GETTING YOUR FOOT IN THE DOOR

"I think that people who have inspiration in an area must see themselves in a particular role in that arena. I think that if people develop their particular talents and make themselves available to the world by being persistent and if they have what it takes, they'll make it into the business. Right now, we're really looking for talented people. We feel it is a talent-driven business. Because we're into content, we are looking for talented people, and I think that is going to drive the future of the company.

or

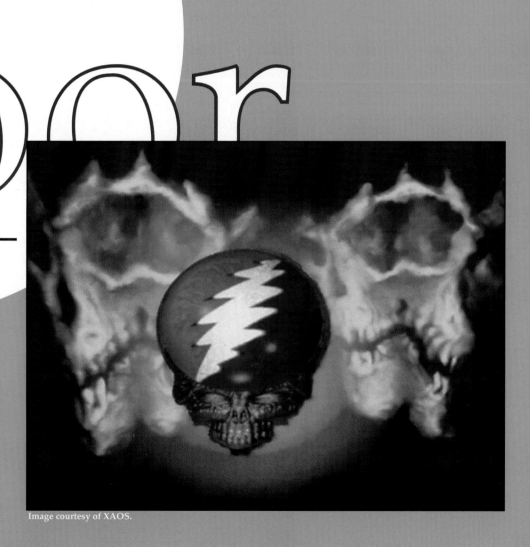

Image courtesy of XAOS.

"Even a global village type of shop may develop; that is, the shop is not geographically located but is on an Internet type of network. You could have collaboration between specialists in Australia, Greenland, Scotland, and Japan. You could create an entire project where no one ever meets each other. For the time being, however, our feeling is that human interaction, the ability to meet each other over coffee or in the hall or at lunchtime, the ability to socialize and interact on a human basis, is the reason for our kind of studio. That kind of interaction is why we are."

Edlund concludes, "If someone wants to get into the business and the desire is there, they'll find a way. You've got to bring something of value though; that's the first thing. If you have something to bring to the party, you'll get in."

113

Chapter 5

Interactive Entertainment

Interactive entertainment encompasses video games, multimedia, and other interactive technologies where computer graphics are used. The interactive entertainment industry may be the easiest place to find work for new animators, for a couple of reasons. First, you do not need expensive video equipment, since the animation doesn't need to go to videotape. Second, you as the animator have a lot of creative freedom and are not restricted to exact specifications for your models. If you can create visually stimulating animation, then you can be a successful game animator.

In this, our first application/tutorial chapter, we will interview Cyrus Lum, a highly successful 3-D video-game animator for Crystal Dynamics. Lum explains what's involved in creating 3-D animation for video games, describes how he got started in the business, and makes recommendations about finding work in interactive entertainment 3-D animation. He also offers some great tips

and tricks for character animation and texture mapping. The tutorial for this chapter will teach you how to navigate in trueSpace's 3-D interface, how to create models with geometric primitives, and how to generate animation.

CASE STUDY: CYRUS LUM, CHIEF ARTIST— CRYSTAL DYNAMICS

One of the most successful animators in the field of interactive entertainment is Cyrus Lum, who currently serves as chief artist for Crystal Dynamics. Lum has been working with computer graphics since the early 1980s, when he bought a TRS-80 personal computer from Radio Shack. The resolution was very low on the TRS-80 (only 128x48 pixels), so it wasn't until the mid-1980s, when Lum purchased an Atari ST computer, that he could create color graphics at a high resolution.

Lum explains, "With the Atari ST, I was actually able to draw a dragon and people would say 'Yeah, that looks like a dragon' instead of 'Is it a dog?'." At first, Lum created simple 2-D animation, but then he started playing around with a program called Cyber Studio, which was one of the first 3-D programs for personal computers. Cyber Studio was very basic; it only offered flat shading, with no texture maps or Phong shading. (It was created by Gary Yost and Tom Hudson, who went on to create 3D Studio, one of the most popular, PC-based 3-D animation packages on the market today.) Lum soon lost interest in computer graphics, mostly due to the technical and artistic limitations at the time, and he went to college to earn a degree in engineering.

Image courtesy of Acclaim Entertainment.

REKINDLING THE INTEREST

In 1987, Lum went to a computer-animation film festival and for the first time he saw what computers were capable of. "It was really inspiring," explains Lum. "It was fantastic! I came away thinking, 'My God, you can actually start doing realistic graphics. You can actually start telling a story.' Ever since I was a little kid, I always wanted to make my own movie, to be able to tell a story through pictures. As a kid, I could never afford an 8mm camera, and I didn't have all the workshop tools to create models and everything else to create stories the traditional way. I just didn't have the resources or the money. When the computer came along, I discovered that you have a lot of the resources there in one box. It's really exciting to me that you can actually tell stories with these machines."

117

While Lum was still in college, he had a slow semester in 1989, so he decided to take a job. He was looking for something simple, and on a job board he saw a position for a play tester at a company called Strategic Simulations, Inc. Thinking the job of a play tester would be easy, he applied for the job and got it. He was taken on a tour and introduced to the production department, the designers, the play testers, the programmers, and the art department. According to Lum, "At the time, I was still playing

around with graphics on the Atari ST, doing some animation, so right there the light bulb went off in my head. I said, 'Hey! This might be something to get into.' So after being at the company for may-be a couple of weeks, I started bringing in my animations and showing them to people in the art department—mainly the art director, Tom Wahl." Eventually they decided to give Lum a chance, and they assigned him to convert some Commodore 64 graphics to the Apple IIe. From there he started using the Commodore 64, and after that, IBM compatibles, doing graphics in CGA, EGA, and eventually, VGA.

Many of the early projects that Lum did for SSI involved drawing little animations of characters. The animations were only 2-stage (two frames), and the resolution was very small, sometimes only a few dozen pixels by a few dozen pixels. Still, Lum managed to create fighting dragons and other game characters. Lum explains, "I felt good about those early animations because I was able to obtain a quality that really didn't look like someone who just started in the computer-game industry. I was able to keep up with the other artists who had worked there for a while."

As Lum progressed in his skills, he was able to create larger and larger pieces. Lum continues, "I got the opportunity to do a large-size picture for one game. It was a picture of two dragons fighting in the sky—a red dragon and a gold dragon, fighting among the clouds. I was so proud

of it, and realizing that it was the first one I'd done, I don't know how many of my friends would notice it or even believe that I created it. So in the clouds I scribbled my name upside down, so when you took a look at the picture the normal way you only see the clouds and you might notice something weird happening up in the upper left-hand corner. But if you take the picture and turn it upside down, you'll see my name there: 'Cy Lum.' So that kind of started me into putting little Easter eggs into my pictures so I could say that they are actually mine. That one picture got into a lot of magazines and was even on the back of the box. It got a lot of exposure."

EARLY 3-D ANIMATION

After working at SSI for about four years, Lum found that he still wasn't getting into 3-D graphics the way he wanted to. He had done some small projects for SSI, but the company still seemed to be oriented to 2-D artwork and resistant to 3-D. Then he produced some sample animations for a futuristic space game called "M." Lum explains, "I ended up doing a lot of sequences for 'M,' like a docking-bay animation. I did a lot of 3-D sequences

and some of them showed up on the 3D Studio '92 SIGGRAPH demo reel. Some of these sequences showed spaceships going towards a planet and a pod being dropped out of a bay of another ship."

You can find the two animations for this game on the CD-ROM under the names MSHIP.FLI & MDOCK.FLI.

The "M" project gave Lum the opportunity to really start playing around with 3-D. He tried to create organic-looking models, and he started telling stories with the animation. He did this by incorporating different camera angles, and by altering the movement and positioning of the objects. His work started earning Lum some notoriety in the 3D Studio world, as his animations and renderings were seen on each successive 3D Studio demo reel.

While still at SSI, Lum started his own company, called ACyLum Graphics. He won some 3-D graphics contracts, such as making 3-D models and even subcontracting animation projects from other animators. One contract Lum tried for was an animation for the Monterey, California, Aquarium. The piece called for sharks swimming around in a shark tank. The client wanted to know if sharks could be animated in 3D Studio. Lum explains, "One day I sat down and created a shark, animated it, and showed it to them. It went over pretty good, but the whole project fell through." The piece was spectacular, however, and appeared on the 3D Studio SIGGRAPH '93 demo reel. During this time, Lum also did some work for an educational multimedia company called Knowledge Adventure. Lum did an animation of two dinosaurs (a tyrannosaurus rex and a triceratops) fighting.

You can find the shark animation on the CD-ROM under the name SHARK.FLC.

Back at SSI, interest was lost in the "M" project. It was put on hold and never saw the light of day. Still wanting to flex his 3-D muscles, Lum started looking around for new opportunities. Other game companies were taking a serious interest in 3-D, so Lum went to LucasArts. Ideally, Lum wanted to get out of the video-game world and into television or motion-picture work. Around this time, TriStar Pictures put the word out that they were looking for a hotshot 3D Studio animator to work on motion pictures. They called Lum requesting some sample images and animations. Lum put in his application and waited. While he waited, he turned down all the other offers that came through. The offer from TriStar never came, so after the 1992 SIGGRAPH conference, Lum accepted a job with a new start-up company called Crystal Dynamics.

According to Lum, "It was actually kind of funny, because Crystal Dynamics at the time was looking for someone who was more of a 2-D artist. Being such a new company, they weren't quite sure what kind of games they where going to do, so they weren't concentrating on 3-D or anything in particular. The offices were pretty bare. I had to borrow a VCR just to show them my 3-D demo tape. They didn't think I was what they where looking for, plus I really wanted to get more into 3-D. Eventually, however, they gave me a call and said 'Yes, we've decided what we are going to do. We are going to make a race-car game and do it all in 3-D.' They had remembered me and what I was able to do, and so I jumped aboard."

EDUCATION

Lum's formal education had little to do with computer graphics. He explains, "Most of the courses in college I took—and actually my whole back-ground—has always been in

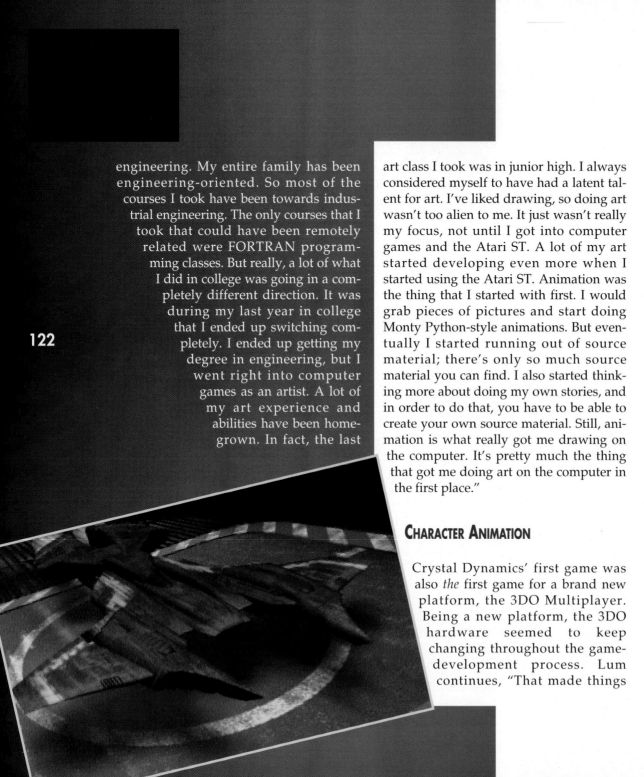

engineering. My entire family has been engineering-oriented. So most of the courses I took have been towards industrial engineering. The only courses that I took that could have been remotely related were FORTRAN programming classes. But really, a lot of what I did in college was going in a completely different direction. It was during my last year in college that I ended up switching completely. I ended up getting my degree in engineering, but I went right into computer games as an artist. A lot of my art experience and abilities have been home-grown. In fact, the last

art class I took was in junior high. I always considered myself to have had a latent talent for art. I've liked drawing, so doing art wasn't too alien to me. It just wasn't really my focus, not until I got into computer games and the Atari ST. A lot of my art started developing even more when I started using the Atari ST. Animation was the thing that I started with first. I would grab pieces of pictures and start doing Monty Python-style animations. But eventually I started running out of source material; there's only so much source material you can find. I also started thinking more about doing my own stories, and in order to do that, you have to be able to create your own source material. Still, animation is what really got me drawing on the computer. It's pretty much the thing that got me doing art on the computer in the first place."

CHARACTER ANIMATION

Crystal Dynamics' first game was also *the* first game for a brand new platform, the 3DO Multiplayer. Being a new platform, the 3DO hardware seemed to keep changing throughout the game-development process. Lum continues, "That made things

kind of scary. We were playing with a lot of different techniques. We had both interactive 3-D and pre-rendered 3-D in the same game." For a game called Crash 'N Burn, Lum mainly used 3D Studio for the modeling and rendering.

From aliens to human cyborgs to nasty troll-like creatures with big appetites, Crystal Dynamics makes heavy use of 3-D graphics for character animation. Lum provides some insight on how this got started: "Originally, all the characters for the game Crash 'N Burn were to be actors, but at the time we were a new company and we were also new to the whole idea of getting quality actors and a director to create quality content. So a lot of what came out of that were really goofy characters, poorly acted. One character was to be a cyborg. We tried videotaping a person in the make-up the costumer made. The costume itself was just a *Terminator 2* rubber mask ripped in half with tubes stuck all over it. This was then glued to the person's face. The second the person started speaking, the glue started coming off and his cyborg mask traveled all over the place on his face. I took that opportunity and sat down to create a 3-D character. I modeled a human head with all the cyborg parts, and then I took some of the original dialog and animated the 3-D head to act to the dialog. Well, it worked out very well."

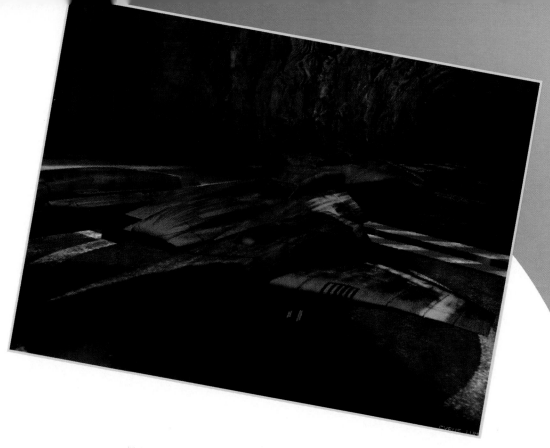

to handle all of our 3-D in real-time, so the only way to do this was to go for limited polygon models. I ended up developing some techniques that allowed us to really capture the detail of the larger models (those with more polygons) and use them on smaller models (with less polygons) yet still keep the detail."

Lum explains how to do this: "First, build the full size polygon model. For example, the '30,000-polygon dragster car from hell.' I would then take pictures from the top, sides, and maybe the front depending upon where the parts of the car were. Once I took these pictures, they become the texture maps I would place on the limited-polygon car."

Lum continues, "To build the limited-polygon car, I traced the outside edges of the 30,000-polygon car to create a basic 3-D shape. The final limited-polygon cars ended up looking more like tanks, but at least they were more-or-less skeletons for holding up a texture map. Next I would place texture maps on top of the polygon models; also, I would sit down and play around

Lum continues, "The dialog made it kind of fun because the cyborg really didn't have a mouth. It was covered by a grill, so most of the acting was done with the hands and with the left eye. When the cyborg would say, 'Come on! Take my offer!' the hand would gesture and his eyebrows would move around. That worked out very well, because I showed the possibility of being able to take this character and have him say other things without having to do any more animation. Also, considering he had no mouth, it was pretty easy to make generic gestures. To make these gestures, I animated him acting out Elvis songs like 'Love Me Tender.' I also used the Pledge of Allegiance. It all worked out very well and was fun."

MODELING FOR REAL-TIME 3-D

The new 3DO platform is leading a new trend of putting high-powered graphics capabilities into video-game systems. This means that once the 3-D models are defined to the system, the computer can animate them on-the-fly for high-speed graphics. This is affecting the way that computer animators do their work, as Lum explains: "We did a lot of modeling for the 3-D objects that the 3DO would generate in the game. However, the thing about 3DO is that even though it's a more powerful system than Nintendo's SNES, it still can't handle 30,000 texture-mapped polygons in real-time. Still, we needed it with the texture maps and make sure the edges matched up. The end result was that you would get something that looked like a 30,000-polygon model with just a few dozen polygons. We were able to get the quality into those models as well as the performance for the 3DO."

GAME MOCK-UPS

124

Today, developing a best-selling video game can be an expensive proposition. Some games run up into the $3-4 million range for development costs. This is another area where 3-D graphics can help out. Lum explains: "3D Studio really came in handy in the beginning of Crystal Dynamics' history, because a lot of what it takes to get started is money. Getting people to invest means you have to sell them on the idea. What I ended up doing with 3D Studio was actually mocking up Crash 'N Burn. This was about a month after I started at Crystal Dynamics. I mocked up a race track, a few cars, a dashboard, and other items. What I would do is put the cars into a little movie

where you're actually one of the cars and you're shooting at the other car. I made explosions going on and other special effects. It showed the investors what kind of game we were trying to accomplish. So it was basically a mock-up of game play. I put it together about four months before coding actually started on the game, so it was a great way to show people and investors what we had in mind. It gave everybody an idea of where we were going and got people confident. One of our potential investors saw this demo and we were able to secure about $2 million from them. Now I think the company is invested with $17 million, so we've come a long way. But back then, that $2 million really made a difference."

LIP-SYNCING CHARACTERS

Crystal Dynamics' next release was called Total Eclipse. Here Cyrus Lum took his character-animation capabilities and enhanced them to create human characters with a lip-synched audio track. However, after running into serious problems, the lip-sync was cut, as Lum explains: "Actually it was a kind of funny story. The characters were a commander and his ensign. Initially I had everything lip-synched, with moving lips in the animation. I tried to take the dialogue that we'd had a voice actor perform and then break down the timing. At that time, I really didn't have any kind of sophisticated sound system or any type of time code. All I had was a DAT tape and the clock that was on the DAT player. But you can use

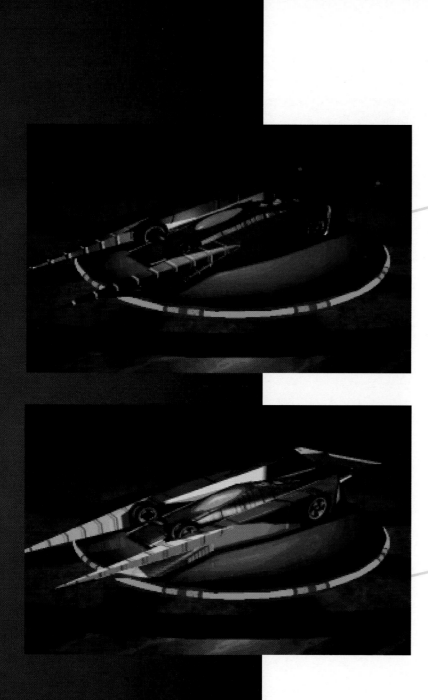

that to at least get whole sections of sentences and try to match up the pause time when characters aren't talking. I was able to get some dialog to match up, but when we played it back, it didn't turn out all that good. Some parts matched up, some parts didn't. What we ended up doing was putting microphones in front of the character's mouths. We also did a re-sync of the sound by having another voice actor act to the existing animation. That end result worked out pretty well."

After working on Total Eclipse, Lum realized the importance of lip Syncing in video-game animation, "I ended up taking a very long look at what was going on with lip-syncing. Lip-syncing seems like the future, at least in computer-game art, where you'll be doing a lot more audio with the visuals. One good tip I picked up from another animator is that when you have your voice actor performing the lines, get a video camera in there and also have a time code stamped onto the video. Actually record the actor saying the lines; then you can take that footage back to your animation studio and see exactly what the mouth positions are with the voice, because you have the time code. This serves as a good reference."

Another digital sleight-of-hand you can use for lip-syncing involves shooting the actors' faces from the front as they speak the dialog. You can then scan the video footage in, frame-by-frame, and map it on a generic 3-D head as an animated texture map. Thus, for every frame of animation you render, you will get a sequential frame from the original video mapped onto the

125

generic face. All you have to do then is ensure that the animation frames play back at the identical speed of the original video footage, and you can dub the audio right in. The only trick to this is that when you film the actor speaking the dialog, the actor's head must remain perfectly still; otherwise the texture map will appear to jostle around on the generic head when the animation plays back.

For the texture maps of the commander's face in Total Eclipse, Lum used one of Crystal Dynamics' producers, John Horsely. Lum used some pictures taken of Horsely and then took them into Fractal Design Painter to age it a little. Lum peppered his hair and added wrinkles to age the face. Then he mapped the altered image onto his 3-D face model and Horsely was thus immortalized in the game.

The next project for Crystal Dynamics was a game called The Horde. Set in medieval times, the game makes extensive use of digital video sequences and 3-D character animation. When The Horde was started, Crystal Dynamics was still only using PC-based 3-D software, such as 3D Studio and Playmation. Playmation worked well for character animation, and so it was used to animate all the game characters during gameplay. It was during this time that the company purchased some Silicon Graphics equipment and started using Alias Power Animator. Power Animator enabled Lum to perform high-quality lip-syncing, since the software allowed him to record audio and visually sync it with the animation.

The character animation was so successful that Lum was able to mix live video with a computer-generated character. This happens at a point in the game were a horde monster shows up to battle the star of the game, the actor Kirk Cameron.

IT'S THE STORY, STUPID

When asked what his specialty is, Lum replies, "When it comes down to it, I like to go more for concept. I don't concentrate on any one technique. What's most important to me is telling a story and being able to use computers to allow me to tell that story. I think it's the concept that gives me the drive, the creativity, that I put into modeling, texture mapping, or animation. I think that if it comes down to a specific thing about 3-D, it would probably be the animation. Animation is what got me into computer graphics in the first place. Animation even got me into art. What's kind of funny is that, in the future, creating animation will turn from key-framing to something more like puppetry, where you'll be using sensors and other motion-capture techniques to control your character. This will really get it to move around with true realism. Then key-framing, instead of being the main heart of the animation process, will probably be used more as the final editing or fine-tuning process of the animation."

TEXTURE MAPPING TIPS AND TRICKS

If there's one thing that characterizes Lum's animation, it's a strong attention to detail. Lum explains: "I definitely believe in texture mapping. I like to go for things that are more organic in nature. I like to do computer art that doesn't necessarily look like computer art, things that don't look shiny and clean like most computer art. I like some realism, or hyper-realism, or something in there that gets people away from thinking the art is computer-generated. It's like I said before—I'm really into concept. I use texture maps to try to break up the look of a computer-generated image. A lot of times I use 3D Studio and Alias with atmosphere effects like fog or glows, just to soften the edges. This helps get the background to bleed or blend into the foreground elements. I like to make it so everything's not always in focus and well defined."

126

Lum continues: "I tend to hand-paint a lot of my texture maps. I just like doing that, because as an artist I really want to have control over it. I mostly use Fractal Design Painter to paint my textures. I'll paint textures that you can also use as bump maps like animal skins. I also try to color it up, so it might have a more natural look to it."

Today, there are a number of texture libraries and CD-ROMs on the market with hundreds of textures on them. While these can save time in some instances, Lum doesn't use them very often. "With the concepts I come up with, I tend to have a different take on things, so the texture libraries don't have the textures I'm imagining. A lot of the creatures that I develop you won't see in model libraries, either. Likewise, a lot of the textures that I might want to use or the colors I want to paint my creatures you won't see in texture libraries. Having the ability to paint and create my own textures and actually model my own objects gives me a lot of freedom to really take what's in my imagination and turn it into a tangible image that people can actually look at. Sticking closely to the original concept helps me create texture maps and models. I ask myself, 'What is the concept that you want to put across?'

"I like trying to put character into texture. For example, if I'm doing spaceships, I might add a lot of rust. By making your own texture maps, you can customize things, put moles or birthmarks on your creatures. On a spaceship, you can put racing stripes where you want, or you can add oil splats. It's a philosophy that was used with the spaceship models in Star Wars. Building this lived-in, weathered look into the ships gives them a history, a personality, character. Even by putting simple grease marks in certain areas on bolts, you can actually give that ship a history. This tells the viewer that the ships are being torn apart all the time; that's why you have all this grease coming out and dents all over the ship. You can develop a whole story out of the textures. Having ships with burn marks or laser blast marks gives it a history, because you can start picturing or romanticizing it, what kind of battles this ship has gone through."

127

FINDING WORK IN THE INTERACTIVE ENTERTAINMENT INDUSTRY

Before an apprentice animator approaches a game developer, Lum recommends doing research on what's currently the state-of-the-art in computer animation for games. You don't necessarily have to look toward broadcast or film animation—just be sure to find out what's going on in the game industry. If you find a company that you are interested in, try their games and take a look at the art. You'll want to fill your portfolio with the style of art they commonly use, art that's relevant to the company. If they are geared towards fantasy, then fill your portfolio with fantasy art. "Everyone is trying to look for artists who are a close match," Lum explains.

Walk and run cycles are great for your portfolio if you are interested in doing animation. Come up with your own characters, because design is important (even if you are more interested in animation itself). In the game industry, when people come in they're expected to pick up a tool and start using it right away. Most companies cannot afford to train people, so they are always looking for someone who understands the overall art style and technical capabilities of their products.

Internships are a good way to enter the business. Many companies offer them. The downside is, internships either don't pay at all or they pay very little. "It really depends on what your confidence level is," Lum says. "If you feel you have what it takes and you just want to get in there, try to go as a natural applicant. But if you're not really sure and you want to see what it's like, going in as an internship really helps out. You don't have all the pressure, and it really gives you an idea of what it takes to be a computer artist in the game industry. A lot of what it takes in the game industry is that you need to be a production artist. What that means is that you've got to be able to take all the pressures of a tight schedule. Especially when it comes down to creativity and when it comes down to implementation. You have to make sure you can handle that; if you're not sure that you can, getting an internship would be a great way to find out."

Lum explains the importance of being an artist first and a computer graphics expert second: "In terms of education, a lot of the trend now days is to grab people who are artists and then train them up on the tools. At Crystal Dynamics, there's a lot of things we take into consideration, and one of them (the most important thing) is that the person who is applying for the art position *is* an artist, someone who actually designs, who actually has the imagination and creativity to really produce something that's unique. Without that, what you have is somebody who is more into implementation. They may know how to use the tools—whether it be PhotoShop, 3D Studio, or Alias PowerAnimator—but if they don't have that creativity behind them, they're limited to what reference material they can find. Considering that in the computer game industry we tackle things like fantasy, sci-fi, weird creatures, and all these monsters, you're not going to find a lot of references on these things. So it's going to be very important that these people are very creative."

Having a strong background in art really helps out, but there are some special cases, and Cyrus Lum himself is a good example. "I think I was lucky. In 1988, it was much easier to get into the game industry, much easier to get in as an intern and to get in as an employee. People were willing to try out everybody. Still, there is no college out there that really has a curriculum set up for computer-game development or computer-game art or anything like that. There's no trade school, no college, nothing like that, so the people that you have in the game industry have very diverse backgrounds."

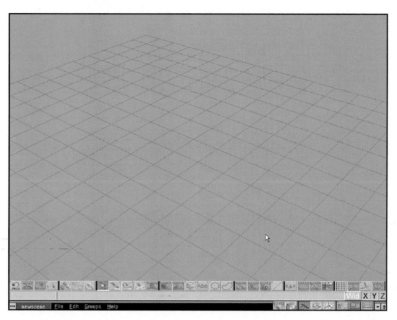

Tutorial Figure 5.1. *The Caligari trueSpace main window showing the 3-D workspace and tool icons.*

TUTORIAL: MODELING AND ANIMATING A SPACE SHIP

In the following tutorial, we will model a 3-D spaceship, apply a texture map to it, and animate it to fly past the camera. All the tutorials from here on will use texture maps that we have provided on the CD-ROM. Teaching you to use image-editing software, such as PhotoStyler and PhotoShop, to create the texture maps is beyond the scope of this book. (To learn more about this topic, see *The Magic of Image Processing* book information in Appendix A, "Resources.")

NAVIGATING IN TRUESPACE

In the first part of this tutorial, we will cover some basics about navigating through trueSpace's 3-D environment. Before starting any of the tutorials from here on, perform the following steps: Load Microsoft Windows, and launch the trueSpace program. This is done by double-clicking on the trueSpace Demo icon. Once the program is loaded, you will see the main window, which is a 3-D perspective view of your workspace. (See Tutorial Figure 5.1.)

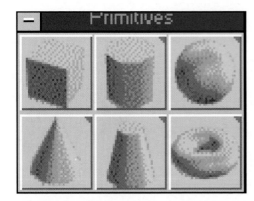

Tutorial Figure 5.2. *The Primitives Panel.*

trueSpace always restores the last file you were working on, and in this demo version, you always see the default scene loaded in the workspace. To clear out the workspace, select Scene from the File menu and then choose New to clear the existing objects. When you do this, you will notice that the current title of the scene in the menu bar located in the lower-left corner changes from "default" to "newscene".

In trueSpace, you can move through the 3-D environment by moving, rotating, or zooming the workspace view. This is accomplished by the Eye Move, Eye Rotate, and Eye Scale icons.

1. Start by left-clicking on the Primitives Panel icon in the Library Group. This will cause the Primitives Panel to appear. (See Tutorial Figure 5.2.)

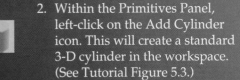

2. Within the Primitives Panel, left-click on the Add Cylinder icon. This will create a standard 3-D cylinder in the workspace. (See Tutorial Figure 5.3.)

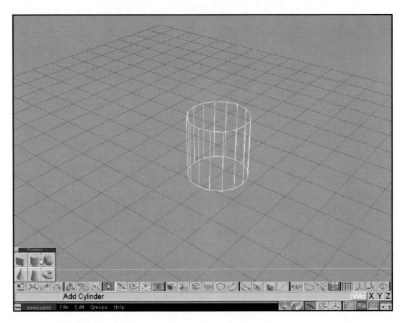

Tutorial Figure 5.3. *Creating a 3-D Cylinder.*

130

3. Next, left-click on the Eye Move icon and then position the mouse anywhere in the workspace. Left-click and drag the mouse forward, backward, left, and right. Notice how you can move around the 3-D environment. To move up and down, right-click and drag the mouse forward and then backward.

4. Now we will try rotating the view point around the object. Left-click on the Eye Rotate icon and then left-click and drag the mouse around. Notice how intuitive it is to rotate the view around the object. By right-clicking and dragging the mouse, you can rotate the view on the third axis. If you get the view too twisted up, you can left-click on the Undo icon as many times as you want until you return to a suitable view point.

5. The Zoom tool enables you to zoom in on your scene without moving the camera. Left-click on the Zoom icon and drag the mouse forward and backward to see how this tool works. Keep in mind, however, that while the other two icons (Move and Rotate) actually move your view point in 3-D space, the Zoom icon simply alters your field of view or eye focal length. This is similar to using a telephoto lens on a camera. If you zoom in, it looks like you are closer, but in actuality you are not. When zooming, it doesn't matter whether you use the right or left mouse buttons.

131

6. At times you may want to quickly check how your scene looks from the top, left, or front. The workspace view can be changed instantly to any of these positions by using the appropriate View Select tool.

The perspective view is the default view for the workspace, so you should see the Perspective View icon in the window group. Left-click on this icon and hold the button down. In about two seconds you will see a pop-up list of icons. These are variants of the View Select tools. (See Tutorial Figure 5.4.) Drag the cursor up to the Front View icon release the mouse button. Notice that now we are looking at an *orthogonal* (showing no perspective) view of the scene from the front. (See Tutorial Figure 5.5.) Also note how the View Select visible icon is now the Front View icon. This is how the variant icons work—the last selected one becomes the top, visible icon.

7. Try looking at our cylinder from the other preset views by left-clicking on the Top View icon and the Left View icon. Do not try the Camera View yet—we will add a camera to the scene later on.

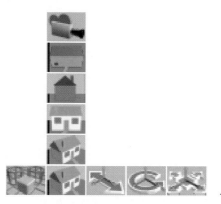

Tutorial Figure 5.4. *The pop-up menus show tool variants.*

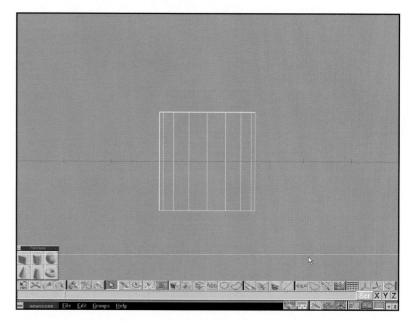

Tutorial Figure 5.5. *The front view of our scene.*

8. Before concluding this tutorial, go back to the perspective view by left-clicking on the Perspective View icon. Then left-click once on the Render Object icon. This will render the current object (in this case, our cylinder). Don't be alarmed by the pink surface. That's just the default material.

MODELING THE SPACESHIP

In the following tutorial, we will create the model of a spaceship. To keep our first modeling tutorial simple, we will construct the spaceship entirely out of geometric primitives. Then we will apply a texture map and assign a background image of stars before rendering some still images.

1. At this point, you should be looking at a single cylinder standing upright in the middle of the screen in perspective mode. First we are going to rotate this cylinder into a horizontal position. To rotate the

cylinder exactly 90 degrees, first turn on Grid Mode by left-clicking on the Toggle Grid Mode icon. This restricts all movement to discrete amounts that are user defined.

2. Next left-click on the Object Rotate icon to activate the icon, and then right-click on it. This will bring up the Coordinates Property Panel for object rotations. (See Tutorial Figure 5.6.) In the Object Coordinates Panel, make sure the Y Axis is turned off and the Object Axis is turned on. Now when we rotate the cylinder, it will only rotate on the X axis.

3. Now left-click anywhere in the workspace and drag the mouse to the left. You may have to drag it a little ways before you see anything happen. This is because Grid Mode is turned on and the object will only rotate at 45-degree angles. Rotate the cylinder so that it is

134

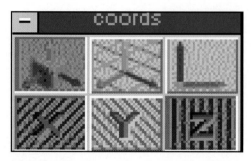

lying horizontally on the reference grid. (See Tutorial Figure 5.7.)

4. We want to make an identical copy of the cylinder, so left-click on the Copy icon. You will not see any changes on the screen. This is because trueSpace made a copy of our cylinder at the exact same location as the existing cylinder. So we must move our copy to a new location. To do this, left-click on the Object Move icon. Place the cursor anywhere in the workspace, then left-click and drag the mouse diagonally down to the right about two notches. (See Tutorial Figure 5.8.) Notice how only one of the cylinders is white and the other is dark blue. trueSpace does this to show you which object or objects are currently active. Any function you select only affects currently active objects. You can left-click on the

Tutorial Figure 5.6. *The Object Coordinates Panel helps control your movement in 3-D space.*

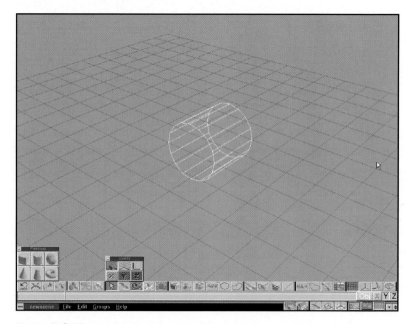

Tutorial Figure 5.7. *The cylinder after being rotated.*

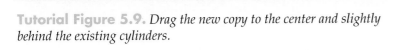

Tutorial Figure 5.8. *Move the new cylinder to the right of the existing cylinder.*

Tutorial Figure 5.9. *Drag the new copy to the center and slightly behind the existing cylinders.*

first cylinder to see it become active and then left-click on the new cylinder to activate it again.

5. Next we will create the ship's wings. First, make sure that the cylinder on the right is the active one, then left-click on the Copy icon again. Left-click on the Object Move icon and drag the new cylinder to the center of the two cylinders and slightly behind them. (See Tutorial Figure 5.9.)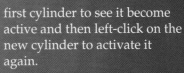

6. Now left-click on the Object Rotate icon to activate the icon, and then right-click on it to access its Coordinates Property Panel. Turn the Y axis on and turn the X axis off. (See Tutorial Figure 5.10.) This will restrict the cylinders rotation to the Y axis. Position the cursor in the workspace, then left-click and

drag the mouse to the right until the cylinder rotates 90 degrees to the right. (See Tutorial Figure 5.11.)

7. To scale the cylinder into the shape of a wing, left-click on the Object Scale icon. Now move the cursor into the workspace, left-click, then drag down and to the right. Keep scaling the object until is has the approximate shape of a wing. (See Tutorial Figure 5.12.) Then right-click and drag to the right until the wing cylinder stretches out to the edge of the reference grid. (See Tutorial Figure 5.13.)

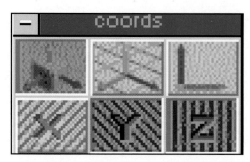

Tutorial Figure 5.10. *This is what your Object Coordinates Panel for object rotation should look like.*

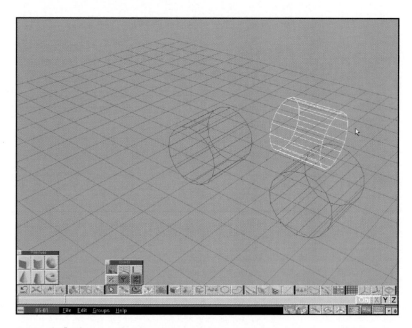

Tutorial Figure 5.11. *This cylinder will become the spaceship's left wing.*

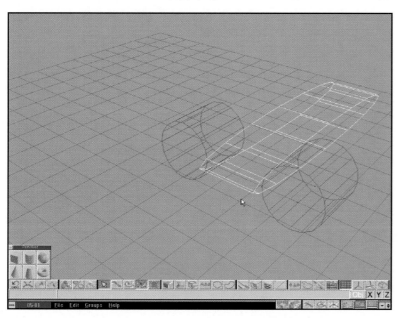

Tutorial Figure 5.12. *Scale the cylinder into the shape of a wing.*

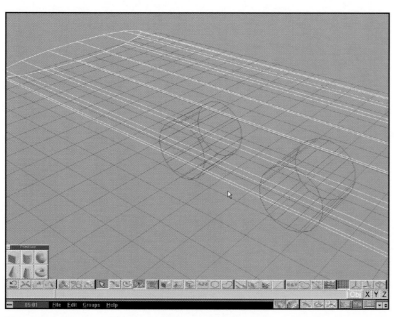

Tutorial Figure 5.13. *Scaling the wing cylinder along the Z axis.*

8. To make our cylinder look more like a wing, we can use the Smooth Quad Divide icon. Just left-click on it once, and the straight edges in our wings will be smoothed out automatically. (See Tutorial Figure 5.14.)

9. Now we'll add a few more details to the ship. In the Primitives Panel, left-click on the Torus icon. This will insert a 3-D torus into our scene. We are going to turn this torus into a smooth tube by scaling it along its Z axis. Left-click on the Object Scale icon, then right-click and drag the mouse forward until the torus turns into a smoothed tube. (See Tutorial Figure 5.15.)

10. Now left-click on the Object Rotate icon, then left-click and drag the mouse down to rotate the cylinder into a horizontal position. (See Tutorial Figure 5.16.)

11. To correctly position the new tube on the edge of the wing, we will need to switch the workspace view to the left view. Do this by left-clicking on the Left View icon. Then left-click on the Zoom tool and left-click on the workspace and drag the mouse down until you can see both tips of the wings at the same time. (See Tutorial Figure 5.17.) You may have to stop dragging and let go of the left mouse button to see where the wings currently are, because trueSpace only updates the currently selected object when moving or scaling.

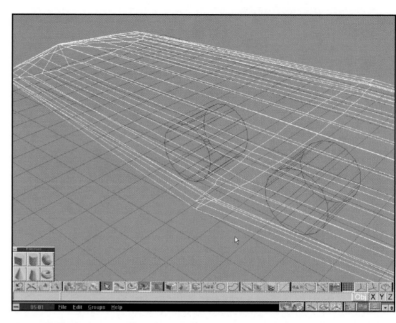

Tutorial Figure 5.14. *The Smooth Quad Divide function smooths out rough edges.*

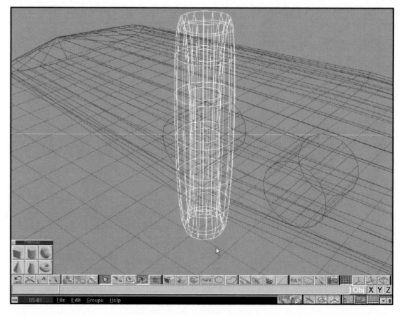

Tutorial Figure 5.15. *Scale the torus up along its Z axis until it looks like a tube.*

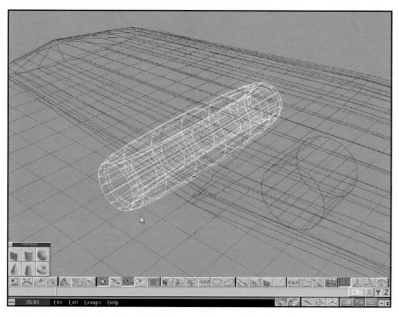

Tutorial Figure 5.16. *This is what your Object Coordinates Panel for object rotation should look like.*

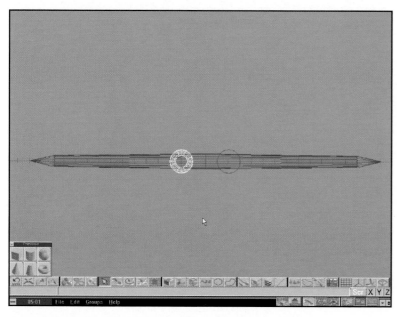

Tutorial Figure 5.17. *Zoom out to see the entire wing.*

12. We are going to put a tube at each end of the wing and then put one in the middle. First, however, we need to make a copy of the wing; do this with the Copy icon. After you've left-clicked once on the copy icon, left-click on the Toggle Grid Mode icon to turn it off. Now we can move and rotate objects freely without being constrained. Left-click on the Object Move icon, then left-click anywhere in the workspace and drag the mouse to the left (but don't click on any objects). Position the tube as if it is hanging from the edge of the wing, make a copy of it, and move the copy to the same position on the right edge. (See Tutorial Figure 5.18.)

139

13. Next left-click on the tube that is still in the middle of the ship and move it to the center of the wing. We will now scale the center tube to make it larger. Do this by selecting the Object Scale icon, then left-click and drag the mouse forward and to the right. As the tube enlarges, keep it circular. (See Tutorial Figure 5.19.)

14. For the final piece of our ship, left-click on the Add Cut Cone icon in the Primitives Panel. First, let's center the cone by left-clicking on the Object Move icon and dragging the cone to the middle of the ship. (See Tutorial Figure 5.20.)

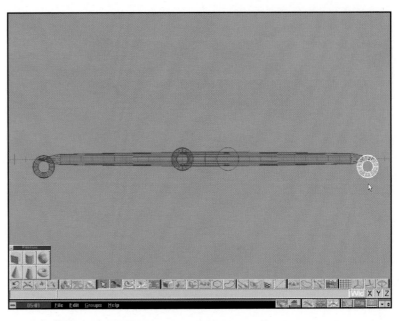

Tutorial Figure 5.18. *Position one tube on each edge of the ship's wing.*

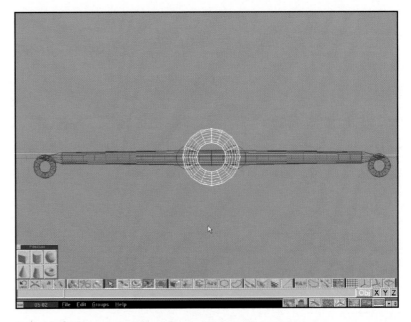

Tutorial Figure 5.19. *After scaling up the middle tube.*

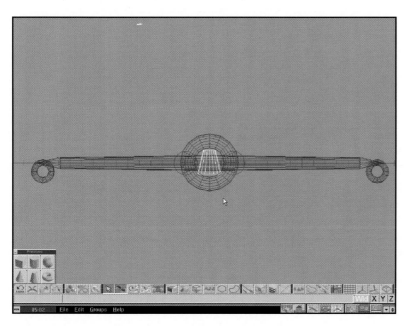

Tutorial Figure 5.20. *The final piece of our ship will be based on a cut-cone primitive.*

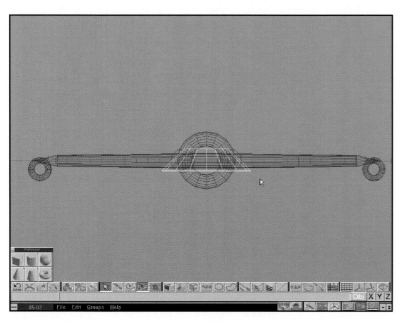

Tutorial Figure 5.21. *The cut cone after scaling.*

15. Now use the Object Scale icon. Left-click and drag the mouse to the right until the cut cone is slightly wider than the center tube. (See Tutorial Figure 5.21.)

16. From the Window Group, select the Top View icon, then left-click on the Zoom icon, left-click anywhere in the workspace, and drag the mouse down until you can see the entire ship. (See Tutorial Figure 5.22.)

17. Choose the Object Scale icon, then left-click and drag the mouse to the right to enlarge the cut cone so it is somewhat proportional. Our ship is finished. (See Tutorial Figure 5.23.)

18. Now we want to assign a surface texture to the spaceship. Left-click on the Material Library icon, and the Material Library will appear. Left-click on the silver sphere with the name Spaceship assigned to it. (See Tutorial Figure 5.24.)

19. After selecting a material, you need only apply it to the parts of your model. To do this, left-click on the Paint Object icon), which may be under the Paint Face icon. Now just left-click on any part of your spaceship model to render that piece in the Spaceship material. After you paint all the pieces, return to the Perspective view by left-clicking on the Perspective View icon.

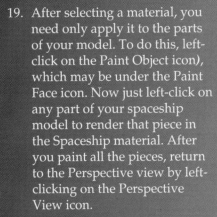

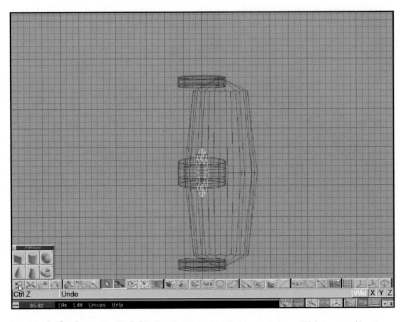

Tutorial Figure 5.22. *Switching to the top view will let us adjust the location and proportions of the cut cone.*

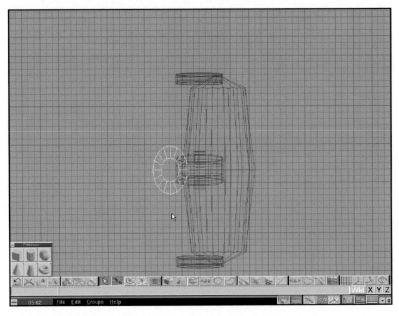

Tutorial Figure 5.23. *Our finished ship.*

Tutorial Figure 5.24. *Selecting the Spaceship material from the Material Library.*

Tutorial Figure 5.25. *The Render Options Panel enables you to choose an image to serve as the background.*

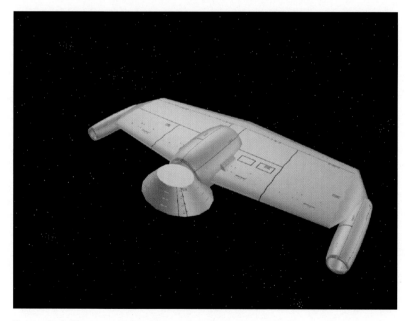

Tutorial Figure 5.26. *The finished rendering of our spaceship.*

20. For the finishing touch, let's add a star background. Right-click on the Render Current Object icon to pull up the Render Options Panel. In this panel, left-click on the wide blank square beneath the word "Background." This will cause a standard Windows file dialog box to appear. Select the file STARS.BMP and left-click on OK. It will return you to the Render Options Panel, and you will now see the name STARS under the Background setting. (See Tutorial Figure 5.25.)

143

21. To see your finished rendering, left-click on the Render Scene icon and the finished picture will be rendered. (See Tutorial Figure 5.26.) Try rendering different views by using the Eye Move, Eye Rotate, and Zoom icons. After you finish rendering the still images, return the perspective view to its original location.

ANIMATING THE SPACE SHIP

In our final interactive entertainment tutorial, we will set up a 30-frame animation. First, however, we will glue together all of the pieces of our model so we can animate it as one solid unit.

1. Return to the top view by left-clicking on the Top View icon. If you cannot see the entire ship in the workspace, try using the Eye Move and Zoom icons to adjust the view so the entire ship can be seen.

2. Next, left-click the Glue as Sibling icon and you will notice that the cursor changes into a little bottle of glue. Now, whatever object you left-click on will become "glued to" or attached to the currently selected object (the object that is white). Left-click on one of the dark blue objects and notice how it turns white as it is glued to the current object. (See Tutorial Figure 5.27.) Continue doing this until all of the objects are glued together (that is, the entire

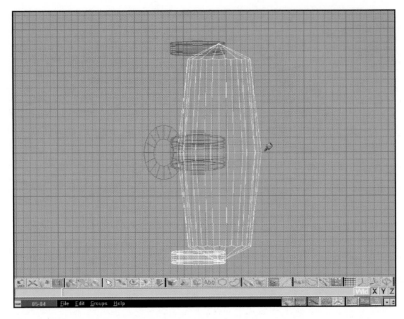

Tutorial Figure 5.27. *Here we have glued the bottom wing tube to the ship's wing. Notice how both are white now.*

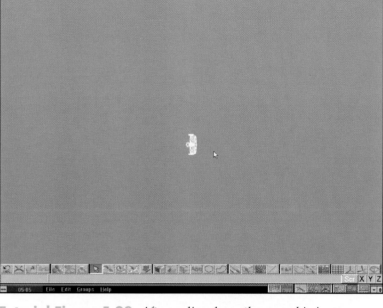

Tutorial Figure 5.28. *After scaling down the spaceship in preparation for its animation.*

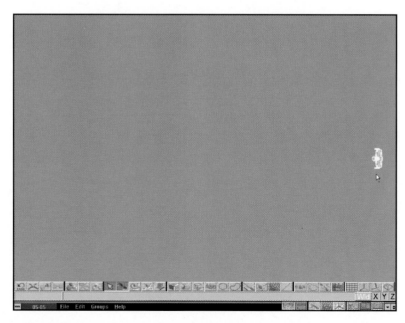

Tutorial Figure 5.29. *Move the ship to the far-right corner of the screen.*

spaceship is white). Once all the objects are glued together, the entire ship can be moved, rotated or even scaled as if it were one object.

3. In order to animate the spaceship flying, we need to zoom out so we have some space to move the ship around. To do this, choose the Zoom icon, left-click and drag the mouse down until the entire spaceship is very small in relation to the screen. (See Tutorial Figure 5.28.)

145

4. Now choose the Object Move icon and left-click in the workspace and drag the spaceship horizontally to the right side of the screen. (See Tutorial Figure 5.29.) This will be the starting point of our animation. From here the ship will fly toward the perspective view.

5. To create an animation, you first have to left-click on the Animation Tool icon in the Animation Group. This brings up the Animation Panel. (See Tutorial Figure 5.30.) The Animation Panel enables you to specify how many frames you want in your animation. (Note: The demo version of trueSpace only allows up to 30 frames in an animation.) It also enables you to use standard VCR-type controls, such as play, fast forward, rewind, and record.

6. Position the cursor over the Scroll Frames icon in the control panel, then left-click and drag the mouse to the right until the number of frames equals 30. (See Tutorial Figure 5.31.)

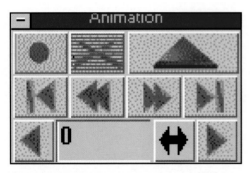

Tutorial Figure 5.30. *The Animation Panel allows you to use standard VCR-type controls to create or edit animation.*

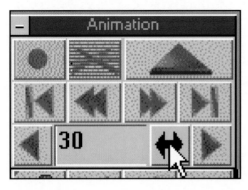

Tutorial Figure 5.31. *Change the number of frames to 30 by typing in the number or by left-clicking and dragging the scroll frames counter until it reaches 30.*

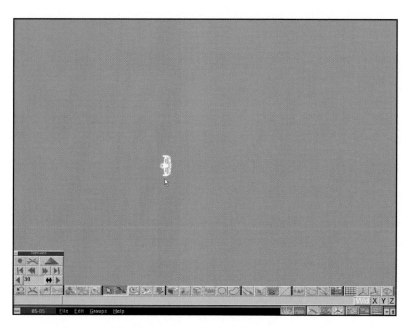

Tutorial Figure 5.32. *Move the ship to the left side of the center of the screen.*

7. To set the motion for our space-ship, left-click on the Object Move icon, then left-click in the workspace and drag the space-ship horizontally back to the center of the screen, just a little further left than it originally was. (See Tutorial Figure 5.32.) This will be the ending point of our animation. By moving the ship a little past the center of the screen, we guarantee that it will fly past the perspective view and not stop right in front of the perspective view.

8. Before going to the perspective view, left-click once on the Play Animation icon in the Animation Panel to see the motion of the spaceship from frame 0 to frame 30. Notice how the ship travels from the start-ing point to the ending point of the animation.

 9. Left click the Return To Start icon and the ship will jump back to its starting position in frame 0. Now let's look at the animation in perspective by returning to the perspective view. Left-click on the Perspective View icon in the Window Group. Don't be surprised that you no longer see your ship—it's off in the distance where we moved it earlier.

10. We need to rotate the perspective view so we can see the ship as it flies towards us. Do this by left-clicking on the Eye Rotate icon and dragging the mouse down and left until you can see the ship in the upper-right corner of the screen. (See Tutorial Figure 5.33.) To see the animation in perspective, left-click once on the Play Animation icon in the Animation Panel. All that's left now is to render the animation sequence to disk.

11. To render the animation to disk, left-click on the Render Current Object icon and hold the button down until the variants pop up, then drag the mouse up to the

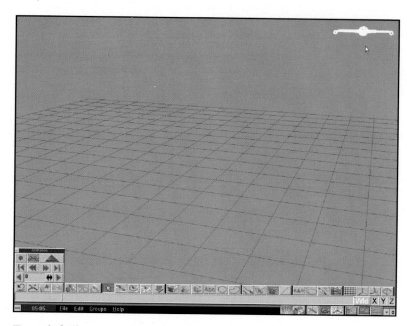

Tutorial Figure 5.33. *Rotate the view until you can see the ship in the upper-right corner of the workspace.*

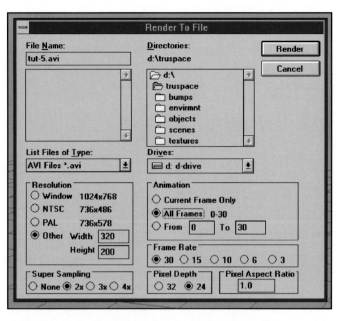

Tutorial Figure 5.34. *The Render To File dialog box.*

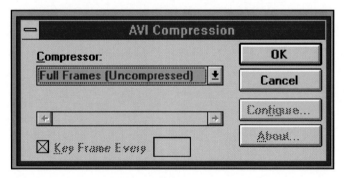

Tutorial Figure 5.35. *The AVI Compression dialog box allows you to choose compression options for your AVI files.*

Render Scene to File icon. You will now be presented with the Render To File dialog box. First, choose the output file type as "AVI Files *.avi", then enter the name **tut-5.avi** as the filename. Make sure that "All Frames" is selected in the animation box and that the frame rate is set to 30 with a pixel depth of 24. For super sampling (anti-aliasing), you can choose none or 2x; however, the more super sampling you use, the longer the time it will take to render. When you have your settings similar to those in Tutorial Figure 5.34, left-click on the Render button. When you are presented with the AVI Compression dialog box (see Tutorial Figure 5.35), verify that the compression is set to "Full Frames (Uncompressed)" and left-click on OK. At this point your animation will render to a Video for Windows AVI file. It can be played back using the Microsoft Media Player.

Extra Projects:

The following are a few suggestions for more hands-on modeling and animation practice.

- Create a new ship using various geometric primitives.

- Assign different materials to different parts of the ship.

- Try creating a different animation by rotating or moving the ship or perspective view to a new position.

- Load the KLINGON.OBJ model and add it to the scene.

Chapter Summary

In this chapter we have given you an overview of computer animation as it is used in interactive entertainment. We have also explained how to model using geometric primitives, assign surface textures, and create and render animations. In the next chapter, we will look at computer animation as it is used in the judicial system.

Chapter 6

Forensic Animation

154

Forensic animation is perhaps both the easiest and the hardest type of animation to create. It is easy because photo-realism is not necessary. It is very difficult because many of the images and movements must be absolutely precise. With other forms of animation, the worst thing that can happen from a mistake is that you lose a client. With forensic animation, a mistake might send someone to jail—or worse.

Computer animation is becoming increasingly popular in the courtroom because of its ability to simply and clearly illustrate technical and complex issues. It is commonly used for patent claims, vehicle collisions, product liability, structural analysis, and manufacturing processes. However, with its increasing popularity, it is even finding its way into other areas,

such as medical claims and even murder trials. The goal in a courtroom is to educate the jury, and computer graphics provides one of the best ways to do this.

In this chapter we will interview Don Pence, a successful forensic animator and co-owner of Video Law Services, Inc. He shares some tips and tricks on creating forensic animation, and he warns of some specific pitfalls. Pence also walks us through a typical forensic animation job and explains how he goes through the bidding process. In our tutorials, we will re-create a freeway accident involving a semi truck and a Camaro.

The full animation from this murder trial can be found on the companion CD-ROM.

CASE STUDY: DON PENCE, VIDEO LAW SERVICES

Don Pence is the co-founder and co-owner of Video Law Services, Inc. a video-production service for lawyers that specializes in accident re-creation. Originally, Pence came from the field of set design, construction, and lighting for motion pictures, video, and theater. Explaining how he got started with forensic work, Pence says, "I got interested in it because it seemed to be a place where I could apply my previous knowledge of design and because I had a good feel for some spatial relationships within the geometric universe as it is."

Video Law Services, Inc. is eight years old. Pence and his wife, Michaela Miller-Pence, concentrate on video production and they provide suggestions or guide lawyers in the best ways to present certain evidence and in the creation of various types of videotape evidence for accident re-creation. This involves going out to the accident site, setting up a scene, and shooting it with a motion-picture camera at 1/3 or 1/4 speed.

Amiga. I think it's probably a bit more cost-effective to do this on the computer at times, although it can be a little tedious because model-creation time is always going to cost the most in that type of thing. Still, compared to doing a video re-creation, where you must procure vehicles and run them, as well as the cost of using drivers, computer animation can be much less expensive." Today, Video Law Services, Inc. uses Commodore Amiga computers to create its animations.

GETTING STARTED IN COMPUTER ANIMATION

There wasn't a particular animation that got Pence interested in creating it himself. "I've always been intrigued by the use of computer graphics and this style of communication," he says. He feels that communication in general is speeding up. "TV commercials are becoming shorter and shorter. Back when I was in the commercial production business, we did some spots that were two minutes long, which is almost unheard-of today. Now it's not unusual to see 10- and 15-second spots

About five years ago, Video Law Services, Inc. started using computer animation to re-create accidents. Pence immediately liked using his computer to create animation. "I'm not an artist, I'm a mechanic. That lends itself to the science end of animation. Of course, we also want to keep things looking nice, and that we can do easily with the Video Toaster and the

within a commercial break, and they tell quite an adequate story. Commercials are becoming, in my opinion, the artwork of today's society, just because they mimic life so well. Even the little coffee commercials, which run a set of TV spots over a period of years to tell a story, are quite an acceptable medium now."

Pence continues, "Graphics is really our best medium to start communicating that is acceptable to the population as a whole. In forensic graphics and animation, the jury is keyed to it, because every night on the news we're seeing something explained, either a room in the White House or a view of the Capitol Building. We're seeing computer graphics used to explain different situations by charts and graphs. There are studies that show that the average person watches 6-1/2 hours of television per day and the average home in the United States has about 1.3 television sets in it currently. The population as a whole feels that television is a valid form of communication, and over 70 percent of them find they learn something from television. So all

of the pointers are there; it's easy to become enthusiastic about it."

Pence taught himself 3-D animation with an older Amiga program called VideoScape, which was written by Allan Hastings. Pence explains, "At the time, we basically had to go out and measure vehicles and enter the data point-by-point. The motion files were created the same way, which wasn't all that tough, since it doesn't take a licensed engineer to figure it out; the math's been around at least 500 years. Concepts of drag coefficients, acceleration, and deceleration have been around for years. There's nothing tricky, magical, or mystical about what we do; it's simply applying numbers to an object to re-create the pattern or path that it took. It's gotten much better recently, with the advent of newer personal computer systems and software. The Amiga platform as a whole works faster, and the operating system is less prone to crashing, which certainly makes it easier than it was five or six years ago, when we started."

Describing his background, Pence explains: "Most of the background I've got as far as mathematics and physics comes from high school and college-level courses that I took in geometry, algebra, some trigonometry, and a little calculus. Most of the trigonometry and calculus that I use has basically been self-taught."

Video Law Services, Inc. has animated a great variety of projects, including medical illustrations, surgical procedures, aircraft accidents, automobile accidents, and many others. Pence says, "A couple years back, we did a lot of motorcycle accidents. We did five or six motorcycle cases in one year. It's fun stuff for me to do, just from the aspect of creating the incident and making it make sense, creating something that communicates to others the complexities of the numbers."

Pence explains the utility and visual appeal of animated information. "If I had to go to the jury and explain the conservation of momentum, and explain why this vehicle was at this particular point and where energy was expended during metal crushing, and things like that, it wouldn't be nearly as effective a case. Get a jury after lunch and they're ready to sleep, not learn or relearn their math lessons from 10th grade. The jury is there to learn something and serve a public function, and at the same time, because it is a new and interesting experience, some might be entertained by the new experience. I use that word guardedly, because I'm sure it would cause a lot of flak in court, but in any situation where you are teaching a human being, you've got to entertain them somewhat."

Typical projects come to Video Law Services, Inc. through attorneys. "An attorney will basically call us and say, `I've got this situation: Two cars collided, one was pulling a trailer. The first car was passing the trailer and bumped it, which sent both sets of vehicles out of control' (What we call an unstable situation). `Those vehicles came to a position of rest or stabilized. Then another vehicle traveling at 65 to 67 miles an hour, approximately 10 seconds after the first non-stable incident happened, ran into the second vehicle. At the same time, a tractor trailer was able to avoid the accident and a small car was able to avoid it as well. There was variable-to-clear visibility, no wet pavement, not a bright night but moderate night.'"

Pence will then take a look at reports and statements provided by the attorney, read through the depositions, and determine an overall price for the project. (See the section on "Bidding a Forensic Animation.") If the job is accepted, the attorney sends the engineering data, the witness statements, photographs of the accident scene (if there are any), and anything else applicable to the case.

157

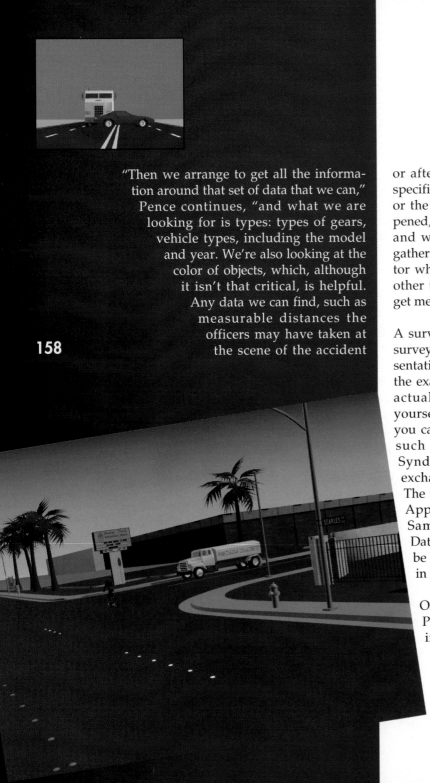

"Then we arrange to get all the information around that set of data that we can," Pence continues, "and what we are looking for is types: types of gears, vehicle types, including the model and year. We're also looking at the color of objects, which, although it isn't that critical, is helpful. Any data we can find, such as measurable distances the officers may have taken at the scene of the accident or after the fact, is important. We want specific measurements of the intersection or the interstate where the accident happened, any landmarks or reference points, and what we can't find, we go out and gather. We might go through an investigator who is near the scene if it's not local; other times, we'll send somebody out to get measurements."

A survey crew can be hired to do a land survey of the area to get an accurate representation of the topography. You can get the exact measurements for vehicles from actual cars and then do the modeling yourself, or if you are in a time crunch, you can buy 3-D objects from producers, such as ViewPoint DataLabs and Syndesis, or you obtain objects in an exchange through associations such as The Society of Forensic Arts (SFA). (See Appendix A for contact information.) Sample 3-D objects from ViewPoint DataLabs, along with other models, can be found on the companion CD-ROM in the \models directory.

Once all the data has been collected, Pence starts putting the information into the computer. "I start running numbers to check the engineering accuracy of the scene. Along the way, I check with an engineer to make sure the corrections are viable and acceptable to him. If I see something that I feel is possibly miscalculated, then I will confer with the engineer and work it out. Finally, when everything is correct, we apply the motion file to the objects and start rendering. Our rendering is done at standard video rates, 30 frames per second."

BIDDING A FORENSIC ANIMATION JOB

When bidding a job, Pence first looks at the size of the objects, how long it would take to model them, or what it would cost to purchase them if there is a time crunch. Based on the complexity of the objects, the cost will run from as low as $600 to as high as $1,200. Pence feels this range is pretty much the standard across the industry for object creation.

Next he looks at the time it's going to take to generate the motion file. This includes all the research time and checking calculations from the engineer. "This is a big flex area, because depending on how much the

the extra features to the animations, such as texture maps; that's not my strong point. I'm good at the mechanical end of things. To avoid pitfalls, learn what your deficiencies are. For example, I'm not good at reading manuals. I've never been able to really get the meat out of what a program does just by sitting down and reading it. I play with a lot of programs; consequently, I've got a lot of software sitting on the shelf that we don't use. Those are the main pitfalls in getting started as I see it, getting to know what your strong points and weaknesses are and accepting the weaknesses and moving forward with the strong ones. Also, accept the fact that if you're not willing to search out someone who has a lot of experience in various platforms and different programs and is willing to share some of these things with you, it's going to take some time, possibly a year or more, finding a program that works best for you—no matter what the platform is."

engineer has done or hopes to have done by the end of the project, it may be anywhere from $5,000 to $25,000. Rendering time, which is usually minimal, is billed out at $25 to $30 per hour. Then the cost of time and travelling is added if they have to go out of town to get data or documentation."

Pence has a number of good suggestions for first-time animators. "The pitfalls are basically finding out whether or not you really want to do this. It takes a very broad-based person to be able to do it, to do any of the production phases of forensic animation well. I certainly have my shortcomings in certain areas, like adding

There are a number of other pitfalls that Pence mentioned as a warning. For any job, make sure you don't under-bid your work, because you're invariably going to find a spot that's difficult to get through in any project. On the other hand, you don't want to over-bid and price yourself out of the market. Another possibility is that you might over-bid and then do a poor job. That burns the market completely, for you and for the animation business in general.

Pence stresses that a forensic animator's first obligation is to technical accuracy. "You always want to measure the objects more than you feel you need to and check your measurements twice. Like the old carpentry rule: `Measure twice, cut once.' I had a guy walk in the shop once and say, `I cut the board three times, and it's still too short.' That happens sometimes, and it's just one of those things that you're going to get used to. `Measure, measure, measure' is the thing I suggest to everybody. Get more measurements than you think you can ever possibly use. It's going to come to the twelfth hour and you forgot to measure how far apart the stripes down the road are. Not all stripes are exactly the same. They vary from state to county roads to city roads; they're all a little different."

If the animation involves vehicles, find as many resources for models as you can. Sometimes it's tough. The manufacturers don't want to help you, especially if you mention that there's litigation involved. Video Law Services, Inc. is currently talking to Mazda's attorneys in Japan to see if they can set up a database of Mazda vehicles. Mazda, apparently, doesn't like that concept very much. Pence explains an interesting legal issue arising from his work: "In the process of getting car data, I've found that car-body styles are intellectual property, and intellectual property is becoming a big issue now. That's a subject that has come up in talks with Chevy, Mazda, and Ford. That's another reason they're not giving out drawings and plans of vehicles, since it's an intellectual property and they really have the right to say how it's used—period, end of story."

FORENSIC ANIMATION: TIPS AND TRICKS

There are a number of tricks that can make forensic animation easier. Roadway data is increasingly being created for state-run computer databases. In some states, you can get color satellite photos from the state highway or transportation department. All of these things are measured to scale. If your state only has black-and-white aerial photos, they can nonetheless be used, via a technique called *photo-grametry*. With photo-grametry, you take several sets of aerial photographs, and by inputting the altitude and path that the photographer's plane flew, you can derive elevation data, such as the height of trees and other landmarks.

Some state departments of transportation convert all their data into CAD databases, so all the roads in the state are in .DXF style files that can easily be imported into the animator's computer. Also, there are

automobile clubs and magazines dealing with automobile memorabilia that trade old automobile brochures like baseball cards. Many of the auto brochures give the wheel-base size, body dimensions, vehicle weights, the type of transmission, and many other important details. Most importantly, they show the body style. However, you should keep in mind that the brochures are made by marketing people, not somebody who's trying to ensure accuracy, so the illustration or photos may be stretched or slightly off from the accurate dimensions.

Car dealerships can be a fount of information. Because forensic animation is such a new and unique situation, they'll often go out of their way to help you, simply out of curiosity. Some car dealers are even willing to help you find the car so that you can measure it. As forensic animation becomes more popular and people get used to it, car dealers may cease to be such a good source of information, but for now they are very helpful. Motorcyclists and motorcycle dealers are not quite the same way; they are a little more protective of each other and want to know why somebody in the legal industry is looking for this or that kind of bike.

TUTORIAL: CREATING A FORENSIC ANIMATION

In our forensic animation tutorial, we will re-create a freeway car accident in which a semi truck hits a car and knocks it off the freeway. In this tutorial, we will learn how to create objects with the Regular Polygon tool, create surface materials, use multiple views at the same time, create cameras, and animate multiple objects in the same scene. This animation is not based on any real events, so unlike a true forensic animation, we will not have to worry about measurements and accuracy, which would make this tutorial unnecessarily difficult.

MODELING THE SCENERY

1. Begin by starting trueSpace (if it's not already loaded). From the file menu, select Scene, New. If any previous panels were open, such as the Animation panel or the

Primitives panel, you can close them by left-clicking on the Close All Panels icon. With a clean slate, we can begin our new animation.

2. Our first step will be to create a freeway and the grass that surrounds it. To create the grass, make a large square plane by left-clicking on the Regular Polygon icon. This will bring up the Polymodes panel. The number at the bottom of this panel represents how many sides your new polygon will have after you create it. We want a square, so verify that the number of sides is set to "4." (See Tutorial Figure 6.1.) Then, in the middle of the workspace, left-click and drag the cursor to the bottom of the screen. Try to keep the polygon oriented the same as the reference grid. (See Tutorial Figure 6.2.)

Tutorial Figure 6.1. *The polymodes panel allows you to perform Boolean operations on polygons, such as setting the number of sides.*

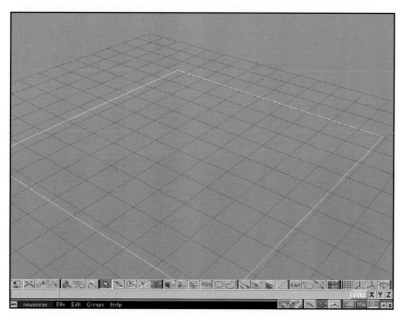

Tutorial Figure 6.2. *Create a large square polygon in the center of the workspace.*

3. Next we want to get a top view of our object. Instead of changing the main workspace view however, we will use a second view. Left click on the New Perspective View icon. This will add a new window in the upper-left corner of the screen. This new perspective view will also have its own Window Group icons, so within this new window, left-click on the Perspective View icon. Hold it down for a second until the variants pop up, and then drag the cursor up to the Top View icon. You should now see the top view in the new window. (See Tutorial Figure 6.3.)

163

4. In the Top View window, left-click on the Zoom icon, then left-click anywhere within the Top View window and drag the mouse down until our new polygon is reduced to the size of an icon in the center of the window. Now we will be able to enlarge it to serve as the

grass field surrounding our new freeway.

5. Before enlarging our polygon, let's first make a copy of it by left-clicking on the Copy icon. We will use one copy for the grass and the other for the free-way. To enlarge the new copy, left-click on the Object Scale icon in the Object Navigation group. Click both left and right buttons anywhere within the Top View window and drag the mouse down until the currently selected polygon is scaled to the size of the window. (See Tutorial Figure 6.4.) This large polygon will become our grass field.

6. To create our freeway, we will scale out the small polygon hor-izontally. To do this, left-click on the Object Scale icon. Then, in the top view window, left-click on the small polygon to select it. Once the polygon turns white, left-click and drag the mouse to the right. Dragging the mouse to the right will increase the horizontal size of the polygon. Scale it out until it is slightly wider than the grass field polygon. (See Tutorial

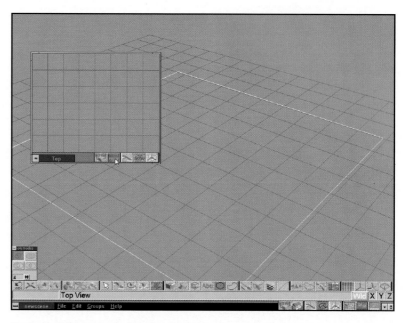

Tutorial Figure 6.3. *You can add up to three perspective views in addition to the main workspace view.*

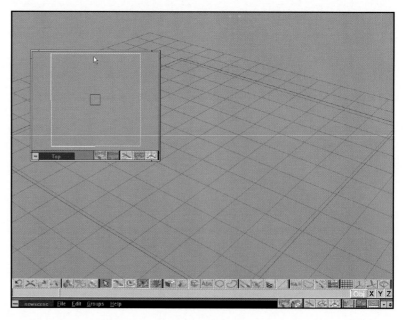

Tutorial Figure 6.4. *To enlarge objects proportionally, click both left and right buttons while you drag the mouse.*

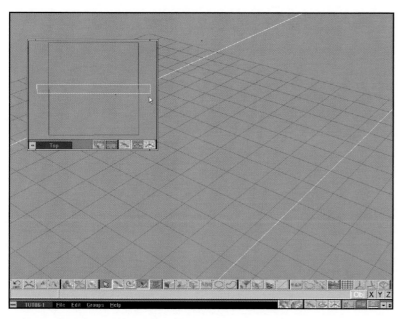

Tutorial Figure 6.5. *Scale the smaller polygon horizontally until it is slightly wider than the larger one.*

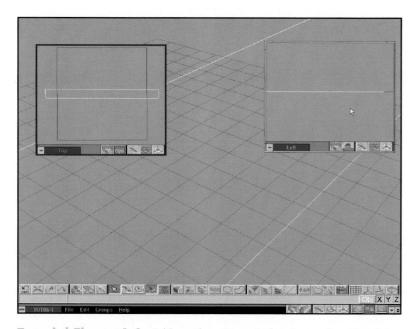

Tutorial Figure 6.6. *Add another view window to see elevation data.*

Figure 6.5.) It will now become our freeway.

7. Since both the grass field and the freeway polygons were created at the same height, we will need to move the freeway up just a little bit so it will render on top of the grass field. To do this, open another window by left-clicking on the New Perspective View icon. This will add a new window just below the current Top View window. After the window appears, left-click on its title bar and drag it to the upper-right corner of the screen. Then within the Window group, left-click on the Perspective View icon. Hold it down for a second until the variants pop up, and then drag the cursor up to the Left View icon. You should now see the left view in the new window. (See Tutorial Figure 6.6.)

165

8. To move the freeway up slightly, left-click on the Object Move

icon. Next, left-click in the Left View menu and drag the mouse slightly upward—just enough so you can see that the freeway is above the grass field. (See Tutorial Figure 6.7.)

CREATING MATERIALS

If you were to try and render our scene now, you would notice that all the objects have a pink material assigned to them. We will correct this by assigning a green color to the grass field and a texture map to the freeway.

1. Begin by pulling up the Materials panels. Do this by left-clicking the Material Library icon. This will display the current library of materials. Next, right-click the Paint Face icon to display the Material Properties panels, which displays a sample sphere and settings that you can change, such as the material's color, mapping, shininess, roughness, transparency, and shader attributes. (See Tutorial Figure 6.8.)

2. Change the default pink color to a green color by left-clicking and dragging the mouse across

166

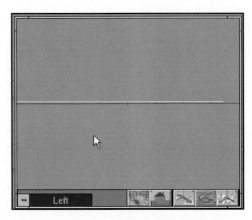

Tutorial Figure 6.7. *Move the freeway up slightly in the Left View to ensure that it renders above the grass field.*

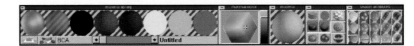

Tutorial Figure 6.8. *The Library of Materials panel and other material properties panels.*

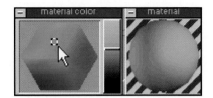

Tutorial Figure 6.9. *Setting the current materials color to green.*

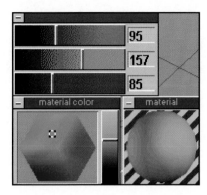

Tutorial Figure 6.10. *Right click on the color cube to get RGB sliders.*

the color cube to about the middle of the green. To get a darker green, drag the vertical color-range selector to the left of the color cube down to a point that is just above the middle. (See Tutorial Figure 6.9.)

Note: If you prefer choosing your colors from RGB sliders, you can right-click on the color cube, which will bring them up. (See Tutorial Figure 6.10.)

3. To save our new material so it can be used later, left-click on the Add Material To Library icon. You will see our new green material (applied to a sphere) added to the current material library. trueSpace will ask you if you want to save your material library when you exit, but it's a good idea to get into the habit of saving it yourself when you add new materials. Do this by choosing the Materials Library load/save

menu, which is hidden between the Remove Material icon and the scroll bar of the Material Libraries panel. (See Tutorial Figure 6.11.)

4. Before applying the new material to the grass-field polygon, we must first select that polygon. Do this by left-clicking on the large polygon in the top view window so that it becomes white and our freeway polygon becomes dark blue. Now, to apply our new material to the grass-field polygon, left-click on the Paint Face icon and hold down the button until the variants pop up. Then drag the mouse up to the Paint Object icon and release the left button. This will paint the polygon green in the top view window.

5. Next, create a material for the road. I have created a texture map that includes the black pavement and stripes commonly found on freeways. (See Tutorial Figure 6.12.) In the Attributes Panel, right-click on the Use Texture Map icon, and the Texture Map panel will appear. (See Tutorial Figure 6.13.) In this new panel, left-

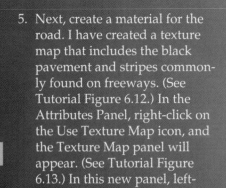

168

Tutorial Figure 6.11. *The Materials Library load/save menu allows you to manage different material libraries for different projects or applications.*

Tutorial Figure 6.12. *The freeway texture map.*

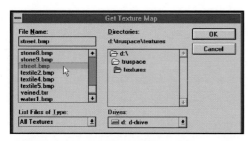

Tutorial Figure 6.13. *The Texture Map panel.*

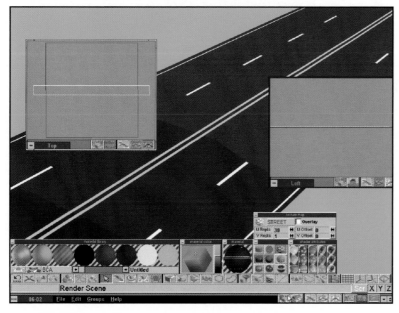

Tutorial Figure 6.14. *The Get Texture Map dialog box.*

click on the name of the current texture map (in this case, it is CHECKER). The Get Texture Map dialog box will appear, enabling you to select a .BMP, .TGA, or .TXR file as the current materials texture. Choose the file STREET.BMP for the texture map and click on OK. (See Tutorial Figure 6.14.) You will see the name STREET appear in the texture map filename box.

6. To apply this new texture to our sphere, just left-click on the Use Texture Map icon. You will notice, however, that the texture map simply contains a small section of a street. By having trueSpace repeat the same text down the length of our freeway polygon, it will give the desired result of freeway stripes. To tell trueSpace how many times to repeat the texture down the length of the road, change the number in the Texture Map panel "U Repts" from 1 to 30.

7. Now simply left-click on the freeway polygon in the top view window to activate it, then click anywhere in the main workspace window to select our perspective view. Finally, left-click on the Paint Object icon and you should see our new street texture map applied to the freeway polygon. To see the grass and freeway rendered together, left-click on the Render Current Object icon, hold it for a second until the variants pop-up appears, then drag the mouse up to the Render Scene icon and let go of the mouse button. The Perspective View will render the scene with the new surface materials. (See Tutorial Figure 6.15.)

USING 3-D DATA SETS

3-D data sets or models can be obtained from a variety of sources, such as the Internet, bulletin boards, commercial CD-ROM libraries, etc. (For a list of 3-D models sources, see Appendix A.) In the following tutorial steps, we will load two models available from ViewPoint DataLabs, a 1983 Chevrolet Camaro and a semi truck. trueSpace allows you to load in

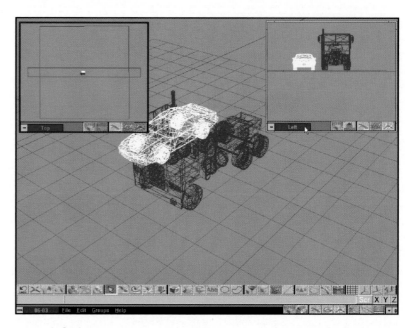

Tutorial Figure 6.15. *After applying the STREET.BMP texture map to our freeway polygon.*

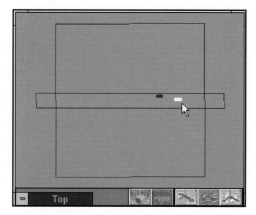

Tutorial Figure 6.16. *After loading the semi truck and Camaro vehicles into our scene.*

3-D objects saved in the following formats: Caligari (.OBJ), 3D Studio Binary (.3DS), 3D Studio ASCII (.ASC), AutoCAD (.DXF), Lightwave (.LWB), VideoScape (.GEO), WaveFront (.OBJ), Imagine (.IOB), and Caligari Amiga (.SOB).

1. Before loading any new models, left-click the Close All Panels icon to close the materials panels and make more room on the screen. You can also move the top view and left view windows further up into the uppe- left and upper right-hand corners. This will give us more working space.

2. To load the semi, choose the File menu and select Load Object. When the Load Object dialog box appears, select the "SEMI.COB" object and left-click on "OK." The 3-D semi truck will appear in the middle of the screen. (See Tutorial Figure 6.16.) Perform the same step again, but this time load the 3-D object called "CAMERO.COB."

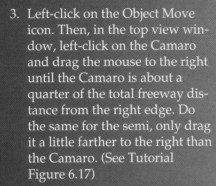

3. Left-click on the Object Move icon. Then, in the top view window, left-click on the Camaro and drag the mouse to the right until the Camaro is about a quarter of the total freeway distance from the right edge. Do the same for the semi, only drag it a little farther to the right than the Camaro. (See Tutorial Figure 6.17)

4. Now create a camera by clicking on the Add Infinite Light icon and hold down the button until the variant pop-up appears. Then drag the mouse up to the Camera Tool icon. This will create a new camera in the center of the various views. We can now switch one of our views to be this new camera view. Left click on the left view window's Left View icon, and from its variants, select the View From Object icon. You'll notice that the view from that window switches to the view that is seen by the new camera. (See Tutorial Figure 6.18.)

5. You rotate cameras as you would any other 3-D object. Left-click on the Object Rotate

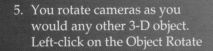

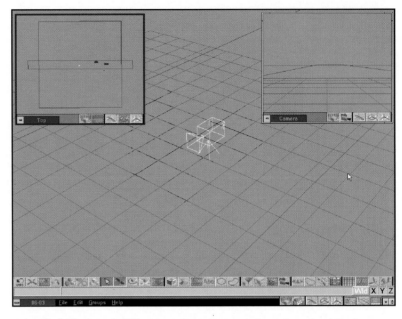

Tutorial Figure 6.17. *Move the vehicles to the right side of the freeway.*

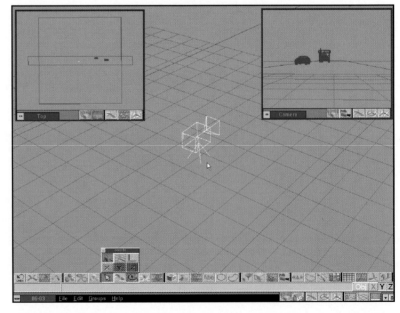

Tutorial Figure 6.18. *Our new camera is facing down the opposite direction of the freeway.*

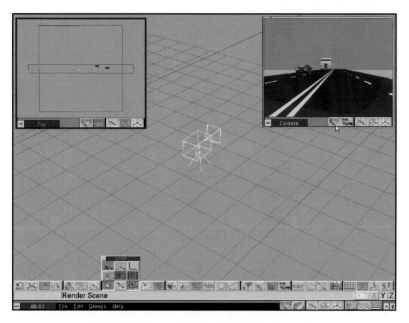

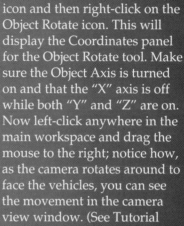

Tutorial Figure 6.19. *Rotate the camera to face the vehicles.*

Tutorial Figure 6.20. *The camera view after rendering the scene.*

icon and then right-click on the Object Rotate icon. This will display the Coordinates panel for the Object Rotate tool. Make sure the Object Axis is turned on and that the "X" axis is off while both "Y" and "Z" are on. Now left-click anywhere in the main workspace and drag the mouse to the right; notice how, as the camera rotates around to face the vehicles, you can see the movement in the camera view window. (See Tutorial Figure 6.19.)

6. In the camera view window, left-click the Render Scene icon from the render variants. You should see the Camaro driving down the freeway in the slow lane, and the semi should be slightly behind it in the fast lane. (See Tutorial Figure 6.20.) (If your vehicles are not in their lanes properly, just use the top view window, and the Object Move icon to reposition them.)

CREATING THE ANIMATION

In this final section of our tutorial, we will re-create the accident where the Camaro spins out into the fast lane occupied by the semi. The semi cannot stop in time, so it smashes into the side of the Camaro, sending it rolling end-over-end into oncoming traffic.

1. Before starting our animation, we need to move the camera back slightly, to give ourselves more room for the animation. In the camera view window, left-click the Eye Move icon. Since this window is a representation of the camera view, any adjustments made to the window will also move the camera. Now left-click anywhere in the window and drag the mouse down. Pull the camera back just a small amount (about the size of a single icon when looking at it from the top view). As you pull it back, make sure it stays above and slightly to the right of the road's center line. (See Tutorial Figure 6.21.) Check this by rendering the scene in the camera view (step 6 from the previous tutorial section).

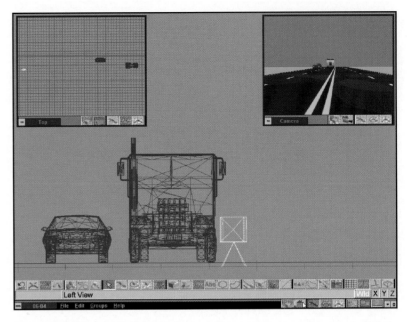

Tutorial Figure 6.21. *Make sure the camera stays above and slightly to the right of the center line.*

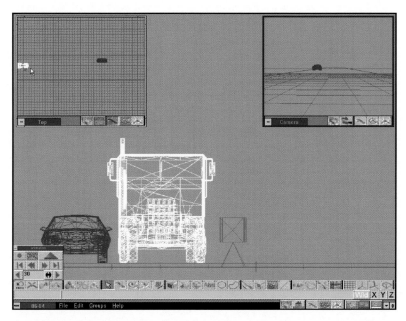

Tutorial Figure 6.22. *Adjust both the top view window and the main workspace window.*

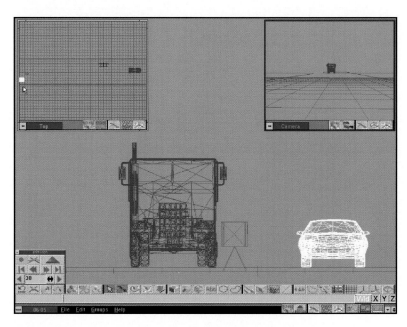

Tutorial Figure 6.23. *Move the truck past the camera.*

2. Zoom the top view window in on the camera and vehicles by using the Zoom icon and the Eye Move icon. Change the view of the main workspace to the left view by clicking on the Left View icon. Then use the Zoom and Eye Move icons to get a good view of the vehicles. (See Tutorial Figure 6.22.)

3. The first vehicle we will animate is the semi, moving toward the camera. Left click the Object Move icon and then left-click the Animation Tool icon, which brings up the Animation panel. In the top view, left-click on the semi so it is the currently selected object (white). In the Animation panel, change the current frame number to "30" and press the Enter key. Then left-click in the top view and drag the semi to the left, just beyond the camera. (See Tutorial Figure 6.23.) After

176

you move the semi, left-click on the title bar of the camera view, then left-click the Play icon in the Animation panel to see your semi animation.

4. Now to animate the Camaro. Left-click on it in any window to select it. After it is selected, in the Animation panel window type in "30" for the frame number and press the Enter key. For the Camaro, move it down the length of the freeway, but move it diagonally across the freeway to the oncoming traffic lanes. (See Tutorial Figure 6.24.) Left click the Play icon in the Animation panel to see your Camaro animation (only the currently selected object will animate).

5. To see all of the objects in an animation move during the playback mode, right-click on the Animation Tool icon. This brings up the Animation Parameters panel, where you can left-click on the Animate Whole Scene button. (See Tutorial Figure 6.25.) Now

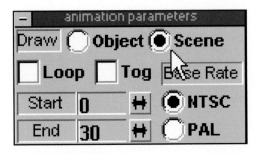

Tutorial Figure 6.24. *Move the Camaro into the oncoming traffic lanes.*

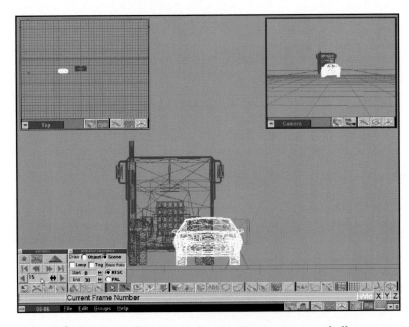

Tutorial Figure 6.25. *The Animation Parameters panel allows you to set defaults for your animation.*

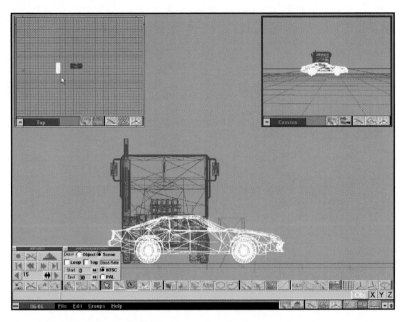

Tutorial Figure 6.26. *At frame 15, the Camaro is quite a ways in front of the semi.*

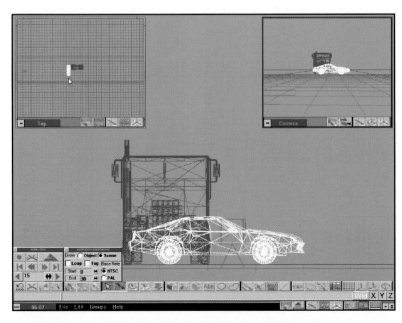

Tutorial Figure 6.27. *After rotating the car to the left 90 degrees.*

when you play back your animation, all of the animated objects move.

6. Next we will set up our first spin, to bring the Camaro into contact with the semi at frame 15. Go to frame 15 by entering the number 15 in the Animation-panel frame-number setting. This causes all the objects to jump to their positions at frame 15. Notice how the Camaro is in front of the semi at this point. (See Tutorial Figure 6.26.)

7. Make sure the Camaro is the currently selected object, and left-click on the Object Rotate icon. In the top view window, right-click and drag the mouse to the right. You should see the car rotating counter-clockwise. Rotate the car 90 degrees so that it is sitting sideways in the highway. (See Tutorial Figure 6.27.)

8. At this point, the car is still too far ahead of the semi, so left-click on the Object Move icon. Then left-click in the top view window and drag the car to the right so that it is touching the semi. Position the rear wheel axle in the center of the semi. (See Tutorial Figure 6.28.)

9. Now go to the next frame of the animation by left-clicking the Advance To Next Frame icon. At this frame we simply want to "lock" the roll of the car because from frame 16 onward, the car will roll over one time. To lock the rotation of the car, left-click on the Object Rotate icon, then left-click on the Record Key icon in the Animation panel. This sets a keyframe for the car's rotation at frame 16.

10. Left-click the Advance To End icon to go to frame 30. Here we will put a roll on the car to flip it over. Right click on the Object Rotate icon, then left-click on the "Y" axis button to turn it off. In the main workspace, which is now the left view, left-click on

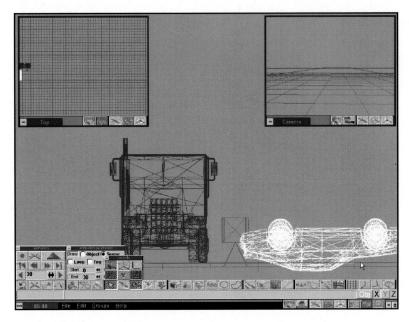

Tutorial Figure 6.28. *Move the car so that it touches the semi.*

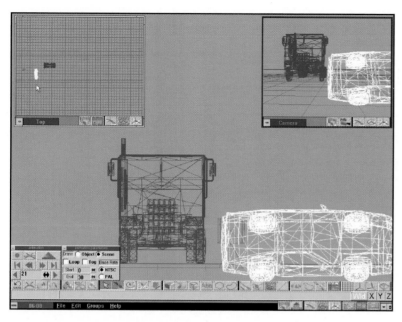

Tutorial Figure 6.29. *Rotate the car forward about 160 degrees.*

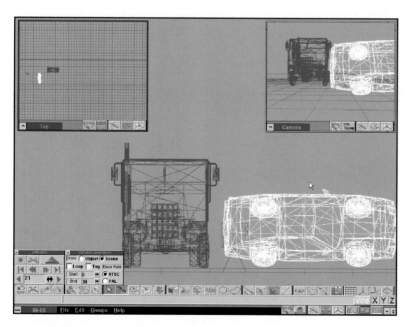

Tutorial Figure 6.30. *After dragging the car ahead of the semi.*

the car and drag the mouse down until the car rotates about 160 degrees—not quite all the way over on its top, but close. (See Tutorial Figure 6.29.)

11. If you play the animation and watch the top view carefully, you will see that the Camaro falls inside of the semi-truck toward the end of the animation. To correct this problem, we need to add a new keyframe. Go to frame number 21 by typing the 21 in the Animation-panel frame-number setting, and press the Enter key. At frame 21, you can clearly see the back end of the Camaro sticking in the side of the semi. To correct this, left-click on the Object Move icon. Then left-click in the top view window and drag the car to the left so that it is ahead of the semi. (See Tutorial Figure 6.30.) This keyframe accomplishes two

180

purposes: First, it keeps the car from falling inside the semi; second, it gives the car a kick of speed right when the semi hits it.

12. At frame 21, you might have noticed another problem. The tires are sinking below the ground as the car rolls on its side. To correct this, left-click on the Object Move icon. Then left-click in the left view and drag the car up slightly, so it is not touching the ground at all. It's OK if it looks like the car's flying in the air for a second after being hit.

13. To render the animation to disk, left-click on the Render Current Object icon and hold the button down until the variants pop up, then drag the mouse up to the Render Scene to File icon. You will now be presented with the Render To File dialog box. First

choose the output file type as "AVI Files *.avi", then enter the name tut-5.avi as the filename. Make sure that "All Frames" is selected in the animation box and that the frame rate is set to 30 with a pixel depth of 24. For super sampling (anti-aliasing), you can choose none or 2x; however, the more super sampling you use, the longer the time it will take to render. When you are ready, left-click the Render button. When you are presented with the AVI Compression dialog box, verify that the compression is set to "Full Frames (Uncompressed)" and left-click on OK. At this point, your animation will render to a Video for Windows AVI file. It can be played back using the Microsoft Media Player.

EXTRA PROJECTS:

Below are a few suggestions for more hands-on modeling and animation practice.

- Adjust the car's movement to create a different type of accident.

- Render the scene from the top and left views.

- Try creating different cameras to view the accident from other angles.

- Animate the camera itself to view the accident while moving.

CHAPTER SUMMARY

Now you should have a good feel for what is involved in forensic animation. We have explained how to create objects with the Regular Polygon tool, create surface materials, use multiple views at the same time, create cameras, and animate multiple objects in the same scene. In the following chapter, we will look at computer animation as it is used in the television industry.

Television

7

chapter

Since its early days, television has provided the "bread and butter" for the computer animation industry. Computer animation is used on television in many different ways including commercials, station identifications, and cartoons. Today, due to the photo-realistic capabilities of animation, it is used in place of traditional special effects techniques such as stop motion and models.

This chapter contains interviews with two individuals from a post production and special effects studio called The Post Group; Jennifer McKnew, a successful animator, and Deborah Ristic, a designer, are both heavily involved in television production. McKnew discusses some interesting points including how to get started in the business and what it was like creating 3-D visual effects for shows such as *SeaQuest DSV*. She also reveals some tips and tricks

on creating photo-realistic surfaces in 3-D. Ristic explains in detail the anatomy of a television 3-D animation project and offers some great suggestions for character animation. In the tutorials, we will create some 3-D text and then focus on getting the most from surface materials using some advanced mapping techniques such as bump, environment mapping, ray tracing, refractions, and shadows.

CASE STUDY: JENNIFER MCKNEW, 3-D COMPUTER ANIMATOR—THE POST GROUP

The Post Group is a special effects, television post production facility that creates special effects and graphics for motion pictures and television. Jennifer McKnew, a 3-D computer animator at The Post Group, has worked on a diverse collection of projects, encompassing visual, effects graphic openings, and logos for broadcast television. Jennifer's involvement in graphic openings has included such projects as "The 45th Annual Emmy Awards." A typical visual effects project for Jennifer might be animating UFOs for the *Unsolved Mysteries* series.

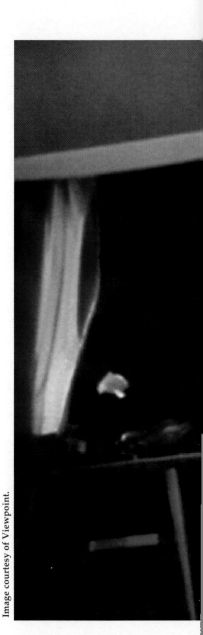

Image courtesy of Viewpoint.

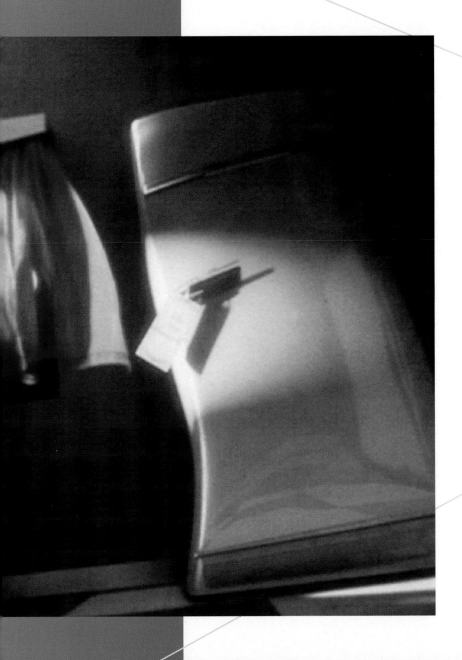

Active within the digital community, Jennifer was recently accepted into the Academy of Television Arts and Sciences (animation section). She is also an active member of the Los Angeles SIGGRAPH group.

Most of Jennifer's work at The Post Group has been generated on the Toaster, using the Lightwave 3-D application. In addition, she uses Electric Image, a Macintosh-based application. Currently, Jennifer is moving into the Silicon Graphics Platform, using the Alias 3D power animator software.

Jennifer cites her grandfather as the person who inspired her. "He is a fine artist who used his artistic skills in the corporate environment. He was able to work in a business atmosphere, yet utilize his artistic jazz. I find the marriage of the corporate and artistic worlds intriguing. I see a continuity of that manner in my professional life."

Another inspiration introduced her to electronic imagery with Pixar's Academy Award-winning computer animated short, "Tim Toy." "My life was greatly influenced from the moment I viewed the animation." Her career aspirations had been discovered and perseverance set loose.

Image courtesy of Wavefront.

GETTING STARTED IN ANIMATION

Originally from Marin County in Northern California, McKnew studied at Sonoma State University for her first year and half. "By fulfilling my general education requirements, I was exposed to many different fields of academia." Jennifer decided to transfer from Sonoma State University and was accepted into UCLA as an English major. Later, she changed her major to Design. Continuing her general education requirements at UCLA, she structured her artistic curriculum in such a way that her courses gravitated toward computer graphics. She acquired her Bachelor of Arts degree from UCLA in Design.

Before graduation, Jennifer was offered a position to build animatics at a company called Animagic. "I was able to generate 2-D animation quickly and cost efficiently with the Amiga. We could provide a client with a selection of animation ideas. I would then convert the data for input to an animation stand, which would replicate the original motion, while at the same time producing the high quality final element on film."

Jennifer continued to create occasional animation tests for features and trailers for Cinema Research Corporation and expanded her duties as an assistant title designer. She then decided to step into the freelance world and began working at Apogee Productions, a visual effects house. "My passion for visual effects led me to Apogee, where I began working with visual effects supervisor, Tim McHugh. He provided me with the opportunity to create visual effects elements by means of computer. Tim had been largely known in the visual effects community for his expertise with traditional optical techniques such as models, motion control, and blue screen. He has been a forerunner in exploring new optical methods like CGI."

Tim and Jennifer created all of the CGI elements for seven episodes of *Unsolved Mysteries*. Elements were created separately to provide for more flexibility during online compositing. For example, the elements consisted of a beauty pass (fully colored UFO shape) and light passes. During the online session, the editors are able to adjust other properties of the image in real-time, such as the color, brightness, timing, and dissolves. The CGI elements

Image courtesy of Wavefront.

were composited over live action at The Post Group, where Jennifer later began working on staff.

Jennifer recalls one of her first 3-D projects at The Post Group. "Graphics were created for several interstitials for The Disney Channel's *Discover Magazine*. The interstitials were short segments within an episode. The show *The Ten Great Unanswered Questions of Science* explored an array of scientific subjects including recreating the evolution of man, simulating the Big Bang Theory, and traveling through an amino acid chain of a DNA molecule. Each graphic was completed in approximately one week."

WORKING AT SeaQuest DSV

After moving on to The Post Group and completing numerous graphics projects, Jennifer was asked to join the visual effects crew for *SeaQuest DSV*. She proceeded to work on the pilot and first four episodes. "My focus involved painting textures that were mapped on the models in each of the sequences. The individual artists applied their unique talents and individual strengths to build a visual effects shot; for example, one individual would model, another surface, and another animate."

FAVORITE PROJECTS

"My greatest passion for computer graphics is visual effects and character animation. I strive to make the impossible conceivable. My favorite projects incorporate vibrant surface design known as hyperrealism. For example, I feel that the surfacing on the 3-D Emmy Award portrayed surface brilliance, due to the texture map's color, saturation, hue, and value. With regard to animation, my favorite projects are ones that allow me to invent a personality for an inanimate object. I recently created a photorealistic jukebox. Traditionally, this inanimate object stands lifeless in the corner of a cafe. But this jukebox conveys its playful personality with exaggerated motion as it dances around."

TIPS AND TRICKS

"It is very important to break the stereotype of computer graphics. Each independent aspect of creating imagery (modeling, surfacing,

lighting, and animating) should not be overlooked. Lacking in one area can break a shot. I often see texture maps that are too clean. Objects should signify that they have been utilized in some capacity and aren't just off the store shelf. For lighting, don't over light objects or use an overabundance of specularity (intensity of highlights). Making things too shiny gives the illusion of plasticity. In the area of animation, add mass and weight to your objects. Too many character animate pieces portray objects as if they are floating. Imagine how heavy the object is and move your object with its natural characteristics. Avoid contrived-looking animation."

COMMON PITFALLS

As each day passes, software matures and improves. "I wish current software parameters were available at my fingertips on projects completed two years ago. Today, projects can be completed more cost efficiently and with fewer steps required to attain a particular look. Looking back at some of my early work is amusing. It's a little like looking at baby pictures. We were just starting out, and boy, have things progressed."

RECOMMENDATIONS FOR NEW ANIMATORS

Jennifer recommends several academic institutions offering computer graphic courses including Ohio State University, Cal Arts, Art Center College of Design, and UCLA or private institutions such as The American Film Institute or The Learning Tree.

"Internships are a good start for beginners and college students. The atmosphere is one where nothing but knowledge surrounds you, ready to be absorbed."

Jennifer's CGI knowledge encompasses several platforms, utilizing various applications. "Would I go through the learning process of each platform again? Absolutely! What I learned on one platform built the infrastructure for understanding a premise on another."

WHAT THE FUTURE HOLDS

Jennifer's career aspirations are to delve into the feature film area (creating 3-D visual effects, main titles, etc.), as well as continuing her involvement in the television broadcast arena. She enjoys being a member of the group of artists that works at The Post Group. "I like the camaraderie we have here. I create 3-D elements that can go into a Harry session or into an online bay for further manipulation. It's the whole team that makes it happen."

Jennifer is passionate about computer-generated imagery. "My enthusiasm is derived from the ability to play with digital crayons and digital clay. I enjoy taking reality to levels where your imagination is your only limitation."

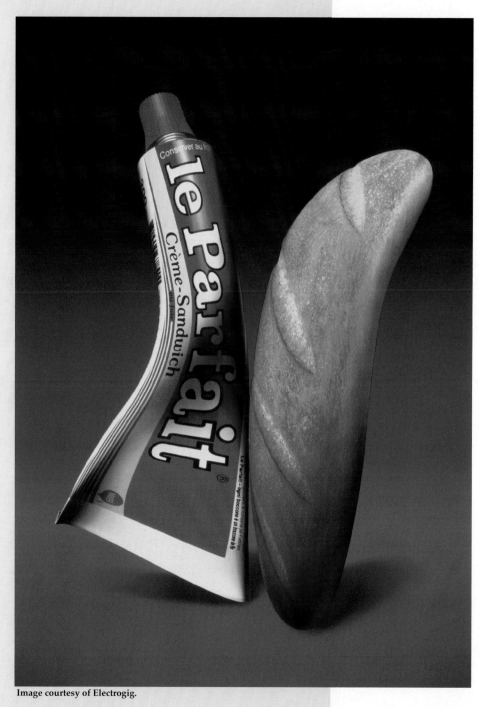

Image courtesy of Electrogig.

CASE STUDY: DEBORAH RISTIC, DESIGNER—THE POST GROUP

Deborah Ristic is a computer graphics artist and designer for The Post Group. She is responsible for helping the clients realize their graphics and effects vision, beginning with the storyboard and ending with the finished product.

BACKGROUND

Ristic's training is that of an artist. She attended Otis/Parsons Institute before the advent of computer graphics and continued her illustration training with some of the film industry's top storyboard artists. After some animation courses, she went on to produce and direct her own animated films.

"I began my career storyboarding music videos, commercials, and feature film projects. After I joined The Post Group eight years ago, I started to storyboard post-production projects, such as title graphics and effects. A large volume of clients I illustrated for needed design input. With my growing knowledge of computer graphics equipment I helped them come up with solutions that balanced their

189

creative needs with their budgets. Gradually, rather than pass the job along after it was boarded, I began using the computer equipment to execute the job."

"An effect often needs the touch of an animator to make things look real and full of character," continues Ristic. "Computers don't give you talent; they're just tools for artists to use. You need people with talent and vision. I mean, really, you can teach a chimp how to work computer graphic machinery (that's my personal philosophy), but you need someone with vision to drive the car."

Ristic recalls, "*Max Headroom* and *Back to the Future, Part II* were a couple of my first big projects." An NBC Sports main title, "World Figureskating Championships," won her an Emmy nomination. Since then, she has worked on "Star Trek: The Next Generation," "Quantum Leap," "Major Dad," and a children's show, "Adventures in Wonderland," for The Disney Channel. "Currently, I'm working on a show for the USA network, "Weird Science."

Ristic does most of her work on a Quantel HARRY and PAINTBOX, which are 2-D graphics computers used for painting, compositing, rotoscoping, editing, and other image processing.

ANATOMY OF AN ANIMATION PROJECT

Ristic is involved with the design and execution of title graphics and visual effects. For example, a client may come in with a 3-D title sequence. The client will either provide a logo or request that one be designed. Ristic will pitch an idea or logo, and after approval, the storyboarding process begins. It is during this time that specifications for the job come into focus: the budget, length of the piece, delivery format, and whether the client will provide footage or The Post Group must shoot their own footage. The action of the animation is storyboarded on paper or animatic, or CGI keyframes are rendered. If the storyboard is too much for their budget, the animation design is scaled back. After storyboard approval, production begins.

"Sometimes if clients know what they want, jobs can be relatively straightforward. A client may say, 'I have my show logo and these titles, and I want them over this footage.' Titles over rolling video don't require too much in the way of specialized computer graphics equipment, so this kind of project can be quickly executed in an online bay. However, should the same client want the titles to come up in some original way or want color washes or textures over the footage or different kinds of layers, I'm in the position to make suggestions and let my expertise enhance the client's ideas or creative direction."

Potential problems can arise when clients come in not knowing exactly what they want, yet having a particular look in mind. "They don't know what they want until they see it. It's my job to get into their heads and extract exactly what it is they want to see," says Ristic. "Other times, we can get full blown into a job, and the client hasn't given us all the information necessary to successfully complete the job on budget or on time. Even if clients are really good at articulating exactly what it is they want, it is always a good idea to have detailed storyboards. It is very prudent and cost effective to be well planned. There's as much pre-production in post-production as there is in regular production."

191

Creating a piece the way the clients see it in their heads is one of the biggest challenges in the whole process. Ristic explains, "Sometimes it is even difficult to realize my own vision. I might have an idea in my head and once I execute it, I find out it's too difficult, or the elements that I pulled are not working together like I thought they would. When a client has a very specific vision in mind, I can produce that vision with the least amount of difficulties, provided that the client can communicate visually with storyboards, examples, and elements. Of course, it's always a treat to have a client with no particular vision in mind, who trusts me to

Image courtesy of Josell Communications.

come up with something appropriate. Then I'm in the driver's seat and I can take that client on a creative journey that's interesting and fun."

Suggestions for Starting Out

192

Ristic feels there are many different angles that a person new to computer animation can approach. "If someone's good at architectural spacing and geometry, that person would be probably better suited for 3-D than digital compositing. If someone is strong in illustration, design, and animation, that person might want to go into the 2-D area and do rotoscoping and 2-D graphics. Someone who's good at timing and cutting might be better doing digital compositing. It's good to analyze your talent and then find the area that is best suited for you. It's important to realize that just knowing how to operate a computer graphics machine doesn't give one talent. It takes true talent and creativity to make machines do what they were designed to do. Computer graphics equipment is just a tool for people with vision to use for creation."

Tips and Tricks

For 3-D animation, Ristic recommends field rendering. "I always like things to be rendered with field motion rather than frame motion if it's not going back to film and just staying in the television format. It doubles the work for 3-D animators since they have to render more frames, but the results always look much smoother; it doesn't have a strobing effect. If the final product goes back to film, then frame rendering is a must since field motion doesn't look good in film. If something is rendered in fields, transferred to film, then back to video, the result can be a strobey, jittery, scan-lined mess. However, if something is rendered in frame motion,

Image courtesy of Josell Communications.

transferred to film, then back to video, there's no problem. With advancing technology, the marriage of film and video is becoming more solid. Film opticals are becoming obsolete. Everything's being done on computer."

Good animation courses are considered very important by Ristic. "Three-D character animation is becoming very popular. A lot of 3-D animators can be very technically hackers, but some of their work lacks life and energy. Traditional animators like the ones at Disney really knew how to capture and exaggerate motion to make an animation fluid, punctuated, and realistic. I remember doing a job where I had to go through some Disney animation one frame at a time, and I was amazed and amused at how exaggerated and distorted-looking some frames were. But put in the context of real-time, the animation was beautiful and believable. The animation had weight and life. By studying the masters of animation, one can learn fluidity in motion. It really makes you appreciate all the hard work that went into those cartoons.

"A lot of art schools and universities offer animation courses. "UCLA has a very well reputed animation department. It's important to get over the fear of putting bizarre, distorted frames in animation sequences. If you make an animated scene of a bouncing ball, and the ball isn't flat when it hits the ground, the animation won't look organic or reactive. If you were to view some high-speed footage of a person falling on cement, you would see the body flatten and spread as it hit the ground. When we create an animation sequence, the tendency is to make every frame perfect because we are only seeing the frame within its own context. But once all the frames are sewn together, we can see that a certain amount of exaggeration in key frames is critical to giving the animation volume and life."

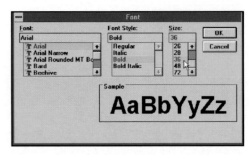

Tutorial Figure 7.1. *You can create 3-D text from any True Type font.*

TUTORIAL: CREATING PHOTO-REALISM

Many projects for television, such as visual effects and graphic titles, are created to look photo-realistic. In this tutorial we will look at photo-realism and how to create it. By creating a 3-D logo and using various surface mapping and lighting techniques, you will learn some of the practical tools for creating photo-realism.

194

CREATING 3-D TEXT

1. Launch trueSpace and choose the File menu and select Scene/New. trueSpace for Windows supports True Type fonts, so it's very easy to create 3-D text. To choose the font and point size, right click on the Text:Horizontal icon. From the Font dialog box, choose Arial, Bold with a size of 36 points and click on OK. (See Tutorial Figure 7.1.)

2. Text can be created in a horizontal or vertical orientation (the default is horizontal text). Left click on the Text:Horizontal

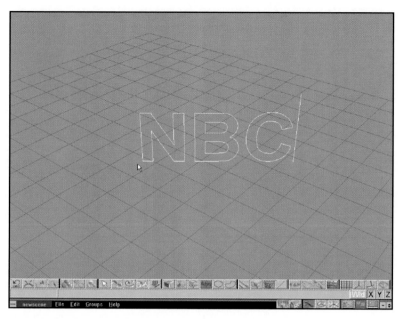

Tutorial Figure 7.2. *Creating vertical text in trueSpace.*

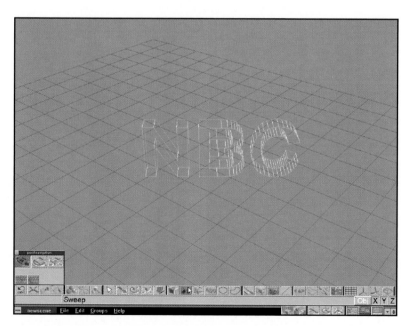

Tutorial Figure 7.3. *Using the Sweep tool extrudes the current object and switches to point edit mode.*

icon and hold the mouse down until the variant popup appears, then drag the mouse up to the Text:Vertical icon and release the button. The cursor will change to an I-bar, indicating that trueSpace is ready to create text. Type in the capital letters, *NBC* and then click the Object Tool icon. (See Tutorial Figure 7.2.)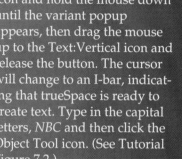

3. Left click on the Sweep icon and our 2-D text will be extruded into 3-D. At the same time trueSpace puts us into point edit mode, allowing us to scale, move, or rotate the currently selected (light green) points, edges, or surfaces. (See Tutorial Figure 7.3.)

4. While we are in point edit mode, we can put a bevel on the front edge of our text. Left click on the Sweep icon and hold the button down until the variants popup appears. Drag the mouse up to the Bevel icon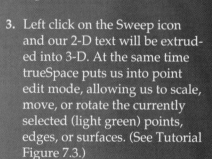

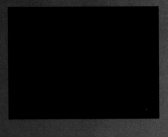

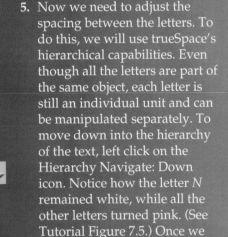

and release the button. When you do this, you will see a small *P* appear next to the cursor and the status line will tell you to "drag to change lift." Click anywhere in the workspace, and drag the mouse around using the left mouse button. Dragging the mouse to the right or forward causes the size of the bevel to increase. Dragging it down or to the left causes the bevel size to decrease. Set the bevel so it looks similar to the bevel in Tutorial Figure 7.4. Click the Object Tool icon to deactivate the bevel mode.

5. Now we need to adjust the spacing between the letters. To do this, we will use trueSpace's hierarchical capabilities. Even though all the letters are part of the same object, each letter is still an individual unit and can be manipulated separately. To move down into the hierarchy of the text, left click on the Hierarchy Navigate: Down icon. Notice how the letter *N* remained white, while all the other letters turned pink. (See Tutorial Figure 7.5.) Once we have moved down into the hier-

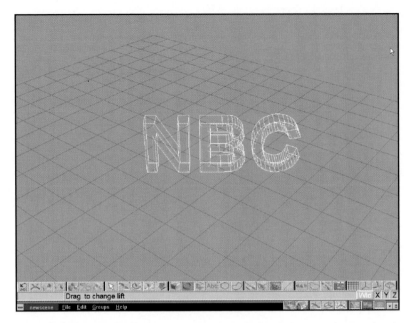

Tutorial Figure 7.4. *Any 3-D shape can be beveled using the Bevel tool.*

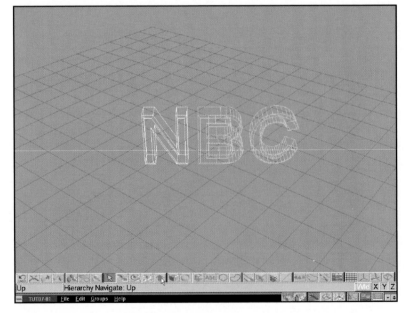

Tutorial Figure 7.5. *The pink objects are connected to the white object through hierarchical relationships.*

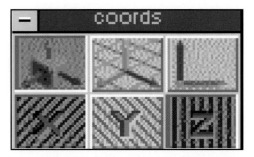

Tutorial Figure 7.6. *Set the coordinates panel to these settings.*

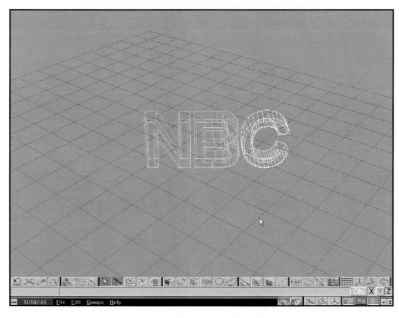

Tutorial Figure 7.7. *After adjusting the spacing of two letters.*

archy, you can use the left and right arrows to move between each letter. Try this now.

6. Using the arrow keys, select the letter *N* as the current letter. Now left click on the Object Move icon, then right click on the same icon to pull up the coordinates panel. In the coordinates panel, left click on the Object Axes icon if it is not already selected. Turn off the Y Axis icon. (See Tutorial Figure 7.6.) This allows you to move the letter *N* to its right along its own X axis.

197

7. To move the letter *N*, left click anywhere in the workspace and drag the mouse to the right until the *N* is close to the letter *B*. Next, press the right arrow twice to activate the letter *C*. Again, left click anywhere in the workspace, and this time drag the mouse to the left until the letter *C* is close to the letter *B*. (See Tutorial Figure 7.7.)

198

8. Before rendering our new 3-D text, right click on the Render Current Object icon. This calls up the Render Options Panel. (See Tutorial Figure 7.8.) If the ray trace option is currently turned on, turn it off by left clicking in the white box to the left of the word.

9. Now we will assign a silver surface material to our new logo and render it to see how it looks. Left click on the Material Library icon to pull up the Material Library panel. On the panel, left click on the silver material. (See Tutorial Figure 7.9.) Before we can apply the material to our object, we must left click on the Hierarchy Navigate: Up icon so the entire logo is selected and not just one letter. Left click on the Paint Face icon and choose the Paint Object icon from the popup variants. This paints our new logo in a metallic silver color. (See Tutorial Figure 7.10.)

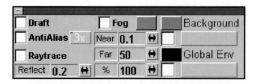

Tutorial Figure 7.8. *The Render Options Panel allows you to control ray tracing, anti-aliasing, and other rendering options.*

Tutorial Figure 7.9. *The Material Library Panel.*

Tutorial Figure 7.10. *After applying the silver material to our new logo.*

BCA   Dull White

Tutorial Figure 7.11. *Select the Dull White material before creating the floor object.*

Tutorial Figure 7.12. *Create a floor quickly with the Regular Polygon tool.*

CREATING LIGHTS

In this section of the tutorial we will create different types of light sources and see how they affect 3-D scenes.

1. So that you can see the effect of our light sources, create a floor for the 3-D logo. Before creating the floor, select the Dull White material in the Material Library panel. (See Tutorial Figure 7.11.) To create the floor, left click on the Regular Polygon icon. Left click at the center of the screen, and drag the cursor to the top of the screen to create a large polygon. (See Tutorial Figure 7.12.)

2. First, we will create a local light, otherwise known as a *point source* or *omni light*. Local lights project light equally in all directions, similar to a light bulb. To create a local light, left click on the Add Infinite Light icon and hold the button down

199

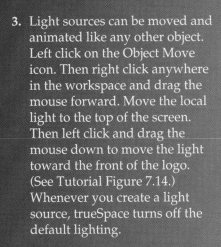

and drag to the Add Local Light icon in the variants popup. A local light is placed in the scene, and the Lights panel appears allowing you to adjust the settings for the current light source. The Lights panel allows you to choose the color of the light, the intensity, whether or not it casts shadows, and the type of falloff. Set the Intensity of Current Light slider close to the top, to increase the brightness of this light. (See Tutorial Figure 7.13.)

3. Light sources can be moved and animated like any other object. Left click on the Object Move icon. Then right click anywhere in the workspace and drag the mouse forward. Move the local light to the top of the screen. Then left click and drag the mouse down to move the light toward the front of the logo. (See Tutorial Figure 7.14.) Whenever you create a light source, trueSpace turns off the default lighting.

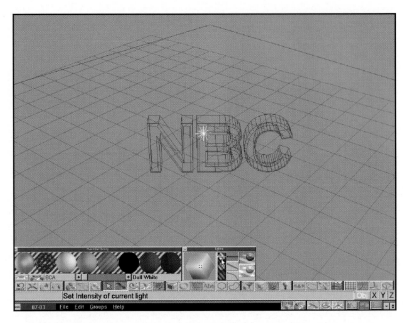

Tutorial Figure 7.13. *The Lights panel appears when you select or create a light source.*

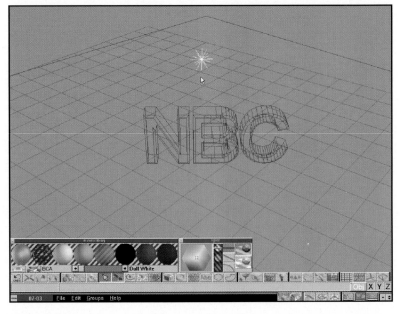

Tutorial Figure 7.14. *Move the light above and to the front of the 3-D logo.*

Tutorial Figure 7.15. *Local lights spread evenly and diminish with distance.*

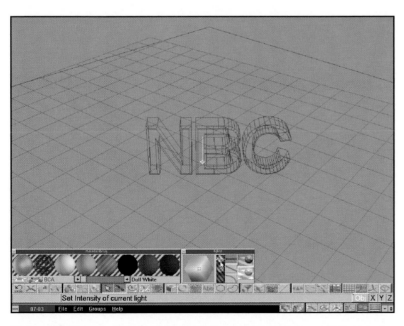

Tutorial Figure 7.16. *Infinite lights simply project parallel rays of light onto the scene based on the infinite lights angle.*

4. Now choose the Render Scene icon from the Render Tools variants. Notice how this light source spreads out evenly and diminishes with distance. (See Tutorial Figure 7.15.)

5. Delete the local light by left clicking on the Erase icon or by pressing the Delete key on the keyboard. Now from the Light Tool variants select the Add Infinite Light icon. Infinite lights cast parallel rays of light from a specified direction. They work very well for simulating sunlight shadows in outdoor scenes. You do not need to bother moving Infinite light sources about the models. As with the local light, set the Intensity of Current Light slider close to the top to increase the brightness of this light. (See Tutorial Figure 7.16.)

6. Now choose the Render Scene icon from the Render Tools variants. Notice how this light source evenly lights the entire scene as sunlight would outside. (See Tutorial Figure 7.17.)

7. Delete the infinite light by left clicking on the Erase icon or by pressing the Delete key on the keyboard. From the Light Tool variants, select the Add Spotlight icon. Spotlights project a cone-shaped beam of light, which works very well for simulating lamps or other directional lights. Notice that the spotlight has a green circle at the base of the cone. This represents the shaded area between the cone's edge and the fully illuminated center. (See Tutorial Figure 7.18.)

To check how well a spotlight covers a scene, you can set a window to view the scene from the light's point of view. Select the light, then use the Camera View icon. You can adjust the light's cone angle and the shaded region interactively with real-time feedback.

Tutorial Figure 7.17. *Local lights spread evenly and diminish with distance.*

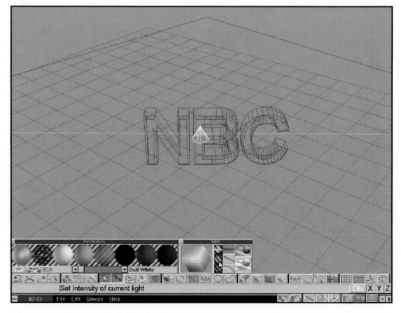

Tutorial Figure 7.18. *Spotlights can simulate light that is projected in the shape of a cone.*

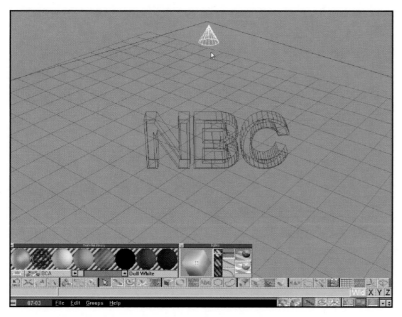

Tutorial Figure 7.19. *Position the spotlight above and just in front of the 3-D logo.*

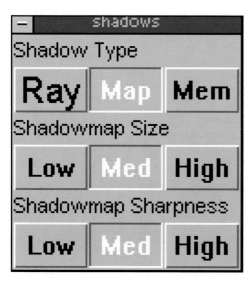

Tutorial Figure 7.20. *The Shadows panel allows you to specify the method used to generate shadows.*

8. Left click on the Object Move icon. Then right click anywhere in the workspace and drag the mouse forward. Move the spotlight to the top of the screen. Left click and drag the mouse down to move the spotlight slightly toward the front of the logo. (See Tutorial Figure 7.19.)

9. Before rendering with this new light source, turn on shadows by left clicking on the Toggle Shadow Casting by Current Light icon. Next right click on the same icon to pull up the Shadows panel. (See Tutorial Figure 7.20.) For Shadow types, you have ray traced shadows or mapped shadows. For local and infinite lights, you must use ray tracing to cast shadows. A faster method of getting shadows, however, is to use shadow mapping. Shadow mapping is only available with spotlights. You can improve the quality of shadow maps by increasing

their size and sharpness (at the risk of increasing rendering time). Since the Shadows panel is set correctly, go ahead and close it by left clicking on the close box.

10. Now choose the Render Scene icon from the Render Tools variants. Notice how spotlights only cast light within the cone. (See Tutorial Figure 7.21.)

To create perfectly sharp and realistic shadows, you must ray trace them.

CREATING REFLECTIONS

In this last section of the tutorial, we will cover the use of advanced mapping techniques, such as reflection mapping, cubic environment maps, bump maps, and transparency maps.

1. To see the advanced materials options, right click on the current Paint Tool. This will bring up (from left to right) the Color

Tutorial Figure 7.21. *The sharpness of Shadow Map can be increased with the Shadows panel settings.*

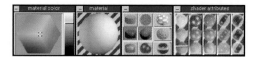

Tutorial Figure 7.22. *The Color Property, Attributes, and Shader Attributes panels.*

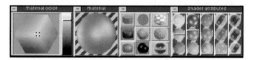

Tutorial Figure 7.23. *The material panels after "Inspecting" the 3-D logo.*

Property panel, the Attributes panel, and the Shader Attributes panel. (See Tutorial Figure 7.22.)

2. The material currently displayed is the last one you selected in the material library. To select a material in your scene, you can either left click on it in the material library or use the Inspect icon in the Paint Tools variants and left click on the object you want to inspect. Use the Inspect tool and left click on the 3-D logo. The current material settings will then be loaded into the various material panels. (See Tutorial Figure 7.23.)

3. Now that we have our 3-D logo material loaded, we will add a reflection map to it. Do this by left clicking on the Use Environment Map icon. Notice that the sample sphere changes

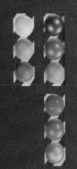

to show the result of a rainbow-colored reflection map. To change the environment map (reflection map), right click on the same icon. A box showing the filename of the current environment map appears. Left click on the filename. The Get Environment Map dialog box appears. Click on the WASTE-LAN.E2-D file and left click on OK. As soon as you do this, the new environment map, WASTELAN.E2-D, is applied to our sample sphere. (See Tutorial Figure 7.24.)

4. Make a few adjustments before applying the new material to our 3-D logo. Drag the Set Material Color slider to the top. Drag the Set Ambient Glow slider all the way to the bottom. Drag the Set Shininess slider all the way to the top. Set the Roughness slider to the middle. (See Tutorial Figure 7.25.) This darkens the reflection slightly and brings out the highlights to make it look richer.

Tutorial Figure 7.24. *The new WASTELAN.ED2 environment map applied to our sample sphere.*

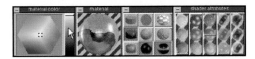

Tutorial Figure 7.25. *Adjusting the various settings can add a richness to our environment map.*

Tutorial Figure 7.26. *Environment maps simulate reflections but don't accurately reflect their surroundings.*

5. Apply the new material to the 3-D logo by left clicking on the Paint Object icon. Then render the entire screen with the Render Scene icon from the Render Tools variants. (See Tutorial Figure 7.26.)

6. An enhancement to environment maps that allows them to reflect their surroundings is the cubic environment map. To create one, the computer first renders a view of the scene from the location of the object. Then the computer applies that rendered image as a standard environment map. Before creating a cubic environment, we need to move our 3-D logo up slightly, because the curve on the bottom of the letter *C* currently drops through and intersects the polygon floor. To move the object up, left click on the Object Move icon. Then left click on the workspace and drag the mouse up slightly. To

create the cubic environment map, make sure the 3-D logo is selected, then choose the Edit menu and select Image Utilities. (See Tutorial Figure 7.27.) Then simply left click on the 2-D Envr Map, enter a filename such as NBC for the cubic environment map, and left click on OK. You will see trueSpace rendering all six views from the position of the selected object.

7. To see our new cubic environment map, simply left click on the filename of the current environment map in the Environment panel. When the Get Environment Map dialog box appears, left click on the NAB file and left click on OK. As soon as you do this, the new environment map, NAB, is applied to the sample sphere. (See Tutorial Figure 7.28.) Cubic reflection maps attempt to solve the problems of accurate reflection, but objects on which they are used cannot reflect themselves.

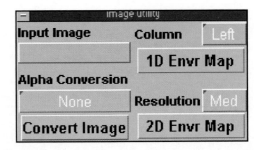

Tutorial Figure 7.27. *The Image Utilities control panel.*

Tutorial Figure 7.28. *Notice how objects that use cubic environment maps do not reflect themselves.*

Tutorial Figure 7.29. *Cubic environment maps can provide a close approximation of accurate reflections.*

8. Apply the new material to the 3-D logo by left clicking on the Paint Object icon. Then render the entire screen with the Render Scene icon from the Render Tools variants. (See Tutorial Figure 7.29.)

9. To get perfectly accurate reflections, you must use ray tracing algorithms. In trueSpace, turn on ray tracing by right clicking on the Render Tools icons. When the Render Control panel appears, right click on the ray trace option to turn on ray tracing. (See Tutorial Figure 7.30.)

10. Next, we want to make some adjustments to our material. First turn off the environment map, since it will be calculated automatically now. Turn the Material Color brightness down to about one-third from the top, drag Ambient Glow to the

Tutorial Figure 7.30. *To turn on ray tracing, use the Render Control panel.*

210

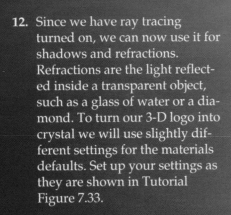

middle, drag the Shininess down to one-third from the top, and drag the Roughness all the way down to the bottom. (See Tutorial Figure 7.31.)

11. Apply the new material to the 3-D logo by left clicking on the Paint Object icon and immediately press Esc to halt the preview. Then render the entire screen with the Render Scene icon from the Render Tools variants. (See Tutorial Figure 7.32.)

12. Since we have ray tracing turned on, we can now use it for shadows and refractions. Refractions are the light reflected inside a transparent object, such as a glass of water or a diamond. To turn our 3-D logo into crystal we will use slightly different settings for the materials defaults. Set up your settings as they are shown in Tutorial Figure 7.33.

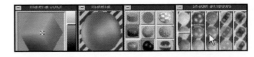

Tutorial Figure 7.31. *The settings for our new ray traced scene.*

Tutorial Figure 7.32. *The rendered scene using ray tracing. Notice the logo reflecting itself on the inside edges of the letters* C *and* N.

Tutorial Figure 7.33. *The settings for creating a photo-realistic refraction effect.*

Tutorial Figure 7.34. *Refractions are easy to create with ray tracing.*

13. Once you get the parameters installed correctly, press the right arrow key to select the spotlight. When the spotlight is selected, use the Lights panel to right click on the Toggle Shadow Casting by Current Light. In the Shadows panel, left click on Ray for ray traced shadows.

14. Apply the new material to the 3-D logo by left clicking on the Paint Object icon and immediately press Esc to halt the preview. Then render the entire screen with the Render Scene icon from the Render Tools variants. (See Tutorial Figure 7.34.)

15. Finally, we come to bump mapping. To start, we will alter our material to use a standard environment map. From the Attributes panel, select Use Environment Map. Left click on the environment map name and

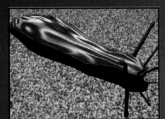

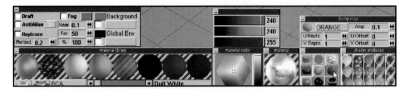

Tutorial Figure 7.35. *Use these settings when preparing the bump mapped texture.*

choose WASTLAN.E2-D from the dialog box and press Enter. Turn off the ambient glow, roughness, transparency, and refraction by dragging the sliders all the way down to the bottom. Drag the shininess slider all the way up to the top. (See Tutorial Figure 7.35.)

16. Right click on the Use Bump Map icon to pull up the Bump Map panel. In this panel we want to set the filename to ORANGE.TAB (if it isn't already that name). Set the Amplitude to .1. In the Render Control panel, turn off ray tracing by left clicking on the checkbox.

17. Apply the new material to the 3-D logo by left clicking on the Paint Object icon and immediately press Esc to halt the preview. Then render the entire screen with the Render Scene icon from the Render Tools variants. (See Tutorial Figure 7.36.)

Tutorial Figure 7.36. *Bump mapping can make objects look less "computerish."*

EXTRA PROJECTS

Following are a few suggestions for more hands-on photo-realism practice.

- Try using bump and opacity maps.

- Create your own texture, opacity, and reflection maps using an image editing program.

- Render an animation of the object with any type of reflective surface.

- Create lights with different colors.

- Create a 3-D flashlight with a spotlight shining out to simulate the flashlight's light.

- Create a 3-D UFO with animated spotlights shining out.

CHAPTER SUMMARY

Television, as a main consumer of computer animation, certainly holds a lot of opportunity for new animators. With the increasing bandwidth of cable television, TV content will come to be in great demand, and this should increase the market demand for television animators. In this chapter we have discussed what it takes to get started and stay in broadcast television animation production. In the tutorials, we create some photo-realistic images using advanced texture mapping techniques. In Chapter 8, "Visualization and Architectural Animation," we discuss what it takes to make a living creating animation for architectural animations and product visualizations.

Image courtesy of SDSU Supercomputing Center.

Archi-
tectural

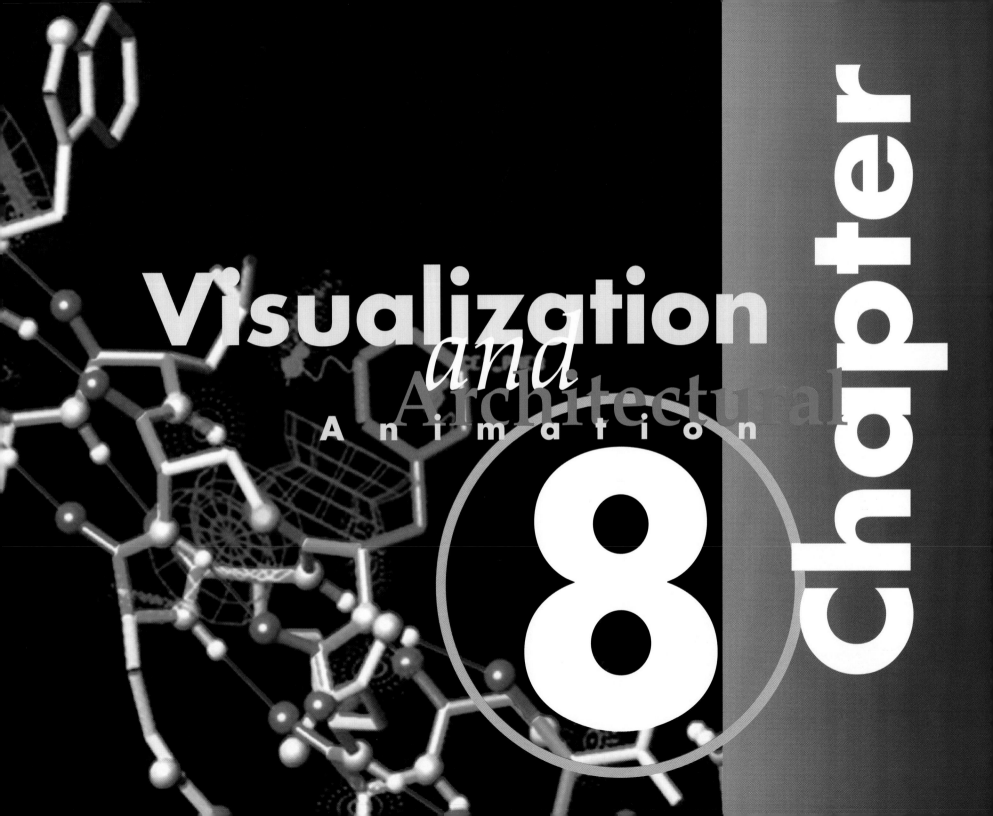

Visualization *and* Architectural Animation

A n i m a t i o n

Chapter

8

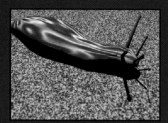

Architecture and visualization are two fields where the computer animation industry plays a big part. Architectural animations usually involve creating walk-throughs of building designs, along with high-resolution still images rendered from the models. Visualizations typically involve the same types of animation. Usually visualizations are of smaller objects than buildings, so the scene is viewed from the perspective of flying around the outside rather than the inside.

In this chapter we interview David Carroll, owner of Support Services, an animation house and service bureau specializing in visualization and architectural animation. We discuss common problems animators face when creating visualizations, suggestions on bidding animation projects, tips and tricks for lighting your 3-D scenes, and other information. In the tutorial, we take the product specifications for the Sony CD-ROM drive, and model it in trueSpace using Boolean operations and other techniques.

CASE STUDY: DAVID CARROLL, OWNER— SUPPORT SERVICES

David Carroll has worked on a variety of animation projects for both architectural and visualization. Carroll's architectural animation of a Caribbean resort won first place in the 1993 CADDIE Awards for Presentation Professionals in Animation.

Image courtesy of View by View.

"The Caribbean resort project was nice because it was a lot of people working together on a single project," Carroll says. Other projects Carroll has worked on include an operating room visualization that featured various operating room equipment, ceiling mounted lights, and other complex details. The piece was used as a sales tool; even though the equipment exists, it's difficult to transport it to show to clients. Carroll explains, "They were having a hard time letting the doctors see how the pieces could move around." The animation was able to convey the information better than any other method. Another job that Carroll worked on was some visualization of a Disneyland attraction, the megamedia show *Fantasia*. They wanted to see how their new attractions would look, so Carroll created a "walk-by" animation.

At Support Services, Carroll uses only IBM-compatible personal computers and Autodesk's 3D Studio. "I'm constantly looking at new packages, but unfortunately, most of the packages I've gotten only make me appreciate 3D Studio that much more." Carroll also runs a service bureau, creating video output for other animators. He records to a Sony laserdisc recorder and then transfers that to a Betacam format. Carroll also has the ability to output to standard with S-Video, VHS, or whatever is needed by the client. When animators come to Support Services to have their animation frames laid out to tape, they usually bring Colorado tape backups in QIC-80 format. They're inexpensive and most of the people who can't afford recording gear can afford an Exabyte backup drive. Carroll usually charges between 35 and 50 cents per frame for transfer fees. Recently Carroll has been doing some three-dimensional digitizing as a service to other animators.

THE EARLY DAYS

Carroll first started making money in computer graphics in 1989, but he was using it and creating animation three years earlier, and before that he got into graphics on the PC. According to Carroll, "Working on computers put me through college and allowed me to get a photographic degree. However, I was working on computers in the airline industry when I remember seeing a scanned image of a rose on the main-frame. I was really impressed. Of course, it was only a 256-color scan back in 1982. I've always been impressed with computer graphics; that's what I gravitated to from day one." Carroll did a lot of work in 2-D animation: "I did a Mitsubishi touch screen kiosk that toured the country with the automotive shows. Some things the client wanted were three-dimensional in nature, so I was kind of looking that way, both for that project and for personal interest. Carroll looked at the different PC-based 3-D animation programs on the market, but they were just too expensive for him. "I read an article on 3D Studio when it was about to be released, so I was at the dealership the day it came out, and I bought it on the spot," he explains.

ART FIRST, TECHNOLOGY SECOND

Carroll feels that getting an internship is a good way to get started, but he does have some reservations about it. "It's hard to find a company that is really willing to do that, because a lot of people just don't have time to be bothered. When beginners intern,

they have to expect to do work for free—not just get free machine time. Also, the best people I find are not the computer people; they're the artists, the traditional cell animators. You can teach just about anybody how to use the computer, but to teach a computer person how to be an artist...that's kind of a skill you either have or you don't. You can, though, always improve if you don't have any artistic skill to begin with. Still, oftentimes it's quite hard to produce good-looking work no matter how good the software is.

"Knowing how colors work really helps," continues Carroll, "knowing how to work with them. If a person can do it with pen and paper then they'll be able to do it in the computer. But if they can't do anything good on paper,

they'll probably have a hard time doing it in the computer. Computer graphics is just a new media. The fundamentals are the same; you still have composition, you still have design, you still have to deal with lighting issues. All of that comes into play. You can be the best technical person with computers but not know anything about art, and yes, you can make the program do stuff, but if the colors don't work, it won't look good."

BE PREPARED FOR RE-DESIGNS WITH VISUALIZATION

There is always some level of risk in creating 3-D animation for something that doesn't exist, but Carroll offers some pointers, "If you're doing visualization, when the product hasn't been built yet, what you're doing is trying to help the client see what the product is going to look like before they spend the money to have a prototype done. Once they have a prototype, it's certainly better to have something that you can hold and look at. We certainly deal with things better that way. When you work with a visualization, count on time, extra time, for dealing with the client so they can change things as they see it. Often they haven't even seen it before. Sure, they've seen the blueprint or a mechanical drawing of it, but many times it'll get done and then they can look at it and say, `Yes, you're right; it doesn't quite look right. We should put a blue

stripe here, or we should tone this down and bring this feature forward a bit.' So that re-design process can actually be a discipline in itself."

HOW CRITICAL IS VISUALIZATION ACCURACY?

When creating visualization animation, TV actually gives you a very wide latitude. Carroll explains, "You can look at one set and an object might look pink; look at it on another set and it might look a little green. There are very few sets that are adjusted right. Most clients usually don't know much more than we do, so they trust you. Of course, you always want to do the best. I tend to be as accurate as I can using a calculator when working in 3D Studio and figuring things out. But occasionally, it gets back to the budget. I have to ask myself, `Do I go out and measure it or do I just rough it out?' A lot of times roughing it out is just as good. And it should be good; we're just trying to get a small impression of the item. I tend to produce very accurate work, almost to the point of its being a detriment, because of the time involved. Sometimes, I'll look at something and say `Hey, do I want to actually take this over to the 3-D digitizer and digitize it to plus or minus 16,000ths of an inch? Do I really need that?' Sometimes you do, sometimes you don't. Even when you do that, you can still run into problems with the scanner. The biggest things controlling detail and accuracy are the budget at the beginning of the project and the client toward the end of the project."

Carroll continues: "The accuracy needed depends on the client. I try to protect myself in case the animation goes out and then people get the product and aren't happy with it. They might come back, look at the animation, and say, `Oh, it's not accurate.' You don't want to get into any false or misleading advertising situations. Then again, your contract should protect you from that sort of thing. A lot of times I put these things in my contracts and people come back and ask why it's in there. As soon as I explain it to them, though, they understand. When I do that, I phrase the contract in such a way that their signing does not give me the right to do anything malicious. I can't go in and intentionally make incorrect designs or give false data. So I'm not trying to get out of all responsibility, but I am trying to limit my liabilities so they are relative to the reimbursement that I receive for the project."

RIGID STEEL
PASSENGER CAGE

DE IMPACT
EAMS

ANTI-LOC
BRAKES
AVAILABL

Image courtesy of Viewpoint.

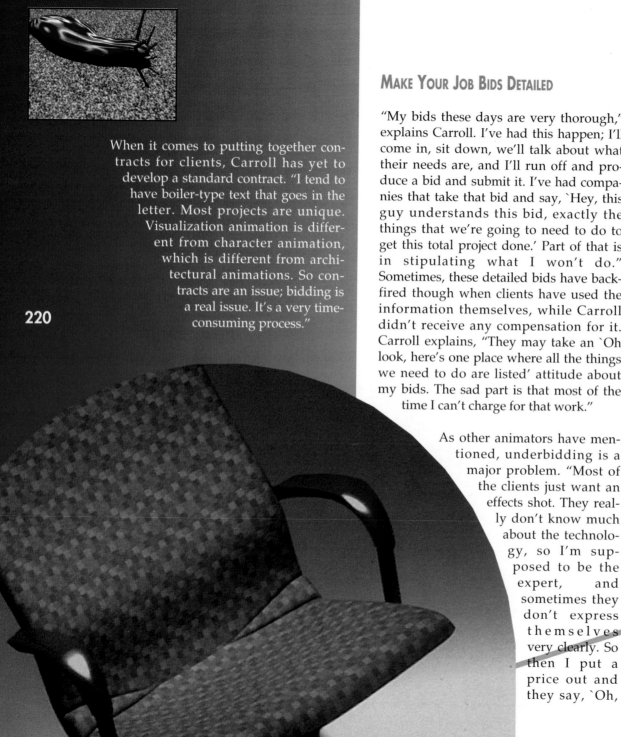

When it comes to putting together contracts for clients, Carroll has yet to develop a standard contract. "I tend to have boiler-type text that goes in the letter. Most projects are unique. Visualization animation is different from character animation, which is different from architectural animations. So contracts are an issue; bidding is a real issue. It's a very time-consuming process."

220

MAKE YOUR JOB BIDS DETAILED

"My bids these days are very thorough," explains Carroll. I've had this happen; I'll come in, sit down, we'll talk about what their needs are, and I'll run off and produce a bid and submit it. I've had companies that take that bid and say, `Hey, this guy understands this bid, exactly the things that we're going to need to do to get this total project done.' Part of that is in stipulating what I won't do." Sometimes, these detailed bids have backfired though when clients have used the information themselves, while Carroll didn't receive any compensation for it. Carroll explains, "They may take an `Oh look, here's one place where all the things we need to do are listed' attitude about my bids. The sad part is that most of the time I can't charge for that work."

As other animators have mentioned, underbidding is a major problem. "Most of the clients just want an effects shot. They really don't know much about the technology, so I'm supposed to be the expert, and sometimes they don't express themselves very clearly. So then I put a price out and they say, `Oh,

this is what we meant.' So the biggest thing I've learned is to write my proposals more as limits than possibilities. Never leave anything out, so when a person gets a proposal from me, it tells them not just what I'm going to do, but it also clearly states what I'm *not* going to do."

Carroll provides an example: "There was a company coming to me wanting some furniture animated, so I gave them a quote and based it on the information they gave me. But then, the level of detail they wanted just kept getting higher and higher. It turned out they didn't even have any plans for their furniture. They didn't have any samples that I could get my hands on, no model numbers, or anything. So in order to get my job done, I had to do a lot of *their* job. And it just got to be a lot more expensive than I originally anticipated. I got the job done and the client was happy, but I put a lot more work into it than I had planned, probably three times as much. One result was that the next time they asked me to do a job, they expected the same price, even though they knew I had lost money on the first job."

AVOID THE TEMPTATION TO EXPERIMENT WHEN THE CLOCK IS RUNNING

Telling a client that you can do something that you've never done before is a dangerous game. "I know it's attractive to people, including myself," says Carroll, "because there are always things you'd like to try. Things that are kind of playing in your

Image courtesy of Computer Design Inc.

mind. If you are working professionally, you don't often have time to experiment. Every now and then you'll accept a job thinking, `Great, this will give me an opportunity to play with something new.' One of the big problems is that sometimes it's more complex and difficult than you expected. When you try something new, you are relying on software or features that you haven't tested completely. When you try new software or features during a project and something doesn't work, you're in a real world of hurt. You're committed to a project deadline."

Carroll provides an example of one of his first projects. "I did a lot of prototyping up front so I could show the client what it would look like. It was some animation that was going to be computer based. I showed it to them in low res, 320×200, and they wanted it to be crisper. I said,`Sure, no problem,' but when I popped it into high

resolution, the computer couldn't display it fast enough to keep the image from ripping or tearing. Then I tried to fix it, putting more frames in with less movement per frame, which didn't help. I went round and round on that. I finally finished the project, but it ended up being one complex image that took about 120 hours to generate. I practically had to paint each pixel by hand!"

PRODUCING CLEAN GEOMETRY

Producing clean geometry, 3-D models without an excessive amount of faces or vertices, is always an important concern with any low-end platform like the PC, Mac, or Amiga. The larger the geometry of a model, the more memory and time it will take to render. We've had the privilege of working with Carroll on an animation project, and clean geometry is something he excels in. He explains, "I try to understand exactly how much geometry is needed to create the illusion of a real object."

Carroll continues, "For instance, if the object doesn't get that close to the camera, yet you model it with dense geometry, then you are increasing your render time needlessly. However, if the camera is going to get close to an object, you need to determine how much detail you want to put into the geometry and how much is needed to create that illusion."

Carroll explains how he once animated a galloping 3-D horse. "I took the Edward Muybridge motion study of the horse running and scanned it. Next, I chopped up the pictures into frames and made it into a digital animation file. Then I colored the right hoof. I put a little spot in it so I could tell at any frame which leg was which. Then I pulled that animation in and used it as a basis to match my geometry to. I ended up with a horse that looked very realistic."

Carroll continues, "A lot of people talk about using Muybridge work as a starting point, but scanning and converting it into a digital animation file worked really well."

221

Image courtesy of View by View.

LIGHTING TIPS AND TRICKS

With a background in professional photography, Carroll has some good tips for lighting effects. "There are two things that can make animation stand out. One thing is sound. A lot of us tend to do animation, and we get this image to look great. But once we put it on a demo tape and send it out without sound on it, it's nothing. If you've ever watched a demo reel without sound, you don't know what to do with your ears. It definitely becomes noticeable. Even if you just take some music and record it with your animation, then it's not noticeable. But a soundless demo is horrible."

222

Carroll continues, "Another thing is lighting. A good understanding of the way light works or photographic lighting works really helps. One of the key things to make animation look more realistic for outdoor scenes is to tint the light slightly blue. Because sunlight is more of a whitish light, the scene is getting a lot of reflective light. When that light comes from a sky which has more of a blue tint to it, you can get a more realistic outdoor coloring that way."

Carroll says, "Instead of using yellow for an indoor animation, you'll want to use a little more reddish tint, maybe slightly orange. Many times you don't see these things because your eye corrects these images automatically. Fluorescent lights are weird because they are not even across the spectrum, but they are kind of bluish-green."

"A good way to see lighting color is to use your camera without a flash and take pictures indoors under different lighting," Carroll explains. "If you use slide film, you'll see it more. If you use film, the developer may color correct it, and you won't see the true color. By using slide film, the color correction is less likely to happen. You can have an outdoor shot and an indoor shot and can look at them right next to each other and you can actually see the difference in color. When

Get It on Your Demo Reel

"I almost always say I have the rights to show the work I create under contract, and a lot of times people will want that stricken," explains Carroll. "They'll say they have an objection to this clause. If so, then I'll strike it. But when I strike it, I normally charge for it. If you're working for two years on projects and can't use them on your demo reel later on, you have nothing to show for your work. Plus, work goes out of date so quickly, you have to show it. You don't have time to create things just for a demo. It takes a long time to put a good demo together."

Watch Your Budget

Carroll stresses the importance of budget. "People underestimate budget. Every project, I don't care what it is, has a budget in it and that budget is going to affect how good the work is. I haven't met an animator yet who can look back on a piece of animation they've done and say, `It's perfect. I couldn't fix it up any better. I couldn't make it nicer.' You can always improve upon it. It all comes down to budget. The budget involves time, as in how much time you can spend on a project before moving on. If you're doing something for a client, the budget involves money. At that point, you're doing this professionally and you're doing it to get paid. So even if it's your first job and you're doing it at a low cost to get established, there's still a budget. Part of the budget is `How much equipment can I throw at this project.' You can do ray tracing and all that kind of fun stuff, but doing so drastically increases the amount of render time. A lot of people don't understand that. When looking at somebody's demo tape, you almost need to see a budget with it. When you look at some of the things on a demo tape, you might think, `Well, that could be better' but that's not what they paid for," concludes Carroll.

Tutorial: Modeling with Dimensional Accuracy

In this tutorial we will take the specifications for a Sony CD-ROM drive and create a computer model to the correct scale using the Object Properties panel. In the process, you will learn how to work with Boolean operations on polygons, customize the grid mode, and animate cameras.

you're doing animation, you don't want to do it as strong as that because the eye naturally corrects for some of it. Even if you apply a little tint, the eye will still correct the image a little bit. Although you're watching it on the screen, you'll get the feeling that `Hey, I'm indoors' because you can tell it is from an artificial light source as opposed to sunlight."

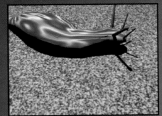

CREATING DIMENSIONALLY ACCURATE MODELS

1. Launch trueSpace, and from the File menu, choose Scene/New. If there are any panels open on the screen, left-click on the Close All Panels icon.

224

2. Our model will be composed of two main parts: the case and the face plate. Start by creating the case. Left-click on the Primitives Panel icon and left-click the Add Cube icon. This will create a perfectly square cube in the middle of the workspace. (See Tutorial Figure 8.1.)

3. To alter the dimensions of the cube to fit the exact dimensions of the CD-ROM case, we will use the numeric input capabilities by right clicking on the Object Tool icon. This will call up the Object Property panel. (See Tutorial Figure 8.2.) The numbers in the Object Property panel can represent any type of value. In this tutorial we will say they represent 100 millimeters.

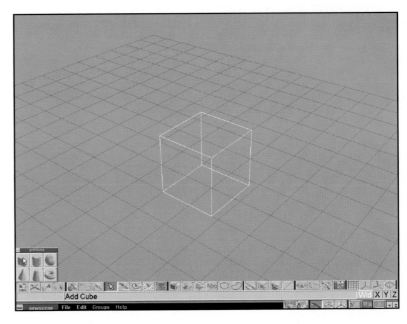

Tutorial Figure 8.1. *This cube will become the case of the CD-ROM drive.*

	X	Y	Z	Name
Location	0.000	0.000	0.000	Cube
Rotation	0.00	0.00	0.00	# faces
Scale	2.000	2.000	2.000	6

Tutorial Figure 8.2. *The Object Property panel allows you to enter numeric values to set object dimensions.*

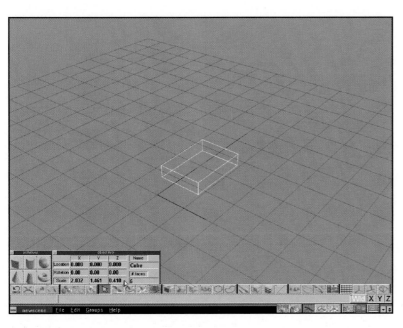

Tutorial Figure 8.3. *After entering the correct scale for the CD-ROM case, the square primitive snaps into shape.*

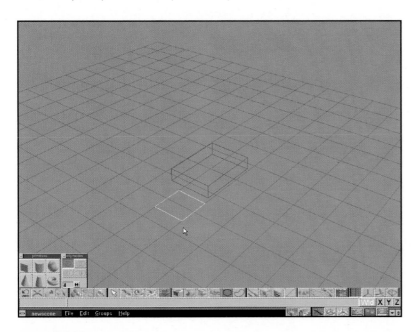

Tutorial Figure 8.4. *Draw a square polygon in front of the CD-ROM case.*

4. In the Object Property panel enter the following values for the scale: **2.032** for X, **1.4605** for Y, and **.41.4** for Z. (See Tutorial Figure 8.3.)

5. Now left-click on the Regular Polygon icon to create the face plate. Before creating the polygon, however, turn on grid mode by left-clicking on the Toggle Grid mode icon. Now with the Regular Polygon icon still active, left-click in front of the case and drag the mouse down until a small, square polygon is created. (See Tutorial Figure 8.4.)

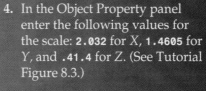

6. To correct the dimensions of our new polygon, right-click on the Object Tool icon to call up the Object Property panel. In the Object Property panel, enter the following values for the scale: **.425** for X, **1.485** for Y,

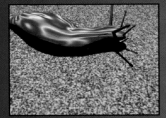

226

and leave *Z* at **0**. (See Tutorial Figure 8.5.)

7. Now we are going to adjust our view so we can work on the detail of the CD-ROM drive. Left-click on the Top View icon, then left-click on the Look At Current Object icon. Next, left-click on the Zoom tool, and left-click and drag forward in the workspace to zoom in on the face plate. Lastly, left-click on the Object Rotate icon, then right-click anywhere in the workspace and drag the mouse to the right until the face plate rotates to horizontal.

8. First, left-click on the Close All Panels icon to clean up the screen. Now we will create some Boolean holes in the face plate before we sweep it into a 3-D shape. Left-click on the Regular Polygon icon. Notice that since we already have a regular polygon selected, the Boolean options are available for creating new polygons. We need to temporarily turn off the grid mode before starting, however, so left-click on the Toggle Grid Mode icon to turn

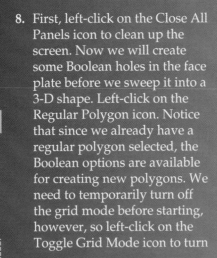

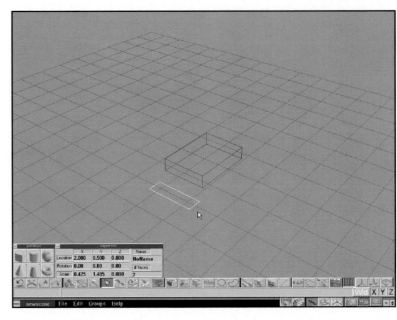

Tutorial Figure 8.5. *After entering the correct scale for the CD-ROM case, the square primitive snaps into shape.*

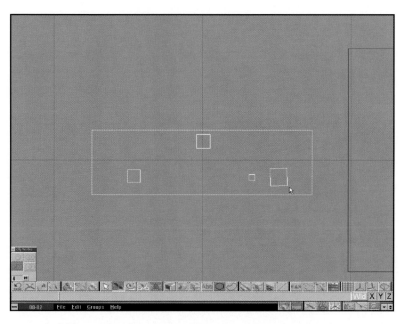

Tutorial Figure 8.6. *Cut four holes in our face plate at these locations.*

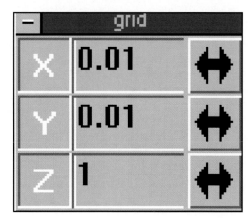

Tutorial Figure 8.7. *The Grid panel allows different grid spacings depending on the tool currently selected.*

it off. On the Poly Modes panel, left-click on the Subtraction icon. Now any polygons we draw with the polygon tool will be subtracted or cut out from the currently selected polygon (in this case, our face plate). Using the left mouse button to drag, draw four small squares in the configuration shown in Tutorial Figure 8.6. Don't worry if your boxes come out a little crooked; we will fix that in the next step.

9. By using Point Edit mode along with grid snap, we can adjust our holes to match the holes needed in the CD-ROM face plate. Turn grid mode back on by left-clicking on the Toggle Grid Mode icon. Right-click on the Toggle Grid mode icon to bring up the Grid panel. The Grid panel lets you adjust the snap spacing for the grid mode. (See Tutorial Figure 8.7.) When the Grid panel appears, set the X and Y values to 0.01.

10. Now from the Point Edit tools variants, left-click on the Point Edit:Vertices icon. This allows us to move the vertices of our holes to any new location. Once you enter a Point Edit mode, the Point Navigation panel appears. (See Tutorial Figure 8.8.) You will also notice the cursor now has a small *P* next to it to indicate that you are in Point Edit mode.

11. Click on the edge vertex of each of the squares and drag them to the positions shown in Tutorial Figure 8.9. You must left-click on the vertex once to select it (they turn bright green when selected), then left-click again to drag it. If you wish to drag more than one vertex at the same time, hold down the Shift key while you select new vertices. You can also use the Point Scale and Point Rotate tools in addition to the Point Move tool. When you finish adjusting the vertices, turn off Point Edit mode by left clicking on the Object Tool icon.

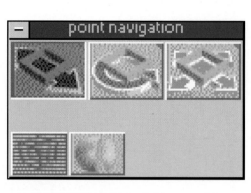

Tutorial Figure 8.8. *The Point Navigation panel lets you move, rotate, or scale points, edges, or faces.*

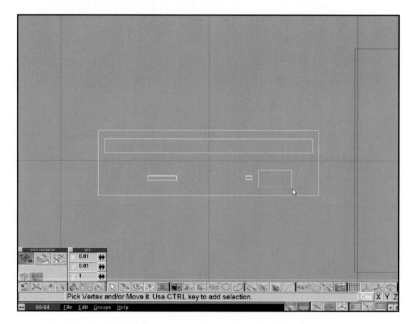

Tutorial Figure 8.9. *Drag the vertices of each hole to these positions.*

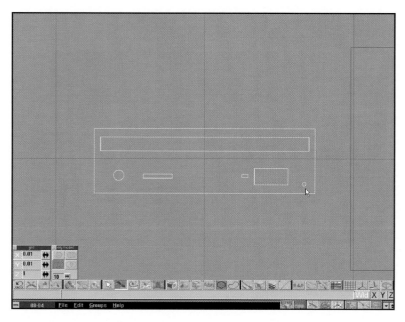

Tutorial Figure 8.10. *Draw two holes at the position shown in the vertices.*

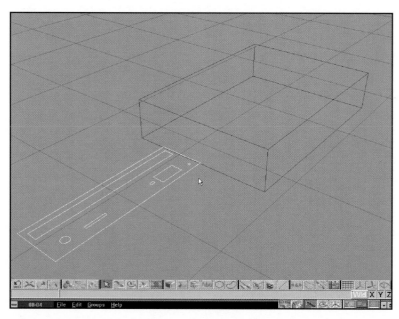

Tutorial Figure 8.11. *Move the perspective view closer to the face plate with the Eye Move tool.*

12. There are two more holes to put in our face plate, but these holes are round. Left-click the Regular Polygon icon and then adjust the number of sides in the Poly Modes panel to 10. This allows us to cut two small, circular holes in our face plate. Verify that the Toggle Grid mode icon is turned off. Make sure the Subtraction icon in the Poly Modes panel is still on, and draw two holes at the positions shown in the specifications. (See Tutorial Figure 8.10.)

13. We are now ready to Sweep the face plate into 3-D, but before you do, switch the main workspace view back to perspective by left-clicking on the Perspective View icon. Then use the Eye Move icon to move the view a little closer to the face plate. (See Tutorial Figure 8.11.) Do this by dragging the mouse forward while holding

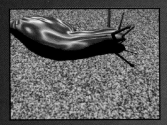

the left button and dragging the mouse backward while holding the right mouse button.

14. To extrude our face plate into 3-D, left-click on the Sweep icon. Left-click and then right-click on the Object Tool icon. This will take you out of Point Edit mode. Then load the Object Property panel. (See Tutorial Figure 8.12.)

15. To scale the height of the face plate back to normal, enter the dimension **.049** for the Z height in the Object Property panel. (See Tutorial Figure 8.13.)

16. Before putting the two pieces together, we will apply surface materials. The case will use a dark gray and a shiny silver material, while the face plate will use a plastic off-white color. Close the Object Property panel and left-click on the Material Library icon. Then right-click on the Paint Face icon and the material attributes

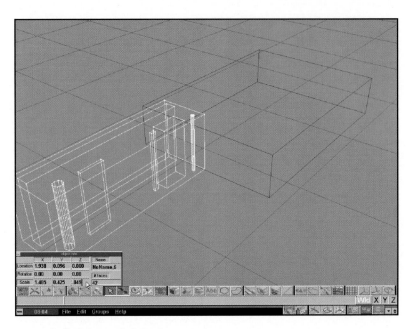

Tutorial Figure 8.12. *The Object Property panel allows us to specify the height of the face plate.*

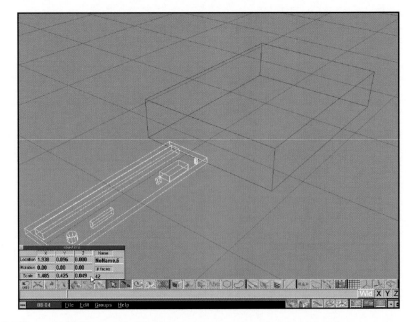

Tutorial Figure 8.13. *After entering .049 for the Z height.*

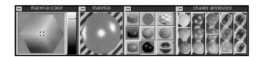

Tutorial Figure 8.14. *The shiny silver material for the CD-ROM case.*

Tutorial Figure 8.15. *The material library allows you to permanently store surface materials.*

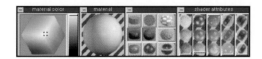

Tutorial Figure 8.16. *The surface attributes for the face plate.*

will appear. First let's create a shiny silver. Drag the material color selector to the center so it selects the color white. Next, left-click on the Metal shader button, then adjust the shader attributes to match Tutorial Figure 8.14.

17. Left-click on the CD-ROM case, then left-click on the Paint Object icon to paint the case with our new material. When it finishes, left-click on the Add Material to Library button so we can keep a copy of it. Left-click in the material name box and enter **Shiny Silver**. (See Tutorial Figure 8.15.)

18. We want to paint the face plate off-white, so using the material attributes, create a new surface material with the settings shown in Tutorial Figure 8.16. Afterward assign the new material to the library by leftclicking on the Add Material to Library button.

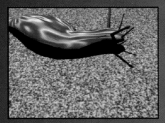

19. From the material library choose the material, Flat Black. Then left-click on the Paint face icon and paint the front of the case. (See Tutorial Figures 8.17 and 8.18.) To paint the back side of the case, use the Eye Rotate icon.

20. Now let's rotate the face plate up to the CD-ROM case. First, turn grid mode back on by left clicking on the Toggle Grid mode icon. This ensures that we rotate the face plate the exact number of degrees. Next, left-click on the Object Rotate icon and right-click and drag the mouse to the left. Right-click Object Rotate to pull up the coordinates panel. Turn off the Y axis. Left-click and drag the mouse down to rotate the face plate up into the correct orientation. (See Tutorial Figure 8.19.)

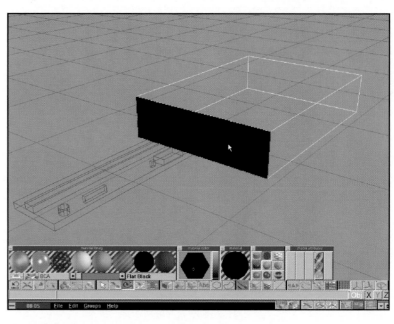

Tutorial Figure 8.17. *Painting the front of the case.*

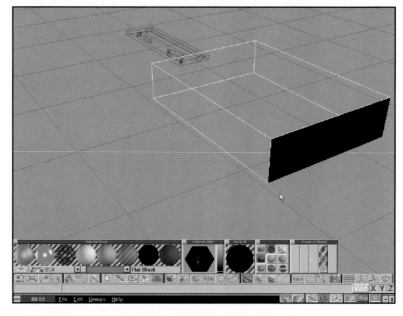

Tutorial Figure 8.18. *Painting the back of the case.*

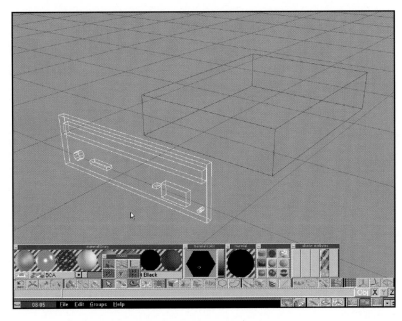

Tutorial Figure 8.19. *After rotating the face plate to its correct position.*

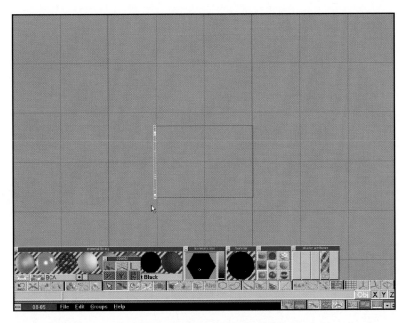

Tutorial Figure 8.20. *Positioning the face plate on the case in the Top View.*

21. To position the face plate correctly, right-click the Object Move icon and turn on the Object Axes. Left-click on the Top View icon. Once in the top view, use the Object Move icon to position the face plate on the case. (See Tutorial Figure 8.20.)

22. Left-click on the Left View icon. Once in the left view, use the Object Move icon to position the face plate squarely on the case. (See Tutorial Figure 8.21.)

233

23. Now we will add the missing buttons to our CD-ROM player. Before creating any new geometry, select the face plate material in the material library. Left-click on the Primitives Panel icon. Left-click on the Add Cylinder and Add Cube icons. This generates large geometric primitives for us to use. (See Tutorial Figure 8.22.)

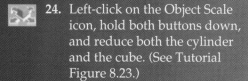

24. Left-click on the Object Scale icon, hold both buttons down, and reduce both the cylinder and the cube. (See Tutorial Figure 8.23.)

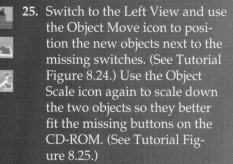

25. Switch to the Left View and use the Object Move icon to position the new objects next to the missing switches. (See Tutorial Figure 8.24.) Use the Object Scale icon again to scale down the two objects so they better fit the missing buttons on the CD-ROM. (See Tutorial Figure 8.25.)

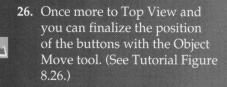

26. Once more to Top View and you can finalize the position of the buttons with the Object Move tool. (See Tutorial Figure 8.26.)

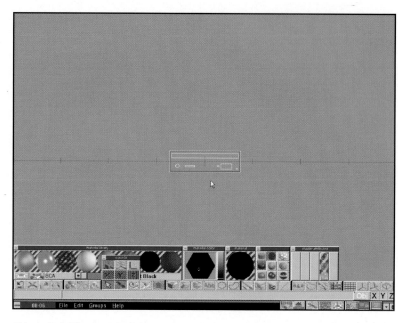

Tutorial Figure 8.21. *Positioning the face plate on the case in the left view.*

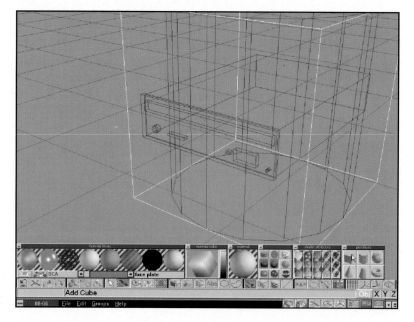

Tutorial Figure 8.22. *Adding two new geometric primitives to our scene.*

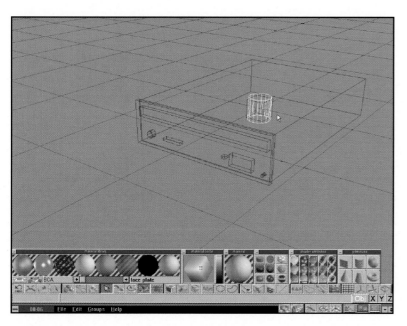

Tutorial Figure 8.23. *Reduce the two new objects with the Object Scale tool.*

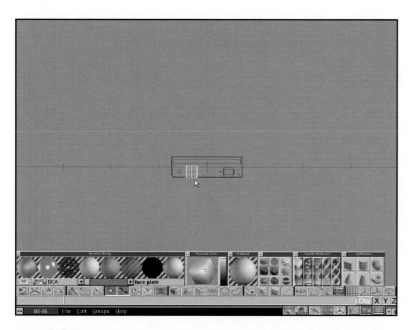

Tutorial Figure 8.24. *Reposition the buttons from the left view.*

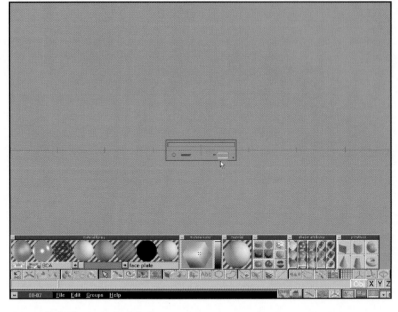

Tutorial Figure 8.25. *Scale the objects down just a little more and they will be perfect.*

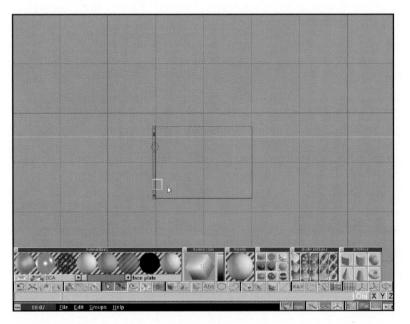

Tutorial Figure 8.26. *Positioning the buttons from the top view.*

Extra Projects

Below are a few suggestions for more hands-on visualization and architectural animation practice.

- Alter the CD-ROM drive's colors and create more sample images.

- Assign bump maps to the surfaces to give them some texture.

- Create a table to set the drive on and light it with different types of lights.

- Set up and render close-up fly-bys of the CD-ROM drive.

- Duplicate the drive and modify each one slightly.

Chapter Summary

Visualization and architectural animation are both good fields to get started in as a computer animator. With more and more designers and architects using CAD software, the popularity of 3-D simulations and animations should increase. In the tutorial, we saw what it takes to model with precise measurements in Caligari trueSpace. As you can see, trueSpace lends itself more toward artistic freeform modeling rather than structured models. However, this should have given you a taste for what engineering-based animation is like. In our next chapter, we discuss creating animation for motion pictures.

237

Motion

9

Motion Pictures

Chapter

Motion picture computer animation is perhaps the highest level that an animator can achieve. It is where the serious money is made and the most advanced technology is used. Computer animation techniques appearing in film usually take a year or more to find their way into television computer animation or other fields.

In this chapter we will interview Mark Dippé, special effects supervisor for Industrial Light & Magic (ILM.) Dippé has worked on such notable feature films as *The Abyss*, *Terminator 2*, *Jurassic Park*, *The Flinstones*, and many others. In the tutorials, we will create a simple character animation of a slug and learn how to use the Animation Project window.

Image courtesy of National Video Center and Telezign (a Division of National Video Center/NY).

CASE STUDY: MARK DIPPÉ, VISUAL EFFECTS SUPERVISOR—INDUSTRIAL LIGHT & MAGIC

Mark Dippé was introduced to computer graphics in the mid-1970s. By 1979, he knew that CGI was what he wanted to do. Animation back then was very different from today. There were no commercial packages with easy-to-use graphical interfaces. Everything had to be programmed, and if you were an artist and wanted to do computer animation, you had to "put up with" the technology. During the mid-1980s, Dippé was just starting to do television spots, and toward the end of the '80s, he started working on motion pictures. He went to work for ILM in 1988. Prior to joining ILM, Dippé had always been a freelance worker for various companies. ILM was his first full-time employment as a computer animator.

EARLY INSPIRATION

"Basically, I was involved in experimental film in the '70s," explains Dippé. "I was introduced to computer graphics when someone said, `Hey, look at this!' It was an early computer painting system, and I thought, `Well, that's cool.' It was an experimental thing done in a laboratory. Later on, I met Dick Shoup who created one of the first color computer painting systems at Xerox PARC. I was just one of those guys who is into anything interesting. So I kept up with computer graphics, and around 1978 I saw some of my first realistic-looking images. It blew my mind! These were images of space vehicles. The stuff is pretty primitive looking now, but it was things like photo-realistic teapots. Jim Blinn and some others had made some very interesting surface texture images."

Dippé continues, "It looks primitive now, but back then it was amazing. The thing that really blew my mind was when I saw some of the very early work of Triple-I. They made their *Juggler* film around 1981, but they had some very interesting earlier computer images. Other interesting early work was done at NYIT, and it was so obvious to me that you could create worlds, that you didn't have to follow the laws of nature. It was surrealism brought to life. It was like a physical being, not just a still, painted image. It was obvious to me it was pretty hip."

GETTING STARTED

"I took a couple of classes at the California College of Arts and Crafts (CCAC) with Judy Gillerman. I didn't get a degree in film; I didn't go to a film school. My path wasn't so clear, but I think that's very common because computer animation is such a new arena. It's not such a well-defined thing. Back when I was doing it, I was creating it myself. I think it will become well established and you'll be able to go to school and study computer animation.

"My interests are really in all the creative disciplines. What got me interested in this was that I always wanted to make experimental films. I got involved by taking courses with Judy Gillerman and getting to use an Image Processor (IP), which was a video synthesizer designed by Dan Sandin and Tom De Fanti and the guys at the University of Chicago. Gillerman had one at CCAC."

That early experience at CCAC became one of Dippé's early connections in the world of synthetic imagery. As he explains, "That was kind of connecting me to the world of synthetic imagery or manipula-

Geoff Campbell working on *Jurassic Park*.
Image courtesy of ILM.

241

Mark Dippé working on *Terminator II*.
Image courtesy of ILM.

Steve Williams working on *The Abyss*.
Image courtesy of ILM.

tive imagery, and that was very exciting. I was introduced, by a guy named Lou Katz, to a system called ZGRASS, which was a very early computer animation system. It was inexpensive and simple to use. Again, it was simple in those days; today it would be considered very complex. You could interactively
create

Image courtesy of Sidley Wright MotionWorks and National Video Center. © Miller Brewing Co.

little animations on it, and all of that was very exciting because this was in 1979 and the early 1980s. That was kind of the genesis of my involvement with the new technology in film making and video. Before that I'd only done the regular video projects."

Simultaneously, Dippé learned of Ed Catmull and Jim Blinn at Berkeley. "I heard about these two guys who I'd never met, but I knew of their work. They were some of the inventors of the technology, so I decided to go see if I could use their ideas and work with them, and that's what I did. They were teaching at Berkeley where I studied, and I learned a great deal from them. I was really lucky. It was kind of accidental. They are truly two of the people who created computer graphics, and I was able to study with them for a year or so. Ed Catmull, incidentally, became my adviser. I learned everything I could about computer graphics. I saw the possibilities, and in the early 1980s, I was able to start doing things like ray tracing pictures and other things, allowing me to make photo-realistic worlds."

THE EARLY DAYS OF COMPUTER ANIMATION

The technology was very different compared to today. "At that time you had to do everything the hard way; the technology was brand new. I had to learn how to program, and so I became very heavily involved in technology. My focus was to make pictures. Don't get me wrong; I didn't want to invent computers or anything like that, but back then, that's the way it was. I'm not at all a technophobe; I worked in music with synthesizers in the old days when they had the cable-patched synthesizers. My involvement with that led to video synthesizers. To me, the process was an interesting thing. I became very much interested in that, studying with Jim and Ed.

"Back in 1980, you had no choice but to program. The process was so bare. It was like owning a car in the 1920s when they were first available; you had to know a fair amount about the car just to drive it. The technology itself was so primitive that every day when you made a picture, you invented something new. It was very exciting; you invented things constantly. If you wanted to make an apple, you would confront new visual ideas and new technical problems in the process of trying to make an interesting looking fruit and be inventing constantly. So it was very exciting. That's the environment I was in."

An "Idealist" for Computer Graphics

Dippé, however, discovered some serious roadblocks in the path of his career. "After going through all that and learning how to master the technology and seeing what I could do, it turned out to be a real bummer. Basically, you had to have access to multi-million dollar systems to do anything. Here I was leaving school, wanting to do great art projects and make these fantastic films, and there was no possibility except to go to work for some company that was doing flying logos. At the time, computer animation was used a lot for Station IDs for TV. I was, and I still am, more of an idealist. I said, `No, this stuff is for creating a whole new cinema; it's not to do that kind of hackneyed crud.' So I just dropped out and sort of hung out because nothing was happening at that time."

Dippé continues "My interest in using computers for animation was to do more of what I would call `experimental film making,' but after I finished my studies at Berkeley in 1984 with Ed Catmull, the industry was not well developed. I was a little headstrong; I kind of dropped out and just did a lot of more artistically oriented work, what we called intermedia, such as simultaneous video projections with dancers. I did rather strange video art with subliminal images and photography. I worked with making computer images in that context and did some exhibitions."

Dippé continued to find freelance work around the Bay area with some television stations and various small groups, but something fantastic happened in 1988. "The Abyss was in pre-production and since I was so heavily involved in the area of computer graphics, I pretty much knew everyone who was doing these kinds of things. So Douglas Kay and George Joblove (from ILM) approached me and said, `Hey, Mark, we know you're not a fan of the American Hollywood film, but this is an amazing character animation story, a character animation sequence in a film,' and it was. I was sort of ripe for that kind of change,

so I decided to leave my little cave in the woods in Bolinas. I dropped all that and moved into San Francisco to begin work on this feature film project. My life was changed very dramatically at that point. I had come into the business in a round-about way, like many other people. So I found my way back into the real world, so to speak, because the technology evolved. There was now an opportunity to create a very interesting film sequence using computer animation. Dennis Muren became a mentor of sorts, and he supported me in my work and brought me into a much higher level very quickly. With The Abyss, we were given enough time, enough money, and the right film. So that's what brought me back into the real world."

243

WORK AT ILM

During the past six years at ILM, Dippé has been able to work on a large number of films. Some of his major CGI projects were *The Abyss*, *Terminator 2*, *Jurassic Park*, and *The Flinstones*. He also worked on The *Hunt for Red October*, *Back to the Future II*, *Ghost*, *Arachnaphobia*, *Die Hard II*, and many others. Dippé mentions some of his favorite projects and what made them so. "I still like *The Abyss* a great deal. That was a big change in my life physically, emotionally, and aesthetically. Again, I was working on a big commercial film that was something I never wanted to do. But I liked the imagery so much (and I still like it today); it was so strong that it was

a very positive and powerful influence on what's happened to me so far, and probably will continue to be the future. I think that's one of my favorite projects. Another one is *Terminator 2*. It was a similar kind of feeling. It was a project that was much bigger; it covered a lot more ground, and gave us more opportunity.

"*Jurassic Park*, because it's been such a tremendous success, has shown all the things that computer animators can do, computer animation's power, and its impact on the language of film. It's kind of the evolutionary step in cinema that we're creating here, the new digital cinema. So I just hope to evolve even further in that direction and in creating films. In a larger sense, not just doing visual effects, but creating entire digital films. Hopefully, we are moving in that direction, getting back to my original intent in the first place."

THE BIG CHALLENGES

For Dippé and others at ILM, problems or difficulties don't necessarily make a project unpopular. "When you do something like this (a creative endeavor with time and budget constraints), nothing is ever good enough. Anything I do, when it's done I'm always critical of it. I always want to go back and make it better; I think that's a natural part of the creative process. So it's always hard; it always takes a

lot of time and a lot of effort."

When it comes to technical difficulties or problems, Dippé actually enjoys them. "In terms of difficulty, in visual effects, one of the things I tend to enjoy is a challenge. That's part of what I do here. I read a lot of scripts, and I see some project, and I can visualize how it can be done even though it has never been done before. It's like leaping off a cliff, knowing in your heart your parachute is going to work even though you never used it before. There's a bit of that in what I do here. So it's always very hard; we are always having to invent new things. You're in this corner thinking, `I'm going to make this creature made of water look beautiful and stick people's heads on the end of it!' You just say, `Yes, I can see it, and it looks great,' and you start trying to do it and it's difficult. I think the enjoyable part is that you are up against this great, monumental task. You're trying to bring to life something you see and it's really hard. It's a lot of blood and sweat; it's all that perspiration, as Ben Franklin used to say. But when it's all done, it's a joy.

"To me, the visual effects work I like least (and by the way, in my mind, visual effects is a term that's going to leave the English language because everything is visual effects nowadays), is when we do things that are not the center of attention." Complains Dippé, "For example, in *The Hunt for Red October*, I did a lot of

Labyrinth

animation for floating debris in the water, which doesn't interest me. When I watch the screen, what I did doesn't seem important in the movie. In *The Hunt for Red October*, none of the submarines were filmed under water. All of that water was created digitally; the subs were just filmed in the dark in smoke, and we just added the feeling of water. It's important for the film, but it doesn't connect to me enough. I'm interested in film making, doing things that connect with the audience and tell stories that are emotive and strong. So I would rate the work I do based on how successful that element is."

Other animators, such as Tom Porter at Pixar, say it can be difficult to work under people who don't have a clear vision of what they want. Yet Dippé doesn't run into that problem often. "We have a very unique relationship here at ILM with the directors; we are not the directors of a film, we are the directors of visual effects. But they are very trusting with us. They come

to us because we have great concepts and great designs. So we are involved with designing the look, the characters, the performance, the style. I go down with the crew and actually shoot the film that we use. We shoot our own sequences under the director, of course, but we have a very close relationship with directors and they're very trusting. They come to us seeking that magic that we bring. So it's not such a problem for me. However, I have been in situations where I work with somebody who says, `No, I don't like that, but I don't know what I do like.' It's a very bad situation."

Dippé continues to describe a situation that is difficult. "A situation that is very upsetting is when you have no control over what's happening. Say you have agreed to do something, like make an animal with fur or make something fly like a bird. You've never done it before, and you must finish it in three weeks because the film is going to be released in five. As the animator, you feel it's still not flying right; I'm not talking about the director yelling at you or anything. You're just trying to figure out how in the world you're going to make it work. That's happened to me and it's scary, but fortunately, we've always been able to pull it off. We've always been creative enough

and savvy enough to pull it all together before it's too late."

Film Animation Versus Video Animation

When comparing film to video, Dippé has some interesting thoughts. "The film experience is a much richer one. Having a big screen you are watching in the dark, where you're paying attention to the screen, is a much richer experience than TV. TV is something you can just have on while you're knitting, reading, or eating dinner. TV is, by essence, a throwaway medium, in my opinion. TV is not nearly as enthralling or interesting as film. You have the TV as one source of light in a room with other lights in it. The TV is one element that's talking to

245

you as other people in the room are talking to you. The TV is much more of an environmental element in one's experience than film is. So besides resolution, to me, the whole experience is a much stronger one on film. Film is like going to the opera or theater; you are there to be there. With television, you're in your living room with nothing to do, so you turn it on. It's very, very different in that way."

Even deadlines are different with television work compared to film. "For television work you generally don't have as much time. It's a much shorter projection schedule, the budgets are a lot lower, and the quality demands are not nearly as high. First of all, it's lower resolution but also television is not as demanding a medium. You don't make a *Terminator 2* for a TV movie; you make *Terminator 2* for the big screen. I love TV, but considering the product quality in general, film is a much richer thing in comparison. TV is like fast food, and film is more like fine dining. There really is that difference: production quality, look, style, everything about it. So it's a much shorter production schedule and a tighter budget with TV."

EQUIPMENT AT ILM

For equipment at ILM, they are pretty much exclusively using the Silicon Graphics Platform. "We use Macs a little bit because some software runs on Macs, but basically we need the high-end level. We use Alias for modeling, SoftImage for animation, Renderman for rendering, and Parallax for paint touchup. We also use a tremendous amount of custom software because a lot of things we do can't be done with off-the-shelf software. We have a small software group that creates custom components, sort of puts all the pieces together, and adds the features we cannot buy. We use these custom features in everything: modeling, rendering, and animation."

A SUPERVISOR OF VISUAL EFFECTS WORK

Dippé describes his job. "The role of a visual effects supervisor really varies. Basically, I have the same role as a director except it's limited to the visual effects portion of the film. When I don't have a project, I read a lot of scripts. I have meetings with directors, or producers, or whoever is involved with projects, to talk to them about how to do things, how to make it look good, what the concepts are, the story ideas, everything, the whole gambit. I get involved at really an early level with a lot of projects, but always it depends on the stage of the project at the time I get involved with it.

"Once I've chosen a project, and everyone likes each other, and we're ready to go, then typically, I'm getting involved with the design of everything, the design of the creatures, design of the shots. We work out how we're going to do things, where we're going to shoot stuff. We might have to go to exotic locations; we decide how we are physically going to do it, what kind of crane do we have, what kind of camera, what kind of set, what kind of aerial stabilizing system. All these things we have to go figure out, and I'll be involved with all that as well. I will go actually do the work

246

with the director, doing the plate photography, as we call it. That's shooting the photography that we're going to put our computer animation into."

"Once we've gotten all that photography, we bring it up to ILM and scan it into computers, and then I supervise all the elements that go into it: the computer animation, the modeling, the computer lighting, the computer rendering, the computer compositing. I take all these pieces, when I'm happy with them, to the director, and hopefully he likes them, although usually there are a few things that the director will want to have changed, so we go back and fix them, and they go to final film. Basically, I follow that whole process through from design concept to execution."

RECOMMENDATIONS TO GET STARTED IN CGI

Dippé feels that the most important thing in getting started with CGI is to do CGI. "The number one thing is, do computer animation! Create some pieces regardless of platform and quality. Have pieces on video tape that you made; it's just that simple. Whatever your interest might be, whatever kinds of things you want to do, just create animation that shows that. Just having that desire, having worked with the equipment, or just having gone to school is not going to make the difference. The first thing is to do it.

"I would say, in addition to that, a very sensible approach is to go to a place where it's being done," suggests Dippé. "There are definitely schools that have computer graphics or computer animation programs; there are not that many right now but the numbers are growing. Secondly, just be involved with companies that do that, perhaps with an internship. But again, to me, the critical thing is to work on pieces that show what you've done. That's exactly what I go on."

THE FUTURE OF COMPUTER ANIMATION

What do we have in store for the future? "The next thing we're going to do is make a totally digital leading character. Maybe not a normal man or woman, maybe it's a creature or a superhero, but that's going to be the next step. You see, to me it's making films. I don't care if things are photographed for real or not photographed or synthesized; that's not the issue for me. To me, it's trying to create stories and movies that you cannot create without digital techniques. That's what I'm involved in now. The only reason it interests me is in creating fantastic stories; you go places you've never gone before. I think this film is like a psychedelic drug; it's like opening your mind and your eyes to new kinds of vision, and that's why I'm interested in digital film making.

"It's not because I just want to use a computer. In fact, as time goes on, I use the computer less and less because I'm more in a directorial role. I say, `Let's make our creature a little bit funnier, let's make his wings longer.' I just approach it purely visually, but I understand the medium so well that I'm very effective at that because I can communicate with people who are running the machines. If there is any issue as to what I mean, I can explain it directly to them or show them. It's been a very successful thing for me in that respect.

"Creating digital characters is a big one. I see things like a digital backlot. I agree with that as well; we can create fantastic scenarios that don't exist: alien worlds, alien crafts. We can do things such as combine the body of one actor with the face of another and the voice of yet another. We can take some fantastic actor and digitize him, and preserve him, and keep him young and beautiful forever. We can take Arnold Schwarzenegger and digitize him now, and he can be in a million movies. He will never age, and get saggy, and lose his big muscular pecs. I see a lot of that kind of stuff happening. But again, to me, it's still going to be the kind of stories we envision; that's still a fundamental aspect. So I'm maybe not as gung ho as some people about all of this stuff in reality," concludes Dippé.

247

TUTORIAL: SPLINE MODELING AND CHARACTER ANIMATION

In these tutorials, we will create a simple character animation of a slug and learn how to use object deformation for animation, glue objects together, assign mapping coordinates, and model spline-based objects.

SPLINE MODELING

1. Launch trueSpace, and from the File menu, choose Scene/New. If there are any panels open on the screen, left-click on the Close All Panels icon.

2. Before starting our model, set up both a front view and a left side view. Choose the New Left View and New Top View icons. Position the new windows on the upper-left corner of the workspace. (See Tutorial Figure 9.1.)

3. To model our elegant slug, left-click on the Spline Polygon icon. This puts you into spline mode and brings up the Draw Segments panel. We will first draw a cross-section of the slug

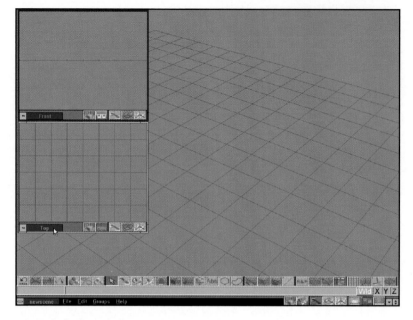

Tutorial Figure 9.1. *Position the left and top view windows in the upper-left corner of the workspace.*

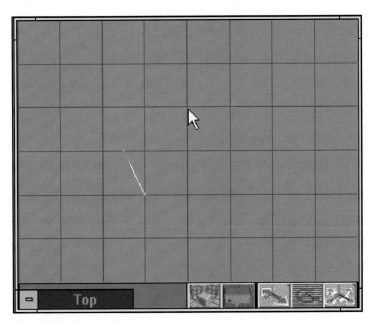

Tutorial Figure 9.2. *Notice that between the spline points there are three segments.*

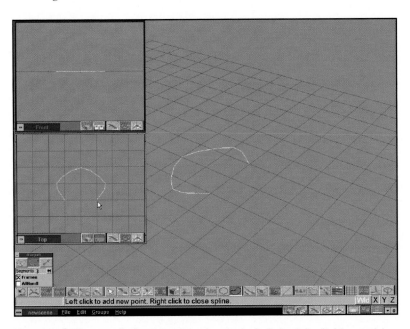

Tutorial Figure 9.3. *Complete the semi-circle by left-clicking twice, creating two more spline points.*

and them use the sweep tool to lengthen it. In the top view, left-click on the intersection of any two grid lines. Move the cursor up and to the left, and left-click at the top center of the current grid square. (See Tutorial Figure 9.2.) The segments between spline points control how smooth the resulting surface will be. You can increase the spline segments by adjusting them on the Draw Segments panel.

4. Left-click two more spline points as shown in Tutorial Figure 9.3.

5. To have trueSpace automatically close our spline, simply left-click on the Object Tool icon.

This causes trueSpace to close off the spline with a straight line. (See Tutorial Figure 9.4.)

6. Before sweeping the new spline, we want to rotate it so it's standing upright. To make the rotation easy, left-click on the Toggle Grid Mode icon. Now left-click on the Object Rotate icon, and right-click on the same icon again to pull up its Coordinates Panel. In the Coordinates Panel, turn off the Y axis button. In the main workspace, left-click and drag the mouse down to rotate the spline cross-section upright. (See Tutorial Figure 9.5.)

7. Turn off the grid mode by left-clicking on the Toggle Grid Mode icon. Left-click on the Object Move icon. Left-click anywhere in the front view and

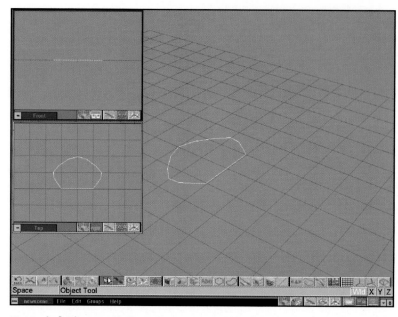

Tutorial Figure 9.4. *Splines cannot be left open, so if you try to end spline mode, trueSpace will automatically close the current spline.*

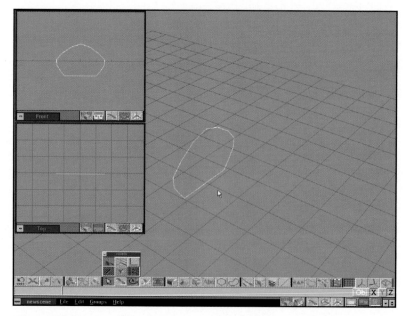

Tutorial Figure 9.5. *Dragging the mouse down will cause the spline cross-section to rotate to the upright position.*

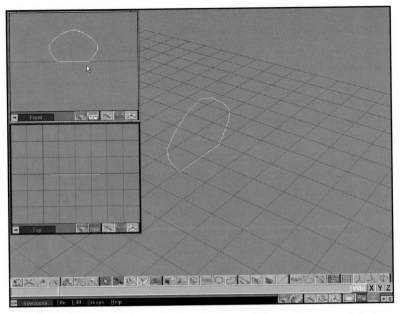

Tutorial Figure 9.6. *Move the spline so its bottom is even with the reference grid.*

drag the spline up until its bottom is even with the reference grid. (See Tutorial Figure 9.6.)

8. In the top view, left-click on the Top View icon, and drag the cursor up to the Left View icon and release. To start sweeping the spline, left-click on the Sweep icon. The spline will expand one level to the right. (See Tutorial Figure 9.7.)

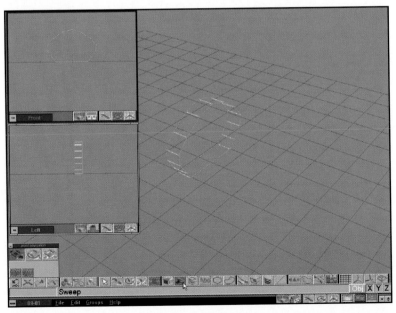

Tutorial Figure 9.7. *Using the Sweep tool puts you in Point Edit mode.*

9. In the left view, left-click and drag the mouse to the right, moving the current level of the spline object to the right about twice the original distance. (See Tutorial Figure 9.8.)

10. Left-click the Sweep icon again, and notice how the new level is created at the same distance that you moved the previous level to.

252

11. Now left-click on the Point Scale icon, and in the workspace window, left-click and drag the mouse down and to the left. Notice how the new level is scaled down slightly. Scale this new level down slightly. (See Tutorial Figure 9.9.)

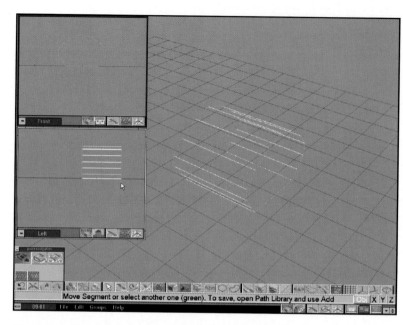

Tutorial Figure 9.8. *Move the new spline level to the right.*

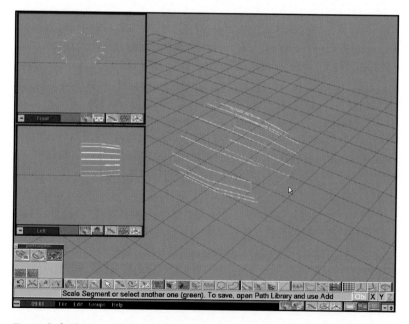

Tutorial Figure 9.9. *Scale the new level down slightly in the workspace view.*

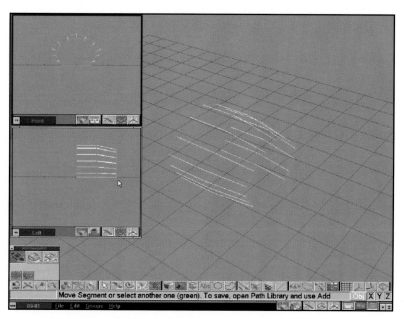

Tutorial Figure 9.10. *After dragging the new level down so it's flat with the reference grid.*

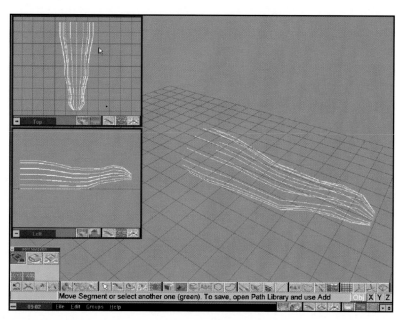

Tutorial Figure 9.11. *Sweep, Scale, and Move the points to create the front half of the slug character.*

12. Before using the Sweep tool again, left-click on the Point Move icon, and in the left view, drag the new level back down so it's sitting on the reference grid. (See Tutorial Figure 9.10.)

13. Repeat steps 10 through 12 until you have created a shape like that in Tutorial Figure 9.11. After a few levels, keep scaling down the current level, but start moving it up higher to form the slug's neck. During these steps, you may need to adjust your views by using the Eye Move icon and the Zoom icon.

253

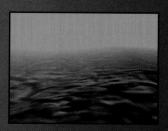

14. Once the trunk and head of the slug are finished, left-click on the Point Edit: Context icon. On the back side of the slug, left-click the cursor on any vertex. (See Tutorial Figure 9.12.) Next, hold the Shift key down and left-click on the next adjacent vertex on the back side of the slug.

15. Hold the Shift key down, and left-click on any vertex on the back side of the slug. Notice all the edges all the way around the backside get selected. (See Tutorial Figure 9.13.) This is because we are in Point Edit: Context mode.

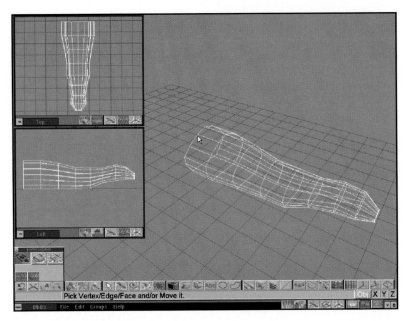

Tutorial Figure 9.12. *In Point Edit: Context mode, you can click on faces, edges, or vertices.*

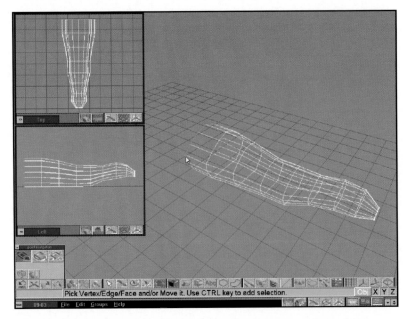

Tutorial Figure 9.13. *Holding the Shift key down when selecting points allows you to select an entire group of connected edges.*

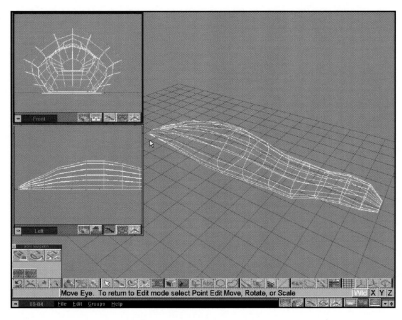

Tutorial Figure 9.14. *Continue to Sweep-Scale-Move the tail cross sections until the slug tail is completed.*

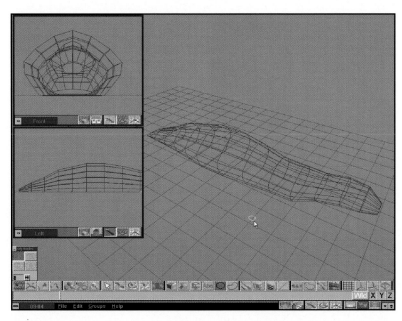

Tutorial Figure 9.15. *By adjusting the number of sides in the Poly Modes panel, you can create any symmetrical shape from a square to a smooth circle.*

16. Left-click the Sweep icon, and the back of the slug will start to extend. Follow the same pattern of Sweep-Scale-Move as described in Steps 10 through 12 until you have a flat, stumpy tail on the slug. (See Tutorial Figure 9.14.)

17. Now we can create the slug's antennae. Left-click on the Regular Polygon icon and in the Poly Modes panel set the number of sides to 8. Then in the workspace window, left-click and drag down to create a small circle. (See Tutorial Figure 9.15.)

255

18. Left-click on the Sweep icon once again to sweep up our circle into the first antenna. In the Point Navigation panel, left-click on the Point Move icon and in the left view, drag the top of the antenna up above the slug's body. (See Tutorial Figure 9.16.)

19. Left-click the Sweep icon again and left-click on the Point Move icon. In the left view, drag the top of the antenna down so it's just above the last level. Left-click the Sweep icon once more for a total of three cross sections at the top of the antenna and one at the bottom. (See Tutorial Figure 9.17.)

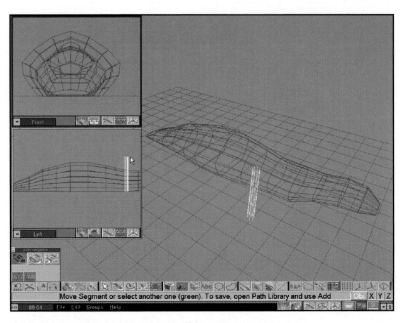

Tutorial Figure 9.16. *Stretch the antenna up slightly.*

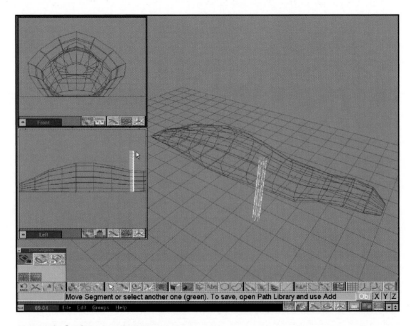

Tutorial Figure 9.17. *Create two more cross-sections, very close together at the top of the antenna.*

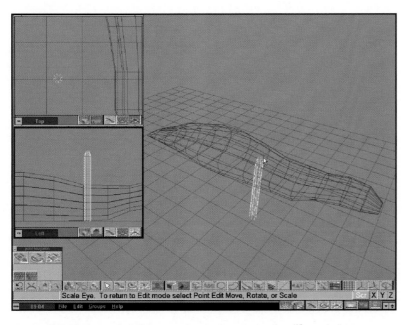

Tutorial Figure 9.18. *Scale down the antenna to about 50 percent.*

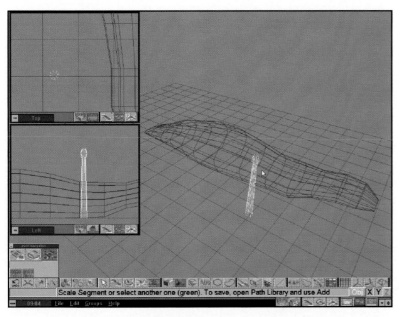

Tutorial Figure 9.19. *By scaling down the top level and the third from the top, we can simulate a slug antenna.*

20. Left-click on the Point Scale icon. In the workspace, click both mouse buttons and drag the mouse down and to the left to shrink the top level of the antenna about 50 percent. (See Tutorial Figure 9.18.) You may need to adjust the Eye Move icon or Zoom icon to get a better view of the antenna.

21. In the Point Navigation panel, left-click on the Point Scale icon. Position the cursor over the third level down and left-click. Notice how a new level is selected. You can now hold down both mouse buttons and drag the mouse down and to the left to shrink the current level (third from the top) of the antenna about 50 percent. (See Tutorial Figure 9.19.)

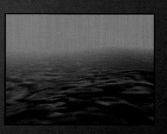

22. To move the antenna onto the slug's head, left-click on the Object Move icon in the top view window, and drag the antenna over to the right side of the head. Next, use the left view to move the antenna up off of the reference grid and onto the slug's head. (See Tutorial Figure 9.20.) You might find it helpful to change the top view to the front view.

23. After the antenna is in its proper position, left-click on the Copy icon to make a copy of it. Left-click on the Object Move icon, and drag the new antenna over to the left side of the slug's head. (See Tutorial Figure 9.21.)

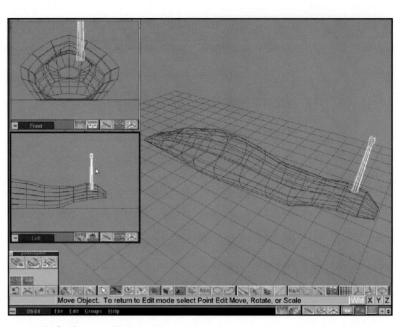

Tutorial Figure 9.20. *Drag the antenna to the correct location on the head.*

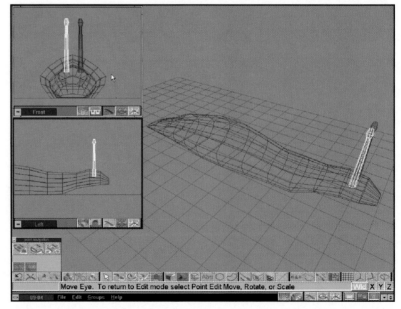

Tutorial Figure 9.21. *Make a copy of the antenna and move it to the left.*

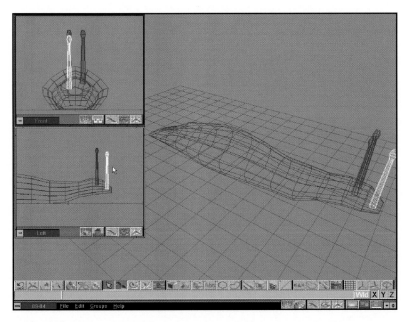

Tutorial Figure 9.22. *Move the new copy to the front of the head.*

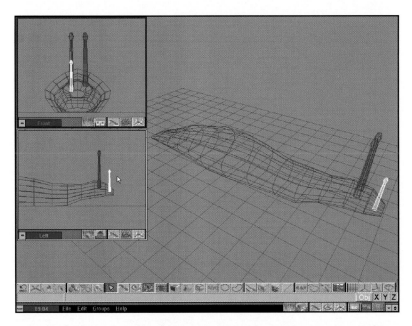

Tutorial Figure 9.23. *Shrink the forward antenna by about half the size.*

24. To make the small front antennae, left-click on the Copy icon to make a copy of the currently selected antenna. From the left view, left-click on the Object Move icon and drag the new antenna to the front of the head. (See Tutorial Figure 9.22.)

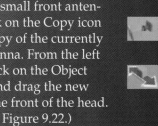

25. Reduce the size of the current antenna by left-clicking on the Object Scale icon. Hold both mouse buttons down and drag the mouse down and to the left to shrink the new antenna and use the Object Move icon to move it down slightly. (See Tutorial Figure 9.23.)

259

26. After the new antenna is in its proper position, left-click on the Copy icon to make a copy of it. Left-click on the Object Move icon and drag the new antenna over to the right side of the slug's head. (See Tutorial Figure 9.24.)

27. To move the antennae into realistic angles, left-click on the Object Rotate icon, and starting with the currently selected antenna, rotate them to the positions shown in Tutorial Figure 9.25. The best way to do this is to use the front and left views while right-clicking and dragging the mouse to set the rotation.

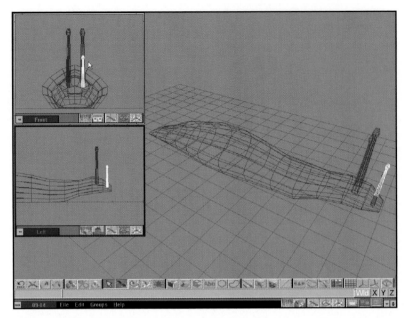

Tutorial Figure 9.24. *Make a copy of the antenna and move it to the left.*

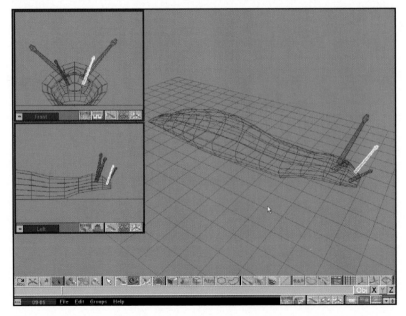

Tutorial Figure 9.25. *Rotate the antennae into these positions.*

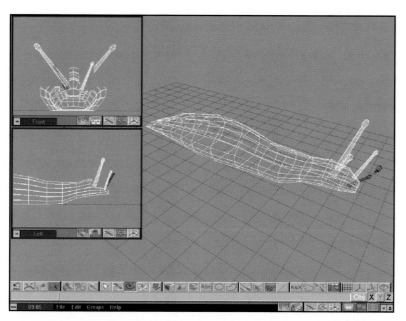

Tutorial Figure 9.26. *Glue the antennae to the body as children.*

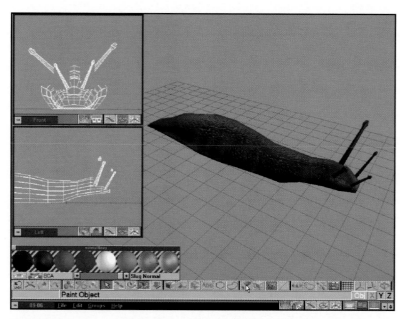

Tutorial Figure 9.27. *Our slug with the Slug Normal material assigned.*

28. Finally, we are going to attach the antennae to the slug's body. Left-click on the slug's body first to make it the current object. Then left-click on each antenna in succession until they are all attached to the body and are selected (white.). (See Tutorial Figure 9.26.)

29. To complete our beautiful slug, we simply need to assign a material to it. Left-click on the Material Library icon and choose the material called Slug Normal (or Slug Psycho if you light bright colors) and then assign it to the slug model with the Paint Object icon. (See Tutorial Figures 9.27 and 9.28.)

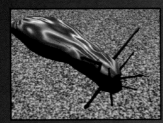

30. You will notice that about half way down our slug, there is a seam in the texture mapping. To correct this, left-click on the UV Projection icon. You will be presented with the UV Map panel. Left-click on the Cylindrical UV Projection icon and then left-click on the Apply button. (See Tutorial Figure 9.29.)

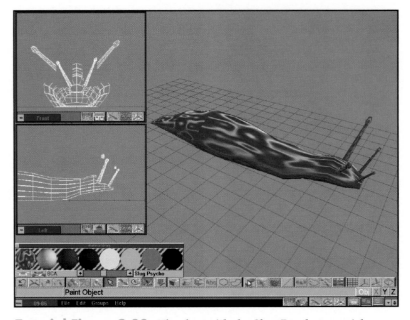

Tutorial Figure 9.28. *The slug with the Slug Psycho material assigned.*

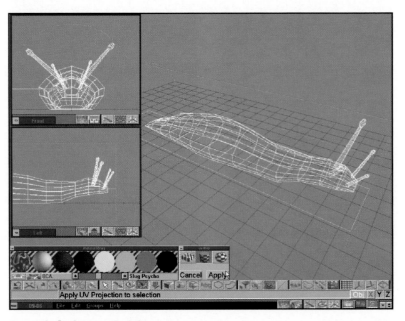

Tutorial Figure 9.29. *Apply cylindrical mapping coordinates to the slug.*

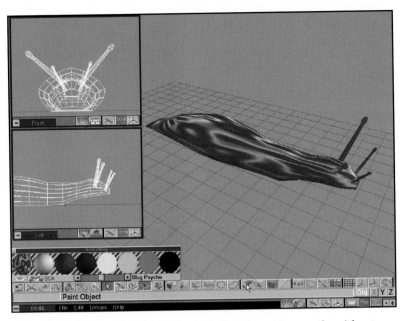

Tutorial Figure 9.30. *Notice how the texture is smooth, without any breaks, after applying new mapping coordinates.*

31. To see the effects of our new mapping coordinates, left-click on the Paint Object icon. (See Tutorial Figure 9.30.)

32. Before creating any animation, build a floor for the slug by left-clicking on the Regular Polygon icon. Then from the Materials Library, choose the Dirt material. Next, set the number of sides in the Poly Modes panel to 4. Left-click in the middle of the screen, and drag the cursor to the top of the screen. (See Tutorial Figure 9.31.)

263

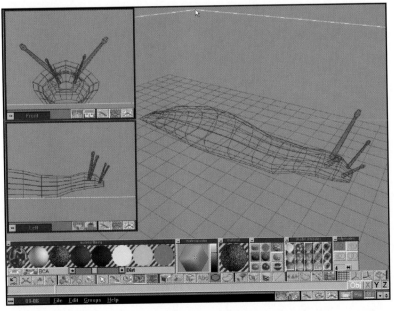

Tutorial Figure 9.31. *Create the floor by dragging the cursor to the top of the screen when creating the floor polygon.*

33. From the Materials menu, select the Sand material, and left-click on Paint Object. Hit Escape and then left-click on the Render Scene icon to see our scene rendered. (See Tutorial Figure 9.32.)

34. To see nice shadows on our scene, left-click on the Spotlight icon. In the left view, left-click on the mouse and drag it above the slug. (See Tutorial Figure 9.33.) Set its intensity to 75 percent and turn on the Shadow Casting icon. When the light is positioned correctly, left-click

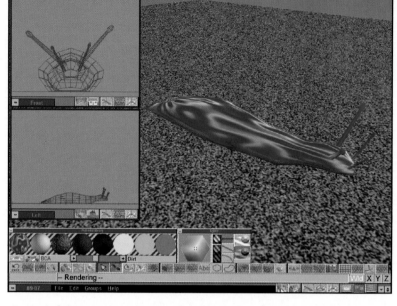

Tutorial Figure 9.32. *The finished model, a spline-based slug.*

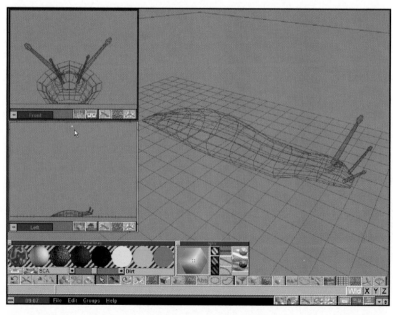

Tutorial Figure 9.33. *Create a spotlight and move it above the slug.*

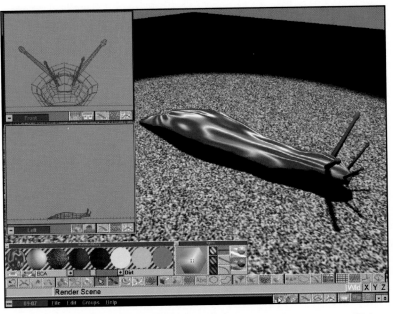

Tutorial Figure 9.34. *Our finished scene rendered with a spotlight and a shadow.*

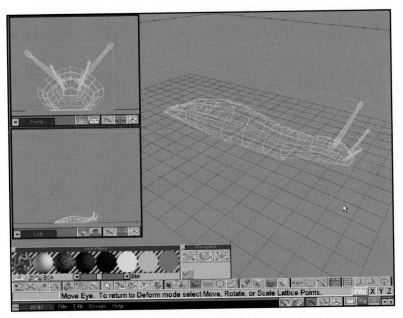

Tutorial Figure 9.35. *The Deform Object tool sets up a deformation lattice around any object.*

on the Render Scene icon to see our scene rendered with shadows. (See Tutorial Figure 9.34.)

ANIMATING DEFORMATIONS

Now that we have created a simplified character and assigned texture maps and setup lighting, we can animate it by using a deformation grid.

1. Before starting our animation, left-click on the slug to make it the active object. Next, left-click on the Deform Object icon, which places a deformation lattice around our slug; the FFD Navigation panel also appears. (See Tutorial Figure 9.35.)

2. So we can better see what we are doing, change the front view window to the top view by choosing the Top View icon. To subdivide the deformation lattice, right-click and drag the mouse to the right until the lattice is divided into four equal parts along the length of the slug. (See Tutorial Figure 9.36.)

3. To select parts of the lattice to pull and deform, left-click on the top center of the front end of the lattice. (See Tutorial Figure 9.37.) Notice how the entire front side is selected.

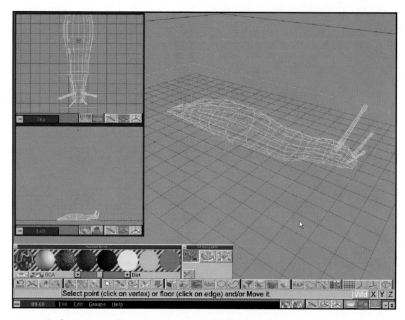

Tutorial Figure 9.36. *Subdivide the lattice along the slug's length.*

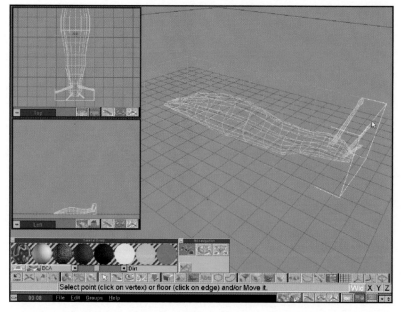

Tutorial Figure 9.37. *Select the front of the lattice by clicking at the top center of the lattice's front.*

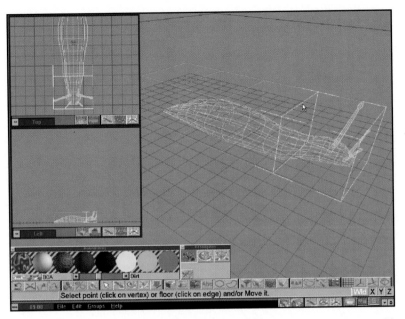

Tutorial Figure 9.38. *Holding down the Shift key allows you to add to the parts of your lattice already selected.*

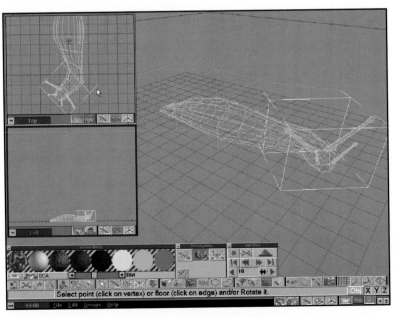

Tutorial Figure 9.39. *Any selected part of the lattice can be manipulated with the tools in the FFD Navigation panel.*

4. Hold down the Shift key and select the second lattice division in the same location. (See Tutorial Figure 9.38.)

5. In the FFD Navigation panel, select the Rotate Lattice Points icon. Left-click on the Animation Tool to bring up the Animation panel, enter the number 10 in the Current Frame Number box, and press the Enter key. Then in the Top View window, left-click and drag the mouse to the left until the slug head rotates to the left about 45 degrees. (See Tutorial Figure 9.39.) Don't worry about the twisting in the slug's neck; we will fix that in the next step.

6. To fix the slug's neck, left-click on the Move Lattice Points icon, left-click in the top window, and drag the selected part of the lattice to the left slightly to straighten out the neck. (See Tutorial Figure 9.40.) Notice how the polygon mesh under the lattice squashes and buckles when it is compressed.

7. To see the result of our deformation, left-click on the Plat icon. It will play back the first 10 frames and stop at frame 10.

8. In the Animation panel, change the Current Frame Number box to 20, and press the Enter key. In the FFD Navigation panel, select the Rotate Lattice Points icon. In the top view, right-click and drag the mouse to the right until the head is looking about 45 degrees to the left. Left-click on the Move Lattice Points icon, then left-click in the top window, and drag the selected part of the lattice to the right slightly to straighten out the neck. (See Tutorial Figure 9.41.)

9. In the Animation panel, change the Current Frame Number box to 30 and press the Enter key. In the FFD Navigation panel,

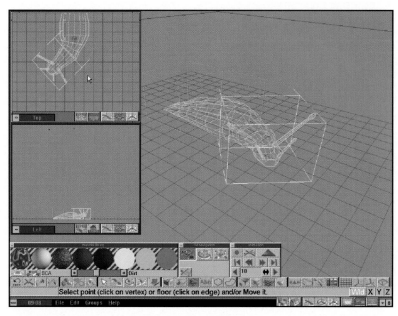

Tutorial Figure 9.40. *The Move Lattice Points tool allows you to move all selected parts of a deformation lattice.*

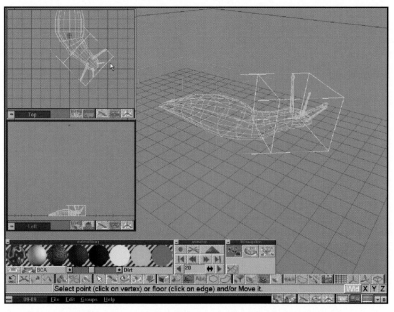

Tutorial Figure 9.41. *At frame 20, rotate the head to the right and move it to straighten out the neck.*

select the Rotate Lattice Points icon. In the top view, right-click and drag the mouse to the left until the head is facing directly forward once again. Left-click on the Move Lattice Points icon, then left-click in the top window, and drag the selected part of the lattice back to the center to straighten out the neck.

10. To see the result of our deformation, left-click on the Plat icon. It will play back all 30 frames and stop at frame 30.

11. To render the animation to disk, left-click on the Render Current Object icon, and hold the button down until the variants pop up, then drag the mouse up to the Render Scene to File icon. You will now be presented with the Render to File dialog box. First, choose

the output file type as AVI Files *.avi, then enter **tut-9.avi** as the filename. Make sure that All Frames is selected in the animation box, and that the frame rate is set to 30 with a pixel depth of 24. For super sampling (anti-aliasing), you can choose none or 2x, but the more super sampling you use, the longer the time it will take to render. When you are ready, left-click the Render button. Then you are presented with the AVI Compression dialog box. Verify that the compression is set to Full Frames (Uncompressed), and left-click on OK. At this point, your animation will render to a Video for Windows AVI file. It can be played back using the Microsoft Media Player.

EXTRA PROJECTS

Below are a few suggestions for more hands-on spline modeling and character animation practice.

- Set up cameras and render the animation from different views.

- Add more antennae to the slug and animate them with repeating motions.

- Copy the slug and animate both slugs crawling.

- Adjust the light sources to simulate day, night, and other conditions.

- Create a fish with animated fins by using the Spline and Sweep tools.

CHAPTER SUMMARY

In this last chapter of the book, we have looked into the cutting edge world of motion picture animation. With the high quality and large budgets of motion pictures, you can be sure that the latest and greatest effects will be seen on the silver screen before any other medium. Mark Dippé helped us understand some of the challenges of working on film projects, and he made suggestions for finding work in the feature film animation. Our tutorial section covered two of the most powerful features of trueSpace: spline modeling and deformation lattices.

I hope this book has done a good job of introducing you to the world of 3-D computer animation and will help you pursue a career in that direction if you choose to do so. In the following appendixes, I have listed a number of resources for getting more information on 3-D computer animation. Make sure you take a look at all the items on the bundled CD-ROM. It will prove to be a good resource for 3-D models, textures, and other software.

Image courtesy of Demografx/Gary Demos/Digital Productions.

Resources

Appendix A

For additional info on computer animation, I have provided the following resource appendix. In it, I have included information on related companies, books, magazines, trade shows, and software developers. This list of resources is by no means exhaustive, but it should help you get more information about the world of computer animation.

BOOKS

The following books provide valuable historical information as well as insights into the computer animation industry.

Clark, David. *Computers for Imagemaking.* Pergamon Press, 1981.

Elliot, Steven, and Phillip Miller, Gregory Pyros. *Inside 3D Studio.* New Riders Publishing, 1994.

Foley, J.D., and A. Van Dam. *Fundamentals of Interactive Computer Graphics.* Addison-Wesley, 1982.

Foley, Van Dam, et al. *Computer Graphics, Principles and Practices*, 2nd Edition, Addision-Wesley, 1990.

Goodman, Cynthia. *Digital Visions.* Harry N. Abrams Inc., 1987.

Fox, David, and Mitchell Waite. *Computer Animation Primer.* McGraw-Hill, 1984.

Hall, Roy. *Illumination and Color in Computer Generated Imagery.* Springer-Verlag Inc., 1989.

Jankel, Annabel. *Creative Computer Graphics.* Cambridge Univeristy Press, 1984.

Leavitt, Ruth. *Artist and Computer.* Harmony Books, 1976.

Lewell, John. *A-Z Guide to Computer Graphics.* McGraw-Hill, New York, 1985.

Lewell, John. *Computer Graphics.* Van Nostrand Reinhold Company Inc., 1985.

Morrison, Mike. *The Magic of Image Processing.* Sams, 1993.

Nelson, Theodore. *Computer Lib / Dream Machines.* T.H. Nelson, 1974.

Rivlin, Robert. *The Algorithmic Image.* Microsoft Press.

Russet and Star. *Experimental Animation.* Van Nostrand Reinhold Company Inc., 1976.

Smith, Thomas G. *ILM, The Art of Special Effects.* Ballantine Books.

Understanding Computers: Computer Images. Time-Life Books, 1987.

Upstill, Steve. *The RenderMan Companion.* Addison-Wesley Publishing Company, 1990.

MAGAZINES

The following is a list of magazines that cover the field of computer animation.

3D ARTIST

Columbine, Inc.
P.O. Box 4787
Santa Fe, NM 87502
Tel (505) 982-3532
Fax (505) 820-6929

ADVANCED IMAGING

PTN Publishing Co.
445 Broad Hollow Road
Melville, NY 11747
Tel (516) 845-2700

ALDUS MAGAZINE

Aldus Corporation
411 First Avenue South
Seattle, WA 98104-2871
Tel (206) 628-2321

COLOR PUBLISHING/TYPEWORLD

PennWell Publishing Company
One Technology Park Drive
P.O. Box 987
Westford, MA 01886
Tel (508) 392-2157

COMPUTER ARTIST

PennWell Publishing Company
P.O. Box 3188
Tulsa, OK 74101
Tel (918) 831-9423

COMPUTER GRAPHICS WORLD

PennWell Publishing Company
One Technology Park Drive

Westford, MA 01886
Tel (508) 692-0700

COMPUTER PICTURES MAGAZINE

Knowledge Industries, Inc.
701 Westchester Avenue
White Plains, NY 10604
Tel (914) 328-9157

CYBEREDGE JOURNAL

1 Gate Six Road #G
Sausalito, CA 94965
Tel (415) 331-3343
Fax (415) 331-3643

DIGITAL VIDEO

Tech Media Publishing, Inc.
80 Elm Street
Peterborough, NH 03458
Tel (800) 441-4403

HIGH COLOR

Imagetech Publications
21 Elm Street
Third Floor
P.O. Box 1347
Camden, MA. 04843

IEEE COMPUTER GRAPHICS AND APPLICATIONS

IEEE Computer Society
10662 Los Vaqueros Circle
P.O. Box 3014
Los Alamitos, CA 90720-1264
Tel (714) 821-8380

IMAGE BASE

Preston Publications
P.O. Box 48312
Niles, IL 60714
Tel (708) 965-0566

IMAGING MAGAZINE

Telecom Library Inc.
12 West 21 Street
New York, NY 10010
Tel (800) 999-0345

IMAGING WORLD

P.O. Box 1358
Camden, ME 04843-1358
Tel (207) 236-6452

MACARTIST

ImageLine Publishing Co.
119E Alton, Suite #D
Santa Ana, CA 92707
Tel (714) 668-1020

MORPH'S OUTPOST

125 Lombardi Lane
Orinda, CA 94563
Tel (510) 254-3145

MULTIMEDIA WORLD

501 Second Street
San Francisco, CA 94107
Tel (415) 281-8650
Fax (415) 281-3915

NEW MEDIA

Hypermedia Communications, Inc.
901 Mariner's Island Boulevard
Suite 365
San Mateo, CA 94404

ON PRODUCTION, INC.

17337 Ventura Boulevard
Suite 226
Encino, CA 91316
Tel (818) 907-6682

PC VR

P.O. Box 475
Stoughton, WI 53589
Tel (608) 877-0909

PHOTO ELECTRONIC IMAGING

1090 Executive Way
Des Plaines, IL 60018
Tel (708) 299-8161
Fax (708) 299-2685

PIXEL MAGAZINE

11 Rue de Faurbourge Poinssoniere
Paris, France 75009
33-1-4246-3010

POST

BPA International
25 Willowdale Avenue
Port Washington, NY 11050
Tel (516) 767-2500

PUBLISH

International Data Group
501 Second Street
San Francisco, CA 94107
Tel (415) 978-3280

RESOLUTION

Resolution Publishing Corporation
21 Elm Street, Third Floor
P.O. Box 1328
Camden, ME 04843
Tel (207) 236-6267

TV TECHNOLOGY

BPA International
P.O. Box 1214
Falls Church, VA 22041
Tel (703) 998-7600

VERBUM

Verbum, Inc.
P.O. Box 12564
San Diego, CA 92112
Tel (619) 233-9977

VIDEO SYSTEMS MAGAZINE

9800 Metcalf
Overland Park, KS 66212-2215
Tel (913) 967-1767
Fax (913) 967-1905

EDUCATIONAL ORGANIZATIONS

AMERICAN FILM INSTITUTE

Advanced Technology Group
2021 North Western Avenue
Los Angeles, CA 90027
Tel (213) 856-7690
Fax (213) 467-4578

ART CENTER COLLEGE OF DESIGN

1700 Lida Street
Pasadena, CA 91103
Tel (818) 584-5106
Fax (818) 795-0819

MASSACHUSETTS INSTITUTE OF TECHNOLOGY

28 Carleton Street
Cambridge, MA 02139
Tel (617) 253-6966
Fax (617) 258-6790

FILM & VIDEO ANIMATION STUDIOS

The following animation studios are active in producing 3-D computer graphics for film, video, and other applications.

ACYLUM GRAPHICS

550 Mansion Park Drive, #306
Santa Clara, CA 95054
Tel (408) 727-2199

ANGEL STUDIOS

5962 Law Place Court
Suite 100
Carlsbad, CA 92008
Tel (619) 929-0700
Fax (619) 929-0719

BLUE SKY PRODUCTIONS, INC.

Alison Brown
100 Executive Boulevard
Ossining, NY 10562
Tel (914) 941-5260

BOSS FILMS

13335 Maxella Avenue
Marina Del Ray, CA 90292
Tel (310) 823-0433
Fax (310) 305-8576

COLOSSAL PICTURES

2800 Third Street
San Francisco, CA 94107
Tel (415) 550-8772

DEMOGRAPHICS

10720 Hepburn Circle
Clovercity, CA 90232
Tel (310) 837-2985

DIGITAL DOMAIN

300 Rose Avenue
Venice, CA 90291
Tel (310) 314-2800
Fax (310) 314-2888

EX MACHINA

22 Rue Hegesippe Moreau
Paris 75018
France
Tel 42-93-2627

FOUNDATION IMAGING

27821 Fremont Court
Valencia, CA 91355
Tel (805) 257-0292
Fax (805) 257-7966

GRAPHX GROUP

30448 Rancho Viejo, Suite 100
San Juan Capistrono, CA 92675
Tel (714) 240-7105
Fax (714) 240-0941

HD/CG NEW YORK

34-12 36th Street
Astoria, NY 11106
Tel (718) 361-1118
Fax (718) 361-1758

HOMER & ASSOCIATES

1420 N. Beachwood Drive
Hollywood, CA 90036
Tel (213) 462-4710
Fax (213) 462-2109

INFORMATION INTERNATIONAL, INC.

5933 Slauson Avenue
Culver City, CA 90230-6550
Tel (310) 390-8611
Fax (310) 391-7724

INDUSTRIAL LIGHT AND MAGIC

Lucas Digital
P.O. Box 2459
San Rafael, CA 94912
Tel (415) 258-2000
Fax (415) 454-4768

KLEISER—WALCZAK CONSTRUCTION COMPANY

8105 Mulholland Highway
Hollywood, CA 90088
Tel (213) 467-3563
Fax (213) 467-3583

LEWIS COHEN & COMPANY INCORPORATED

141 Ruxton Road
Mt. Kisco, NY 10549
Tel (914) 241-3638
Fax (914) 241-7821

LITTLE BIG ONE S.A.

Avenue Ariane 12
1200 Brussels
Belgium
Tel (322) 773-4820

MAGIC BOX PRODUCTIONS, INC.

345 N. Maple Drive, #222
Beverly Hills, CA 90210
Tel (310) 550-0243
Fax (310) 550-7226

MARTIN FOSTER

26292 Eva Street
Laguna Hills, CA 92656
Tel (714) 362-9983

METROLIGHT STUDIOS INCORPORATED

5724 West 3rd Street, Suite 400
Los Angeles, CA 90036-3043
Tel (213) 932-0400
Fax (213) 932-8440

MR FILM

228 Main Street, Suite 12
Venice, CA 90291
Tel (310) 396-0146

PACIFIC DATA IMAGES

650 North Bronson Avenue
Suite 400W
Los Angeles, CA 90004
Tel (213) 960-4042
Fax (213) 960-4051

PIXAR

1001 W. Cutting Boulevard
Richmond, CA 94804
Tel (510) 236-4000
Fax (510) 236-0388

POST EFFECTS

400 West Erie
Chicago, IL 60610
Tel (312) 944-1690
Fax (312) 944-4989

REZ.N8

5834 Hollywood Boulevard, 5th floor
Hollywood, CA 90028
Tel (213) 957-2161
Fax (213) 464-8912

RHYTHM & HUES STUDIOS

910 North Sycamore Avenue
Hollywood, CA 90038
Tel (213) 851-6500
Fax (213) 851-5505

SAN DIEGO SUPERCOMPUTING CENTER

10100 John Jay Hopkins Drive
La Jolla, CA 92122
Tel (619) 534-5000

SANTA BARBARA STUDIOS

201 N. Salsipuedes Street, Suite 300
Santa Barbara, CA 93103
Tel (805) 568-1902

SIDLEY/WRIGHT

953 N. Highland Avenue
Hollywood, CA 90038
Tel (213) 465-9527
Fax (213) 465-9703

SONY PICTURES IMAGEWORKS

Tri-Star Building, Room 372
10202 West Washington Boulevard
Culver City, CA 90232-3195
Tel (310) 280-7603
Fax (310) 280-2342

SUPPORT SERVICES

10612 Sennit Avenue
Garden Grove, CA 92643
Tel (714) 775-3130
Fax (714) 775-1828

TELEZIGN

460 West 42nd Street
New York, NY 10036
Tel (212) 564-8888

THE POST GROUP

6335 Homewood Avenue
Los Angeles, CA 90028
Tel (213) 462-2300
Fax (213) 462-0836

THE PYROS PARTNERSHIP

1201 Dove Street, Suite 550
Newport Beach, CA 92660
Tel (714) 833-0334
Fax (714) 833-8655

THINKING MACHINES CORP.

245 First Street
Cambridge, MA 02142
Tel (617) 234-1000
Fax (617) 234-4444

THREE SPACE

10544 West Pico Boulevard
Los Angeles, CA 90064
Tel (310) 837-4450
Fax (310) 837-4470

TOPIX COMPUTER GRAPHICS AND ANIMATION, INC.

217 Richmond Street West
2nd Floor
Toronto, Ontario M5V 1W2
Canada
Tel (416) 364-6444

TRISTAR PICTURES

10202 W. Washington Boulevard
Culver City, CA 90232
Tel (310) 280-7677
Fax (310) 280-1569

WALT DISNEY FEATURE ANIMATION

1420 Flower Street
Glendale, CA 91221
Tel (818) 544-2504
Fax (818) 840-1930

WARNER BROS., INC.

4000 Warner Boulevard
Burbank, CA 91522
Tel (818) 954-6000
Fax (818) 954-2464

WINDSTAR STUDIOS

525 Communications Circle
Colorado Springs, CO 80905
Tel (719) 635-0422

XAOS COMPUTER ANIMATION & DESIGN INCORPORATED

600 Townsend, Suite 271E
San Francisco, CA 94103
Tel (415) 558-9267
Fax (415) 558-9160

FORENSIC ANIMATION STUDIOS

The following companies specialize in producing forensic animation.

Bio Horizons

1075 13th Street South
Birmingham, AL 35205
Tel (205) 934-2368
Fax (205) 975-6366

Enterprise Design Associates

330 Boston Post Road West, Suite 270
Marlborough, MA 01752
Tel (508) 485-9098
Fax (508) 481-7522

Failure Analysis

139 Commonwealth Drive
Menlo Park, CA 94025
Tel (415) 326-9400
Fax (415) 326-8072

Forensic Productions

4137 East Greenlee
Tucson, AZ 85716
Tel (602) 622-2600
Fax (602) 620-1703

Forensic Technologies Inc.

2021 Research Drive
Annapolis, MD 21401
Tel (410) 224-1480
Fax (410) 266-0765

GeoEngineering

150 Mineral Springs Drive
Dover, NJ 07801
Tel (201) 361-3600
Fax (201) 361-3800

Serious Robots

1101 Capitol Boulevard
Raleigh, NC 27603
Tel (800) 827-0914
Fax (919) 821-0902

Society of Forensic Arts (SFA)

Bulletin Board Service
904.396.0318

Video Law Services, Inc.

1533 Lakewood Road
Jacksonville, FL 32207

Online Services

The following online services can be accessed by almost any personal computer with a modem. These services have discussion groups on computer graphics, and some have graphics software and images that are available for downloading. The following addresses are provided for those who want to subscribe to these services.

America Online

8619 Westwood Center Drive
Vienna, VA 22182-2285
Tel (703) 448-8700

CompuServe

5000 Arlington Centre Boulevard
P.O. Box 20212
Columbus, OH 43220
Tel (800) 848-8199

Delphi

General Videotex Corporation
3 Blackstone Street
Cambridge, MA 02139
Tel (800) 544-4005

GEnie

GE Company
Information Services Division
401 N. Washington Street
Rockville, MD 20850
Tel (800) 638-9636

Icon Associates, Inc.

3221 NW 13th Street
Suite D-1
Gainsfield, FL 32609
Tel (904) 371-8142
Fax (904) 371-2166

Organizations and Conferences

Throughout the year, a number of organizations and professional associations offer conferences and expositions that are of interest to computer animators. Many of these organizations also publish literature and provide services for professionals in the field of computer animation.

Academy of Motion Picture Arts & Sciences

8949 Wilshire Boulevard
Beverly Hills, CA 90211
Tel (310) 247-3000
Fax (310) 859-9619

ACM SIGGRAPH

Annual Conference
and Exhibition on
Computer Graphics and
Interactive Techniques
Smith, Bucklin & Associates
11 West 42nd Street
New York, NY 10036
(310) 274-8787

Conference Management
401 N. Michigan Avenue
Chicago, IL. 60611-9553

ASSOCIATION FOR INFORMATION AND IMAGE MANAGEMENT (AIIM)

1100 Wayne Avenue, Suite 1100
Silver Spring, MD 20910-5699
Tel (800) 477-2446
Fax (301) 588-4838

NATIONAL COMPUTER GRAPHICS ASSOCIATION

2722 Merrilee Drive, Suite 200
Fairfax, VA 22031
Tel (703) 698-9600

SYBOLD SEMINARS

P.O. Box 6710
Malibu, CA 90264-6710
Tel (800) 433-5200

HARDWARE MANUFACTURERS

The following is a list of hardware manufacturers in the field of computer animation.

ACECAD, INC.

2600 Garden Road, Suite 111
Monterey, CA 93940
Tel (408) 655-1900

APPLE COMPUTER INCORPORATED

20525 Mariani Avenue
Cupertino, CA 95014
Tel (800) 776-2333
Tel (408) 996-1010

ATI TECHNOLOGIES, INC.

33 Commerce Valley Drive East
Thornhill, Ontario
L3T 7N6
Canada
Tel (416) 882-2600

COMMODORE BUSINESS MACHINES, INC.

1200 Wilson Drive
Brandywine Industrial Park
West Chester, PA 19380
Tel (800) 66-AMIGA
Tel (215) 431-9100
Fax (215) 431-9465

DIAMOND COMPUTER SYSTEMS, INC.

1130 E. Arques Avenue
Sunnyvale, CA 94086
Tel (408) 736-2000

DIAQUEST, INC.

1440 San Pablo Avenue
Berkeley, CA 94702
Tel (510) 526-7167
Fax (510) 526-7073

DIGITAL PROCESSING SYSTEMS

11 Spiral Drive
Florence, KY 41042
Tel (606) 371-3729
Fax (606) 371-3729

DIGITAL VISION, INC.

270 Bridge Street
Dedham, MA 02026
Tel (617) 329-5400

EASTMAN KODAK CO.

100 Carlson Road
Rochester, NY 14653-9011
Tel (800) 242-2424

EPSON

20770 Madrona Avenue
Torrance, CA 90509-2842
Tel (310) 782-5184

EVANS & SUTHERLAND

600 Komas Drive
Salt Lake City, UT 84108
Tel (801) 582-5847

FARGO ELECTRONICS, INC.

7901 Flying Cloud Drive
Eden Prairie, MN 55344
Tel (612) 942-3366

GENOA SYSTEMS CORP.

75 E. Trimble Road
San Jose, CA 95131
Tel (408) 432-9090

HERCULES COMPUTER TECHNOLOGY, INC.

3839 Spinnaker Court
Fremont, CA 94538
Tel (510) 623-6030

HEWLETT-PACKARD CO.

16399 W. Bernardo Drive
San Diego, CA 92127
Tel (800) 752-0900

IBM CORPORATION

1133 Westchester Avenue
White Plains, NY 10604
Tel (914) 642-5363
Tel (817) 338-2020
Tel (800) 426-3333

JVC PROFESSIONAL PRODUCTS COMPANY

Elmwood Park, NJ
Tel (800) 582-5825
Fax (201) 523-2077

MATROX ELECTRONIC SYSTEMS, INC.

1055 Regis Boulevard
Dorval, Quebec
H9P 2T4
Canada
Tel (514) 685-2630
Fax (514) 685-2853

MITSUBISHI INFORMATION SYSTEMS DIVISION

5665 Plaza Drive
P.O. Box 6007
Cypress, CA 90630-0007
Tel (714) 220-2500
Tel (800) 843-2515
Fax (714) 236-6171

NANAD USA CORP.

23535 Telo Avenue
Torrance, CA 90505
Tel (310) 325-5202

NEWTEK, INC.

215 Southeast 8th Street
Topeka, KS 66603
Tel (800) 847-6111
Tel (913) 231-0100
Tel (800) 368-5441 (sales)
Tel (800) 527-3334 (tech support)
Fax (913) 231-0101

ORCHID TECHNOLOGY

45365 Northport Loop W
Fremont, CA 94538
Tel (800) 7-ORCHID

PANASONIC BROADCAST & TELEVISION SYSTEMS COMPANY

1 Panasonic Way
Secaucus, NJ 07094
Tel (201) 348-7000
Tel (800) 524-8064
Fax (201) 348-5318

RADIUS

1710 Fortune Drive
San Jose, CA 95131
Tel (408) 434-1010

SANYO

Industrial Video Division
1200 W. Artesia Boulevard
Compton, CA 92022
Tel (310) 605-6527
Fax (310) 605-6529

SILICON GRAPHICS, INC.

Silicon Graphics Computers
2011 N. Shoreline Boulevard
P.O. Box 7311
Mountain View, CA 94039-7311
Tel (415) 960-1980
Fax (415) 390-1737

SONY CORPORATION

Sony Drive
Park Ridge, NJ 07656
Tel (201) 930-1000

StereoGraphics Corporation

2171-H E. Francisco Boulevard
San Rafael, CA 94901
Tel (415) 459-4500
Fax (415) 459-3020

Sun Microsystems Computer Corporation

2550 Garcia Avenue
Mountain View, CA 94043
Tel (415) 960-1300
Fax (415) 969-9131

Symbolics, Inc.

8 New England Executive Park
Burlington, MA 01803
Tel (508) 287-1000
Fax (508) 287-1009

Tatung Co. of America, Inc.

2850 El Presidio Street
Long Beach, CA 90810
Tel (310) 637-2105

Tektronix, Inc.

Wilsonville Industrial Park
P.O. Box 1000
Wilsonville, OR 97070-1000
Tel (503) 682-3411

TrueVision, Inc.

7340 Shadeland Station
Indianapolis, IN 46256-3925
Tel (800) 858-8783
Fax (317) 576-7700

Videomedia, Inc.

175 Lewis Road, Suite 23
San Jose, CA 95111
Tel (408) 227-9977

Viewsonic

20480 Business Parkway
Walnut, CA 91789
Tel (800) 888-8583

Wacom Technology Corp.

501 S.E. Columbia Shores Boulevard
Suite 300
Vancouver, WA 98661
Tel (206) 750-8882

Software Developers

The following companies provide computer animation software and hardware.

Adobe Systems Inc.

1585 Charleston Road, P.O. Box 7900
Mountain View, CA 94039
Tel (415) 961-4400
Fax (415) 961-3769
Products: Adobe Dimensions
Photoshop Premiere

Adspec Programming

467 Arch Street
Salem, OH 44460
(216) 337-3325
Fax (216) 337-1158
Product: Aladdin 4D

Aldus Corporation

9770 Carroll Center Road, Suite J
San Diego, CA 92126
Tel (619) 695-6956
Tel (800) 888-6293
Fax (619) 695-7902
Product: PhotoStyler

Alias Research Inc.

110 Richmond Street East
Toronto, Ontario
M5C 1P1
Canada
Tel (416) 362-9181
Tel (800) 267-8697
Fax (416) 362-0630
Products: Alias UpFront
Alias PowerAnimator

Anjon & Associates

Anjon & Associates
714 E. Angeleno, Unit C
Burbank, CA 91501
Tel (818) 377-8287
Tel (818) 566-8551
Fax (818) 566-1036
Product: Playmation

Apex Software Publishing

405 El Camino Real #121
Menlo Park, CA 94025
Tel (415) 322-7532

ASDG, Inc.

925 Stewart Street
Madison, WI 53713
Tel (608) 273-6585
Product: ElasticReality

Autodesk, Inc.

Autodesk, Inc.
2320 Marinship Way
Sausalito, CA 94965
Tel (800) 445-5415
Tel (415) 332-2344
Tel (800) 964-6432 (sales)
Fax (415) 491-8311
Product: 3D Studio

Autodessys Inc.

Autodessys Inc.
2011 Riverside Drive
Columbus, OH 43221
Tel (614) 488-9777
Fax (614) 488-0848
Product: form*Z

Azeena Technologies

P.O. Box 92169
Long Beach, CA 90809
Tel (310) 981-2771
Fax (310) 988-7607
Product: Animation Paint Box

Byte by Byte Corporation

Byte by Byte Corp.
8920 Business Park Drive
Suite 330
Austin, TX 78759

Tel (512) 795-0150
Fax (512) 795-0021
Products: Envisage 3D
Sculptor
Sculpt 3D 3.0
Sculpt 4D 3.0
Sculpt 3D RISC
Sculpt 4D RISC

Caligari Corporation

Caligari Corporation
1955 Landings Drive
Mountain View, CA 94043
Tel (415) 390-9600
Fax (415) 390-9755
Tel (415) 390-9750 (tech support)
Products: trueSpace
Caligari24

Claris Corporation

5201 Patrick Henry Drive
Box 58168
Santa Clara, CA 95052
Tel (408) 727-8227
Product: Claris CAD

Crystal Graphics, Inc.

Crystal Graphics, Inc.
3110 Patrick Henry Drive
Santa Clara, CA 95054
Tel (800) 394-0700
Tel 408) 496-6175
Tel (408) 450-0212 (tech support)
Fax (408) 496-0970
Products: Crystal TOPAS for the Mac
Crystal 3D Designer

Crystal TOPAS
Crystal TOPAS Professional
Crystal Flying Fonts:

Diaquest Inc.

1440 San Pablo Avenue
Berkeley, CA 94702
Tel (510) 526-7167
Fax (510) 526-7073
Product: DQ-Animaq

Dynaware USA Inc.

Dynaware USA Inc.
950 Tower Lane, Suite 1150
Foster City, CA 94404
Tel (800) 445-3962
Fax (415) 349-5879
Product: Dynaperspective

Electric Image Inc.

117 E. Colorado Boulevard, Suite 300
Pasadena, CA 91105
Tel (818) 577-1627
Fax (818) 577-2426
Product: ElectricImage Animation
System

ElectroGIG USA, Inc.

30 E. Huron Plaza, Suite 3807
Chicago, IL 60611
Tel (312) 573-1515
Fax (312) 573-1512
Product: 3DGO

Engineering Animation Inc.

Engineering Animation Inc.
2625 N. Loop Drive
Ames, IA 50010
Tel (800) 324-6777
Tel (515) 296-9908
Fax (515) 296-7025
Products: VisLab
ElectroGIG USA

Expertelligence Inc.

203 Chapala Street
Santa Barbara, CA 93101
Tel (805) 962-2558
Fax (805) 962-5188
Product: ExperLogo

Graphisoft

400 Oyster Point Boulevard
Suite 429
South San Francisco, CA 94080
Tel (800) 344-3468
Fax (415) 871-5481
Product: ZOOM

Hash, Inc.

2800 E. Evergreen Boulevard
Vancouver, WA 98661
Tel (206) 750-0042
Fax (206) 750-0451

Impulse

8416 Avenue North
Brooklyn Park, MN 55444
Tel (800) 328-0184
Fax (612) 425-0701
Product: Imagine

Information International, Inc.

5933 Slauson Avenue
Culver City, CA 90230-6550
Tel (310) 390-8611
Fax (310) 391-7724
Products: ARK Geometry
Hypermation!

Lunar Graphics, Inc.

Lunar Graphics, Inc.
23845 Currant Drive
Golden, CO 80401
Tel (303) 526-2553
Fax (303) 526-7319
Product: Realize Rendering Tool
(V.2.5)

Looking Glass Software Inc.

Looking Glass Software Inc.
11222 La Cienega Boulevard
Suite 305
Inglewood, CA 90304-1104
Tel (800) 859-8500
Tel (310) 348-8240
Fax (310) 348-9786
Product: Cheetah 3D

Macromedia Inc.

Macromedia, Inc.
600 Townsend Street
Suite 310W
San Francisco, CA 94103
Tel (800) 945-4061
Tel (415) 252-2000
Fax (415) 626-0554

Products: Swivel 3D Professional
MacroModel
LifeForms
SwivelMan (Swivel 3D
bundled with
MacRenderMan)
ModelShop II
MacroMind Three-D

NewTek, Inc.

NewTek, Inc.
215 Southeast 8th Street
Topeka, KS 66603
Tel (800) 847-6111
Tel (913) 231-0100
Tel (800) 368-5441 (sales)
Tel (800) 527-3334 (tech suppoort)
Fax (913) 231-0101
Products: Lightwave 3D
Video Toaster

Pacific Motion

Pacific Motion
3145 Geary Boulevard
Suite 265
San Francisco, CA 94118
Tel (800) 208-1515
Tel (415) 221-5581
Fax (415) 221-5582
Product: 3D Workshop

Pixar

Pixar
1001 W. Cutting Boulevard
Point Richmond, CA 94804
Tel (800) 888-9856

Tel (510) 236-4000
Tel (510) 236-4094 (tech support)
Fax (510) 236-0388
Products: Typestry
   Showplace-MacRenderMan
   " " CD-ROM version
   Pixar OneTwentyEight
NetRenderMan licenses:
   UNIX
   Macintosh

PYROS PARTNERSHIP

1201 Dove Street #550
Newport Beach, CA 92660
Tel (714) 833-0334
Fax (714) 833-8655

RAY DREAM, INC.

Ray Dream, Inc.
1804 N. Shoreline Boulevard
Mountain View, CA 94043
Tel (800) 846-0111
Tel (415) 960-0765
Tel (415) 960-0767 (tech support)
Fax (415) 960-1198
Products: addDepth
   Ray Dream Designer 2.0
   DreamNet

REALSOFT INTERNATIONAL, INC.

601 N. Orlando Avenue, #103
Maitland, FL 32751
Tel (407) 539-0752
Fax (407) 539-0976
Product: Real 3D

RENDERSTAR TECHNOLOGY BV

Keizersgracht 448, 1016 GD
Amsterdam, The Netherlands
Tel (31) 20-622-4480
Fax (31) 20-622-4939
Product: RenderStar
   ARE-24

SOFTIMAGE INC.

SOFTIMAGE, Inc.
3510 Boulevard St. Laurent
Suite 500
Montreal, Quebec
H2X 2V2
Canada
Tel (514) 845-1636
Fax (514) 845-5676
Product: Softimage Creative
   Environment (V.2.6)

SPECULAR INTERNATIONAL, LTD.

Specular International, Ltd.
479 West Street
Amherst, MA 01002-2904
Tel (800) 433-7732
Tel (413) 253-3100
Tel (413) 549-7511 (tech support)
Fax (413) 253-0540
Products: Infini-D 2.0
   BackBurner

STRATA INC.

Strata, Inc.
2 West St. George Boulevard
Ancestor Square, Suite 2100
St. George, UT 84770

Tel (800) 869-6855
Tel (801) 628-5218
Tel (801) 628-9751 (tech support)
Fax (801) 628-9756
Products: StrataType 3d:
   StrataVision 3d 2.6
   StrataVision PC
   RenderPro

UNIC INC.

1330 Beacon Street
Brookline, MA 02146
Tel (617) 731-1766
Fax (617) 731-8089
Product: Architrion II

VIEW BY VIEW

View By View
1203 Union Street
San Francisco, CA 94109
Tel (415) 775-6926
Fax (415) 923-1205
Product: Turbo 3D

VERTIGO TECHNOLOGIES, INC.

Vertigo Technologies, Inc.
842 Thurlow Street
Vancouver, British Columbia
V6E 1W2
Canada
Tel (604) 684-2113
Product: Vertigo 9.5

VIRTUS CORP

Virtus Corp.
117 Edinburgh, South Suite 204
Cary, NC 27511
Tel (800) 847-8871
Tel (919) 467-9700
Fax (919) 460-4530
Products: WalkThrough
           WalkThrough Pro
           WalkThrough for
Windows
           Virtus VR

VISUAL INFORMATION DEVELOPMENT INC. (VIDI)

Visual Information
Development, Inc. (VIDI)
136 W. Olive Avenue
Monrovia, CA 91016
Tel (818) 358-3936
Fax (818) 358-4766
Products: Presenter Professional
           VIDI Express Board

VISUALSOFTWARE, INC.

VisualSoftware, Inc.
Division of VisualTechnology, Inc.
21731 Ventura Boulevard, Suite 310
Woodland Hills, CA 91364
Tel (800) 669-7318
Tel (818) 883-7900
Fax (818) 593-3750
Product: Renderize

WARM & FUZZY LOGIC

Warm & Fuzzy Logic
2302 Marriot Road
Richmond, VA 23229
Tel (804) 285-4304
Product: LightRave for the Amiga

WAVEFRONT TECHNOLOGIES

Wavefront Technologies
530 E. Montecito Street, Suite 106
Santa Barbara, CA 93103
Tel (800) 545-WAVE
Tel (805) 962-8117
Fax (805) 963-0782
Product: Advanced Visualizer
(V.3.0)
           IDI Explore

XAOLS TOOLS, INC.

600 Townsend Street, #270E
San Francisco, CA 94103
Tel (415) 487-7000
Fax (415) 558-9886

3-D MODEL SERVICES

ABSOLUTE 3D DIGITIZING CENTER

500 Duchess Avenue
West Vancouver, British Columbia
V7T 1G4
Canada
Tel (604) 925-4300
Fax (604) 922-6560

ACURIS

931 Hamilton Avenue
Palo Alto, CA 94025
Tel (415) 329-1920
Fax (415) 329-1928

C.E. TECHNOLOGY

3630 Ballina Canyon Road
Encino, CA 91436
Tel (800) 654-1138
Tel (818) 981-4121
Fax (818) 905-1292

CRESTLINE SOFTWARE PUBLISHING

P.O. Box 4691
Crestline, CA 92325
Tel (909) 338-1786

DIMENSION TECHNOLOGIES

2800 W. 21st Street
Erie, PA 16506
Tel (814) 838-2184

IMAGINATION WORKS

Imagination Works
644 N. Santa Cruz Avenue
Suite 12
Los Gatos, CA 95030
Tel (408) 354-5067

KETIV TECHNOLOGIES, INC.

6601 N.E. 78th Court, #A8
Portland, OR 97218
Tel (503) 252-3230
Fax (503) 252-3668

MIRO IMAGING, INC.

2257 South 1100 East, Suite 1A
Salt Lake City, UT 84106
Tel (800) 950-6472
Tel (801) 446-4641
Fax (801) 466-4699

NOUMENON LABS

1349 Empire Central #310
Dallas, TX 75247
Tel (800) 959-5227
Tel (214) 688-4100
Fax (214) 688-4101

SCHREIBER INSTRUMENTS, INC.

4800 Happy Canyon Road, #250
Denver, CO 80237
Tel (800) 252-1024
Tel (303) 759-1024
Fax (303) 759-0928

SHARPIO ENTERTAINMENT, INC.

335 North Maple Drive
Beverly Hills, CA 90210
Tel (512) 328-1454
Fax (512) 328-1455

SYNDESIS CORPORATION

P.O. Box 65
235 S. Main Street
Jefferson, WI 53549
Tel (414) 674-5200
Fax (414) 674-6363

VIEWPOINT DATALABS INTERNATIONAL

870 West Center
Orem, UT 84057
Tel (801) 224-2222
Fax (801) 224-2272

VRS MEDIA

7116 S.W. 47th Street
Miami, FL 33155
Tel (305) 667-5005
Fax (305) 662-7915

WIZARD MULTIMEDIA PRODUCTIONS

1710 Zanker Road
San Jose, CA 95112
Tel (408) 436-0100

COMPUTER GRAPHICS RESOURCE LISTING

For a complete list of resources, updated
biweekly, FTP to:
nic.switch.ch
[130.59.1.40]
/info_service/Usenet/periodic-postings.

SIGGRAPH ONLINE BIBLIOGRAPHY PROJECT

The ACM SIGGRAPH Online Bibliography
Project is a database of over 15,000 unique
computer graphics and computational
geometry references in BibTeX format,
available to the computer graphics community as a research and educational resource.

The database is located at siggraph.org.
Users may download the BibTeX files via
FTP and peruse them offline, or telnet to
siggraph.org and log in as biblio and
interactively search the database for entries
of interest, by keyword. For the people
without Internet access, there's also an e-
mail server. Send mail to: archive-
server@siggraph.org

In the subject or the body of the message
include the message send followed by the
topic and subtopic you wish. A good place
to start is with the command send index,
which will give you an up-to-date list of
available information.

FTP SITES WITH COMPUTER GRAPHICS RELATED SOFTWARE

For more information about each of these
sites, see the Computer Graphics Resource
Listing on the CD-ROM.

```
wuarchive.wustl.edu [128.252.135.4]
/graphics/graphics

princeton.edu [128.112.128.1]
/pub/Graphics

alfred.ccs.carleton.ca
[134.117.1.1] /pub/dkbtrace

avalon.chinalake.navy.mil
[129.131.1.225]

omicron.cs.unc.edu [152.2.128.159]
/pub/softlab/CHVRTD

ftp.mv.com [192.80.84.1]
```

harbor.ecn.purdue.edu
[128.46.154.76] /pub/tcl/exten-
sions/tsipp-3.0c.tar.Z

toe.cs.berkeley.edu
[128.32.149.117]
/pub/multimedia/mpeg/mpeg-
?.0.tar.Z

acs.cps.msu.edu [35.8.56.90]
/pub/sass

hobbes.lbl.gov [128.3.12.38]

geom.umn.edu [128.101.25.31]
/pub/geomview

ftp.arc.umn.edu [137.66.130.11]
/pub/gvl.tar.Z

ftp.kpc.com [144.52.120.9]
/pub/graphics/holl91

swedishchef.lerc.nasa.gov
[139.88.54.33] programs/hollasch-
4d

jazz.gsfc.nasa.gov
[128.183.88.159]

zamenhof.cs.rice.edu [128.42.1.75]
/pub/graphics.formats

rascal.ics.utexas.edu
[128.83.144.1] /misc/mac/inqueue

ftp.ncsa.uiuc.edu [141.142.20.50]
misc/file.formats/graphics.formats

tucana.noao.edu [140.252.1.1]
/iraf

ftp.ipl.rpi.edu [128.113.14.50]
sigma/erich

ftp.psc.edu [128.182.66.148]
/pub/p3d - p3d_2_0.tar

ftp.ee.lbl.gov [128.3.254.68]

george.lbl.gov [128.3.196.93]
/pub/ccs-lib/ccs.tar.Z

havefun.stanford.edu [36.2.0.35]
/pub/mpeg/MPEGv?.?.tar.Z

hanauma.stanford.edu [36.51.0.16]
/pub/graphics/Comp.graphics

ftp.uu.net [192.48.96.2] /graphics

freebie.engin.umich.edu
[141.212.68.23]

export.lcs.mit.edu [18.24.0.12]
/contrib

ftp.x.org [198.112.44.100]

life.pawl.rpi.edu [128.113.10.2]
/pub/ray

cs.utah.edu [128.110.4.21] /pub

gatekeeper.dec.com [16.1.0.2]
/pub/DEC/off.tar.Z

pprg.eece.unm.edu [129.24.24.10]
/pub/khoros

expo.lcs.mit.edu [18.30.0.212]

venera.isi.edu [128.9.0.32]
*/pub/Img.tar.z

castlab.engr.wisc.edu
[128.104.52.10] /pub/x3d.2.2.tar.Z

sgi.com [192.48.153.1]
/graphics/tiff

surya.waterloo.edu [129.97.129.72]
/graphics

ftp.sdsc.edu [132.249.20.22]
/sdscpub

ftp.brl.mil [128.63.16.158] /brl-
cad

cicero.cs.umass.edu
[128.119.40.189] /texture_temp

karazm.math.uh.edu [129.7.7.6]
/pub/Graphics/rtabs.shar.12.90.Z

ftp.pitt.edu [130.49.253.1]
/users/qralston/images

ftp.tc.cornell.edu [128.84.201.1]
/pub/vis

sunee.waterloo.edu [129.97.50.50]
/pub/raytracers

archive.umich.edu [141.211.164.153]
/msdos/graphics

apple.apple.com [130.43.2.2?]
/pub/ArchiveVol2/prt.

research.att.com [192.20.225.2]
/netlib/graphics

siggraph.org [128.248.245.250]

ftp.cs.unc.edu [128.109.136.159]
/pub/reaction_diffusion

avs.ncsc.org [128.109.178.23]
~ftp/VolVis92

uvacs.cs.virginia.edu
[128.143.8.100]
/pub/suit/demo/{sparc,dec,etc}

nexus.yorku.ca [130.63.9.66]
/pub/reports/Radiosity_code.tar.Z

ftp.u.washington.edu [140.142.56.2]

zug.csmil.umich.edu [141.211.184.2]

sunsite.unc.edu [152.2.22.81]
/pub/academic/computer-science/vir-
tual-reality

archive.cis.ohio-state.edu
[128.146.8.52] /pub/siggraph92

lyapunov.ucsd.edu [132.239.86.10]

cod.nosc.mil [128.49.16.5]
/pub/grid.{ps,tex,ascii}

ics.uci.edu [128.195.1.1] /honig

taurus.cs.nps.navy.mil

[131.120.1.13] /pub/dabro/cyber-
ware_demo.tar.Z

pioneer.unm.edu [129.24.9.217]
/pub/texture_maps

cs.brown.edu [128.148.33.66]

pdb.pdb.bnl.gov [130.199.144.1]

biome.bio.ns.ca [142.2.20.2]
/pub/art

ic16.ee.umanitoba.ca [130.179.8.95]
/specmark

explorer.dgp.toronto.edu
[128.100.1.129] /pub/sgi/clrpaint

ames.arc.nasa.gov [128.102.18.3]
/pub/SPACE/CDROM

pubinfo.jpl.nasa.gov [128.149.6.2]

spacelink.msfc.nasa.gov
[128.158.13.250]

stsci.edu [130.167.1.2]

charon.er.usgs.gov [128.128.40.24]
/pub/PROJ.4.1.3.tar.Z

cs.ubc.ca [137.82.8.5] /ftp/pick-
up/spline

seq1.loc.gov [140.147.3.12]
/pub/vatican.exhibit

sun.irus.rri.uwo.ca [129.100.7.136]

monte.svec.uh.edu [129.7.2.23]
/pub/bit

ftp.cs.rose-hulman.edu
[137.112.40.250]
/pub/CS_dept/NeXtrad.tar.Z

image.vanderbilt.edu
[129.59.100.16] /pub/morph.tar.Z

willis.cis.uab.edu [138.26.64.2]
/pub/sloan/ContoursRelease.tar.Z

merlin.etsu.edu [192.43.199.20]

laser.elmer.alaska.edu
[137.229.17.151]

charon.elmer.alaska.edu
[137.229.17.254] /pub/DLG_CLG

rtfm.mit.edu [18.70.0.209]
/pub/usenet/news.answers

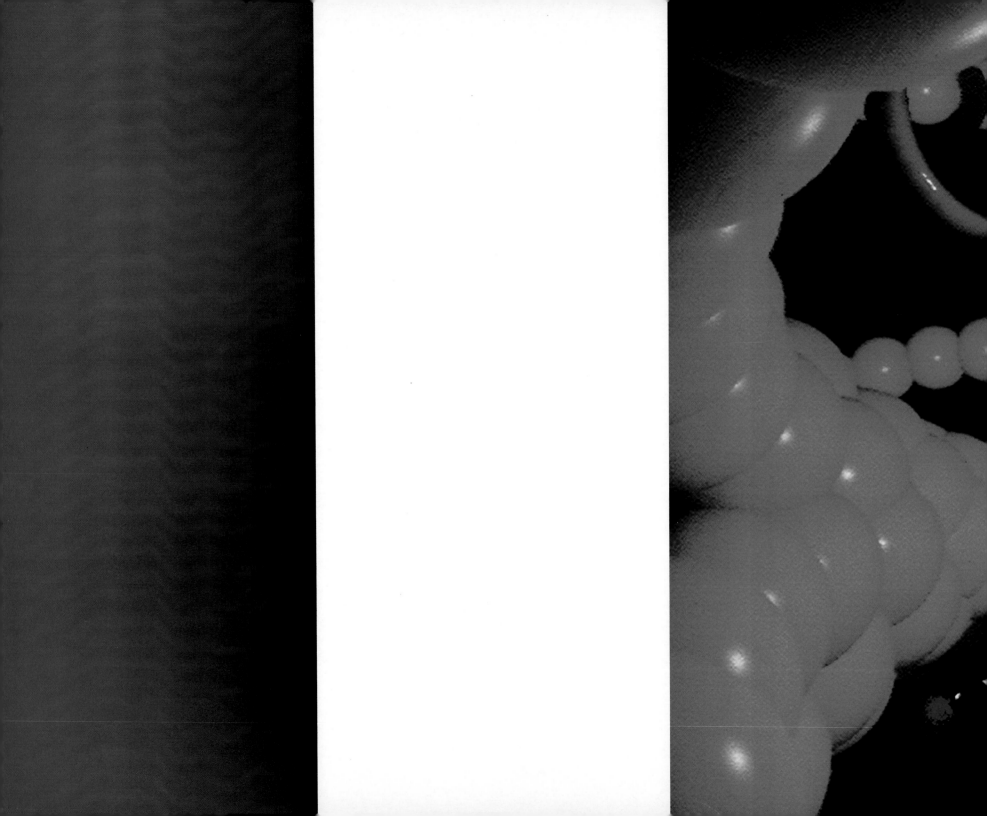

Appendix

B

Troubleshooting

Caligari

trueSpace

The following questions and answers from Caligari should help you solve any problems with Caligari trueSpace.

Q: What kind of system do you recommend?

A: The minimum system is a 386 with 4 MB and a VGA card, but you would be quite limited in what you could do on such a system. For a processor, I recommend at least a 486DX, and for those of you with a larger budget, trueSpace is Pentium-optimized. At least 8 MB is recommended for serious work, and if you are going to use large models or a lot of ray tracing, you should think about having 16 MB or more. An accelerated graphics board (preferably local bus or PCI) makes the program much more enjoyable to use.

Q: What resolution and bit depth do you recommend?

A: Although you can run in any resolution, trueSpace works best in 8 bits (256 colors) at 1024×768. If you run in 16-bit or 24-bit, you will see nicer color output, but your screen refresh will be slower, and the program will require more memory to run. Note that the color information in files created by trueSpace is independent of the color settings of your screen.

Q: What are the advantages of ray tracing, and how do I turn it on?

A: Ray tracing enables some additional visual effects: accurate mirror-like reflections; refraction, or bending of light through objects such as water or glass; and sharp shadows from any light source. You can turn it on from the rendering options panel, which you get by right-clicking on one of the render buttons.

Q: Sounds great! Is there any reason to not use ray tracing?

A: Yes, there are two very good ones: speed and memory. Ray tracing takes considerably longer than rendering without it. Thus if you can design scenes, and especially animations, that do not need ray tracing to look good, you will save yourself a lot of rendering time. Rendering 3-D objects can quickly require a lot of memory when using ray tracing. You can create scenes that are so complex that you will run out of memory when ray trace rendering, but you can render them without ray tracing.

Q: Is there anyway to get ray tracing-like effects without using ray tracing?

A: You can get shadows by using shadow maps without using ray tracing. Shadow maps only work with spotlights, and they are not as sharp as ray trace shadows. If your shadow looks "blocky," you can try increasing the shadow map resolution or decreasing its sharpness. You simulate reflections by using 2-D environment maps. These can be created using the Image Utilities.

Q: Is there anything I can do if my rendering runs out of memory?

A: There are a few things you can try to do to fix this. If you are running other programs at the same time as trueSpace, you may want to exit them before you try rendering. You can try increasing your Windows swap file. You can try to simplify your scene, either by eliminating some objects or by rebuilding some objects so that they contain fewer faces. If you are using texture, bump, or environment maps, see if you can use smaller images as your maps. Many paint programs allow you to shrink an image. If your budget allows, consider buying more memory, especially if you have less than 16M.

Q: How do I set the Windows swap file?

A: To find out about your swap file, open the Windows control panel, open the 386 Enhanced section, and click on the virtual memory button. The recommended size for your swap file is twice the size of your actual RAM if you have enough disk space for this. It's not usually helpful to set the swap file any larger than this.

Q: Why don't my shadows show up?

A: Shadows do not show up in object renders. Ray trace shadows will not show up unless ray tracing is turned on. To set the type of shadow used, right-click on the shadow button on the light panel. The shadow may also not be where you think it is. For spotlight, try setting up a camera view looking down the spotlight. This will allow you to position the spotlight much more precisely.

Q: Why are there strange horizontal lines on my beveled truetype text when ray tracing?

A: Unfortunately, with the bevel function, it is very easy to create self-intersecting geometry, and ray tracing cannot handle such geometry properly. The best solution is to try not to create self-intersections, for instance by using a smaller bevel. If this is not possible, then there is a `fix bad geometry` function, which will attempt to fix self-intersecting geometry. Be aware that after the object is fixed, certain operations (sweep, lathe, slice) will no longer be possible on this object. The Fix Bad Geometry button is on the utility strip in the same popup with Quad Divide and Mirror.

Q: Why do some faces on my object seem to disappear when looking from some directions?

A: If the object was created by point editing a 2-D object to make it into a 3-D object, it may have some flags incorrectly set. Try using the Fix Bad Geometry button mentioned in the last answer.

Q: Sometimes, while rendering, the program starts accessing the hard disk a lot and the speed slows down.

A: You are probably running into paging. This happens when the program requires more memory than you have real RAM and has to use the swap file frequently. The only way to alleviate this is to not use ray tracing, simplify your scene, or buy more memory.

FINAL SUGGESTIONS

Make sure you save your work frequently.

Before you start rendering any large images or long animations, make sure you do some test renderings at smaller resolutions and lower frame rates. This will allow you to spot potential problems quickly.

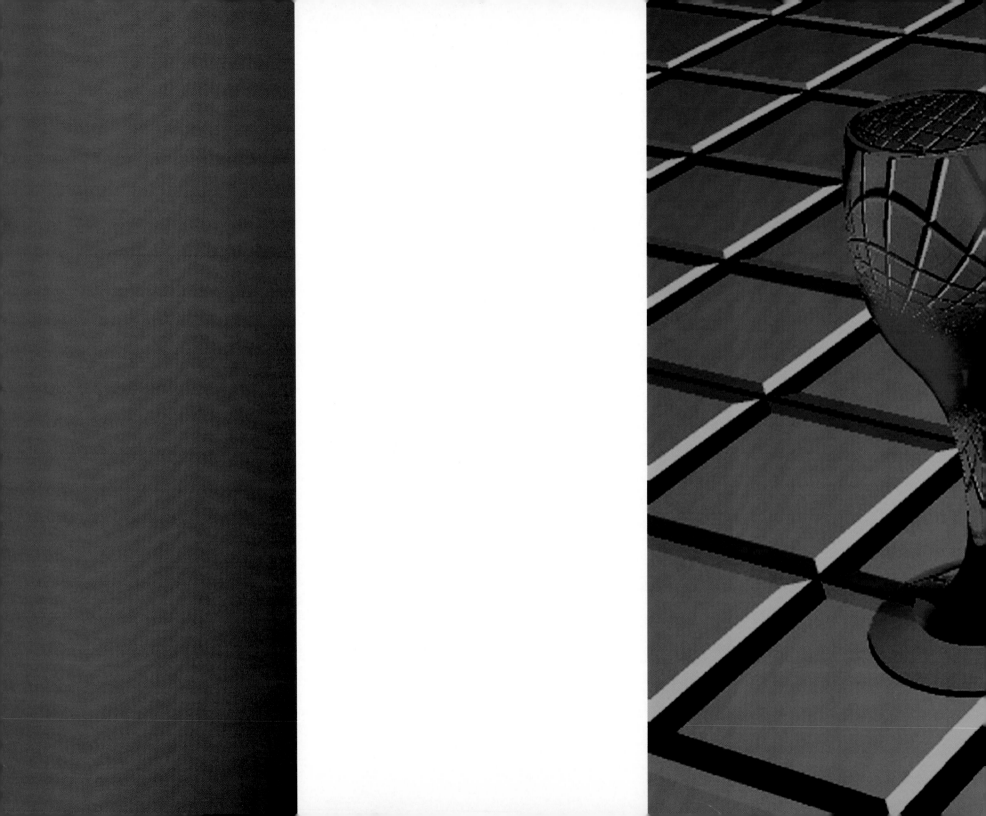

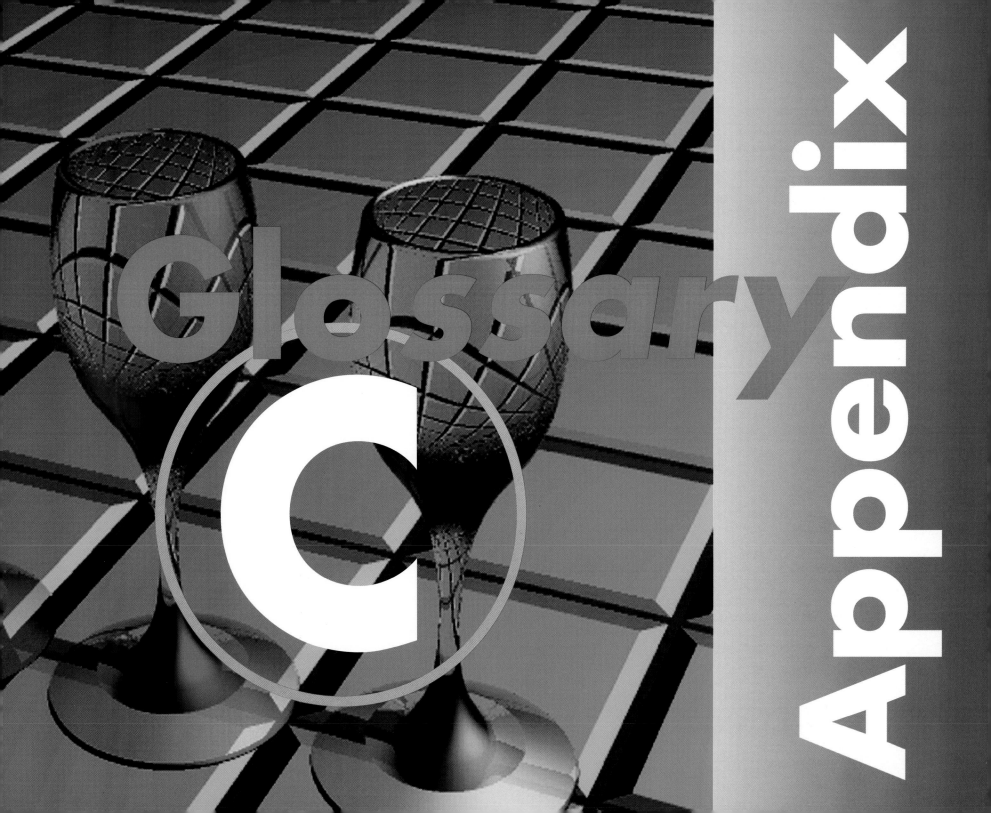

Glossary

Appendix

C

1-Bit Color

The number of colors per *pixel* a particular graphics file can store. 1-bit color means that each pixel is represented by one bit, which only has one of two states or colors. 1-bit pixels are either black or white. (See also **Color Depth**.)

8-Bit Color/Grayscale

8-bit color means that each pixel is represented by eight bits, which can have 256 colors or shades of gray (as in a *grayscale* image). (See also **Color Depth** and **Grayscale**.)

24-Bit Color

24-bit color provides 16.7 million colors per *pixel*. The 24 bits are divided into 3 *bytes*: one each for the red, green, and blue components of a pixel. (See also **Color Depth**, **True Color**, and **Channel**.)

3-D Graphics

The process of creating three-dimensional models within the computer's memory, setting up lights, and applying textures. After you tell the computer from which angle you want to view the 3-D scene, it will generate an image that simulates the conditions you have defined in the scene. 3-D animation involves the same steps but adds to it setting up the choreography, or movement, of the 3-D objects, lights, or cameras. (See also **Texture Mapping** and **Ray Tracing**.)

ACM

Association of Computing Machinery. (See also **SIGGRAPH**.)

Additive Color Mixing

A color model that mixes colors in a way that simulates how light works when you mix different colored lights together. The result is a brighter color as opposed to *subtractive color mixing*, which is mixing different colors of paint together where the result is always darker. (See also **Color Model** and **Subtractive Color Mixing**.)

Alpha Channel

An additional piece of information stored for a pixel that represents the pixel's transparency. An image, composed of many *pixels*, often has a separate channel for red, green, and blue. (See also **Pixel** and **Channel**.)

Ambient Light

The background light or existing luminance of a 3-D scene.

Anaglyph

A technique for producing stereoscopic images. Right- and left-eye views of the image are printed in red and blue colors. The viewer then wears 3-D glasses that contain a red filter on one eye and a blue filter on the other. This forces each eye to see a different image, and the mind builds a three-dimensional scene. (See also **Stereoscopic**.)

Analog

A form of measurement in with the indicator has no fixed state, such as ON and OFF. *Analog* measurements are variable, like the up-and-down motion of a cork floating on the ocean. (See also **Digital**.)

Animation

The illusion of movement caused by the rapid display of a series of still images. When each image differs slightly, and the images are viewed at speeds of over 10 per second, the eye perceives motion.

Anti-Aliasing

The process of smoothing edges where the individual pixels are visible. Anti-Aliasing removes *Stair-Stepping*.

ASCII

American **S**tandard **C**ode for **I**nformation **I**nterchange. A standard code that assigns a unique binary number to each character in the English alphabet along with other special characters.

Aspect Ratio

The height-to-width ratio of an image. (The standard for a TV frame is 4:3.)

BINARY

Having only two states, ON and OFF, or 0 and 1. A light switch could be considered a *binary* switch since it is either on or off and there are no other possible settings.

BIT

A *binary* unit of storage that can represent only one of two values, ON and OFF or 0 and 1 (**BI**nary digi**T**).

BLANKING

The time period that an electron beam in a video display is turned off and reset to its starting position of the next *scan line*.

BLURRING FILTER

A special-effects filter that simulates an out-of-focus photograph.

BMP

A **BitMaP** file. A graphics file format used as a standard for the Microsoft *Windows GUI*. It stores *raster graphics* images. (See also **File Format** and **Raster Graphics**.)

BOUNDING BOX

A square box created by clicking and dragging the mouse. Often used in graphical user interfaces to select an object or group of objects on the screen. (See also **GUI** and **Mouse**.)

BRIGHTNESS

A component of the HSB (Hue, Saturation, and Brightness) color model. For RGB pixels, the largest component value is the brightness. (See also **HSB** and **RGB**.)

B-SPLINE

A mathematical description of a curved surface, using only a few control points.

BURNING

Darkening specific areas of a photograph. Originally used in the darkroom with traditional photographic equipment, this process is now simulated by all image-editing programs. (See also **Dodging** and **Painting Tool**.)

BYTE

A unit of storage composed of eight *bits*. It can store a numeric value from 0 to 255 (decimal) or one letter. (See also **Bit**.)

CCD

Charge **C**oupled **D**evice. A special memory chip that is sensitive to light. The results convert to electrical impulses.

CD-ROM

Compact Disc Read-Only Memory. Ident-ical in size and shape to an audio/music CD, but organized to store computer data instead of sound. A single *CD-ROM* disc can hold over 600 *megabytes*, equivalent to 428 *floppy disks*. (See also **Photo CD** and **Multisession CD-ROM**.)

CEL ANIMATION

Invented by John Bray around 1913, a method of using translucent paper on which to print cartoon backgrounds. Earl Hurd also used the celluloid sheets, but he painted the characters on them so the characters could easily be overlaid on complex backgrounds.

CGI

Computer-**G**enerated **I**magery. A description commonly used for 3-D computer graphics that are used for visual effects.

CHANNEL

One piece of information stored with an image. *True Color* images, for instance, have three *channels*: red, green, and blue.

CHARACTER ANIMATION

The creation of living characters, either by traditional animation means (2-D) or 3-D computer-generated animation.

CHROMINANCE

See **Lightness**.

CIRCUIT BOARD

An electronic board on which computer chips have been laminated. Often called a Printed Circuit Board (PCB).

CLIPBOARD

A temporary storage location. When you use the Cut or Copy commands, the data is stored in the Clipboard. When you use the Paste command, the data comes from the Clipboard.

CLONE TOOL

A popular tool in image-editing programs that allows you to copy small groups of pixels from one location to another. (See also **Painting Tool**.)

CMYK

The four colors used for color printing: **C**yan, **M**agenta, **Y**ellow, and **B**lack. (See also **Color Separation**.)

COLOR CORRECTION

The process of correcting or enhancing the color of an image.

COLOR DEPTH

The amount of color stored in an image expressed in *bits*. An image with a 24-bit color depth can have 16.7 million colors. An image with 8-bit color depth can only have 256 colors or shades of gray. (See also **1-Bit**, **8-Bit**, and **24-Bit**.)

COLOR MODEL

A method of describing color. (See also **HLS**, **HSB**, and **RGB**.)

COLOR SEPARATION

A color image that has been separated into the four process colors (CMYK). (See also **CMYK**.)

COLOR SIMILARITY

How close two different colors are to each other within the respective color model being used. (See also **Color Model**.)

COMPOSITING

The process of merging two or more images digitally.

COMPRESSION

A means by which to reduce the amount of data required to store a computer file. (See also **File Format**, **Fractal Compression**, **Huffman Compression**, **JPEG**, **Lossey Compression**, **LZW**, and **Run Length Encoding**.)

COMPUTER-GENERATED

Created on or by the computer. Any image that was not scanned in from an existing original.

COMPUTER TOMOGRAPHY

A method of *scanning* the human body and producing a computer-generated image. Used in the medical field.

CONTINUOUS-TONE

An image that contains gradient tones from white to black.

CPU

Central Processing Unit. This computer chip is the brains of the computer. It controls all other functions and processes information fed to it by programs.

CRAY

Cray Research, Inc., a manufacturer of supercomputers.

CROPPING TOOL

The cropping tool simulates the traditional method of cropping or trimming photographs. (See also **Painting Tool**.)

CURSOR

A small blinking character on the computer screen that indicates where the next typed character will appear. Often controlled by a *mouse*. Sometimes called the Pointer.

CUSTOM FILTER

A special image filter that can be defined by the user. You enter values on a matrix grid. Those values in turn determine how the filter will affect each pixel in your image.

DATA

Any type of information that is stored in a computer. All data must be in a *digital* format.

DATA PROCESSING

The manipulation of *data* by a computer.

DEFAULT SETTING

Typically used in computer programs to set any variables or values to a common setting.

DESPECKLE FILTER

A special filter that removes any specks from the image. It actually blurs the entire image except for any edges.

DIALOG BOX

Any type of screen in a graphical user interface that displays or requests information from the user. (See also **GUI**.)

DICHORIC FILTER

A special type of optical filter that reflects certain light wavelengths and allows others to pass through.

DIFFUSE LIGHT

Light that originates from a specific source, but scatters in all directions.

DIFFUSION DITHERING

A method of dithering that randomly distributes pixels instead of using a set pattern. (See also **Dithering**.)

DIGITAL

A form of representation in which information or objects (digits) are broken down into separate pieces. Numbers are examples of *digital* information. *Digital* is the opposite of *analog* information, such as sound and light waves.

DIGITAL PAINTING

Creating artwork on a computer directly as opposed to using traditional media and scanning the artwork.

DIGITAL-TO-ANALOG CONVERTER (DAC)

Converts *digital* information, such as numeric data, into *analog* information, such as a sound waves.

DIGITIZING

The process of converting analog information into a digital format. Recording sound into a computer is considered digitizing, as well as capturing video or pictures on a computer. (See also **Scanning**.)

DIRECTORIES

An electronic area on a computer disk for storing data files. Similar to storing letters in a folder. A directory can be considered an electronic folder. (See also **File**.)

DISTORTION MORPHING

A method of morphing that only distorts a single image or sequence without fading into another. (See also **Morphing** and **Transition Morphing**.)

DITHERING

A method of simulating many colors with only a few. By placing a limited number of color dots closely together, the eye blends them into a new color. (See also **Diffusion Dithering**.)

DODGING

Lightening specific areas of a photograph. Originally used in the darkroom with traditional photography equipment, this process is now simulated by all image-editing programs. (See also **Burning**.)

DPI

Dots **P**er **I**nch: a resolution for scanning and printing devices. (See also **Scanning**.)

DRUM SCANNERS

Professional-quality scanners where original transparencies are positioned on a drum. The drum then rotates at high speeds and light is detected by a Photomultiplier. (See also **Photomultiplier**.)

Dye Sublimation

A method of color printing. Colored dyes are heat-transferred to special paper to create photographic-quality color images.

Editing

The process of changing or manipulating data.

Emboss

A common image-processing filter that simulates the look of a picture that is embossed on paper or metal.

Encryption

The process of converting information into codes that cannot be deciphered.

EPS

An Encapsulated PostScript graphics file. This format can store both *raster* and *vector* graphics. (See also **File Format**, **Raster Graphics**, and **Vector Graphics**.)

Equalization

A method of enhancing an image by evenly distributing the color or gray values of pixels throughout the image.

Eye Dropper Tool

An image-editing tool used to select a color from the current image.

Fades

In film or video, the smooth transition from one sequence to another. Often, fades are made to a solid color such as black.

FIF

The Fractal Image Format. A method of storing *raster graphics* and compressing them with *fractal transform* formulas. (See also **File Format**, and **Raster Graphics**.)

File

A collection of data organized on some type of storage media such as a *hard disk* or a *floppy diskette*.

File Format

The specific type of organization a given file uses. Some file formats are strictly for word processing documents; others are for graphics/images. Most file formats support some form of data compression to save storage space. (See also **Compression**.)

Fill Tool

A common painting tool used to fill a solid area with color. (See also **Painting Tool**.)

Flat Shading

One of the first methods used to create a shaded object. Based on the work of a sixteenth-century physicist and astronomer, Johann Lambert. The Lambert Cosine Law dealt with the intensity of reflected light as it strikes an object. This law, when applied to 3-D computer graphics, allows computers to create colored solid objects instead of wireframe models. This method was later improved and is commonly referred to today as *flat shading*. Flat shading colors every polygon in a 3-D object the same color, and that color is varied based on its orientation to a light source. When the polygons or surfaces making up the 3-D object are small enough, flat shading can provide a little realism.

Floating Palettes

Groups of icons that perform functions. They are usually grouped together and can be freely positioned anywhere on the screen with a *graphical user interface*. (See also **GUI** and **Icons**.)

Floppy Disk

A small circular piece of mylar with a metallic coating inside of a plastic cover. Used by computers to store *data*. (See also **Hard Disk**.)

Forensic Animation

Computer graphics used for court cases. These computer graphics are more geared to technical accuracy than to visual aesthetics. They help jurors visualize complex data and issues.

Formats

Any method of arranging data for storage or display.

Fractal Graphics

A term coined by Benoit Mandelbrot in 1975 to describe certain types of geometry. Commonly used to describe irregular, organic shapes that occur in nature, such as coastlines, mountain ranges, and plants.

Fractal Compression

A compression method developed by Michael Barnsley. It reduces images to a series of fractal-based formulas for very high compression levels. (See also **File Format**, **Fractal Graphics**, **FIF**, and **Compression**.)

Gamma

A measure of contrast that affects the middle tones in an image.

Gaussian Blur

A blurring filter that can be adjusted to provide very high levels of blurring. (See also **Blurring Filter**.)

Geostationary Orbit

A type of satellite orbit that exactly matches the rotation of the Earth. This causes the satellite to stay at the same location above Earth at all times. Commonly used for weather imaging satellites such LandSAT. Also known as *Geosynchronos*.

GIF

The **Graphics Interchange Format**. A common graphics format for storing *raster graphics*. This format is made popular by the CompuServe online service and is supported by a number of *hardware* platforms. (See also **File Format** and **Raster Graphics**.)

Gigabyte

A unit of computer storage representing one billion *bytes*. (See also **Byte**.)

Gouraud Shading

A method of shading 3-D objects invented by Henri Gouraud in 1971. It creates the appearance of a curved surface by interpolating the color across the polygons. This method of shading a 3-D object has since come to be known as Gouraud shading. One of the most impressive aspects of Gouraud shading is that it hardly takes any more computations than flat shading, yet provides a dramatic increase in rendering quality. (See also **Flat Shading** and **Phong Shading**.)

Gradient Fill

An enhancement to the fill tool that fills an area with a gradual transition from one color to another.

GUI (Graphical User Interface)

A graphics-based interface between a *user* and the computer. GUIs usually require a mouse-type pointing device. All programs within a GUI look similar, with pull-down menus and scroll bars.

Gray/Color Correction

The process of adjusting the gray or color levels of an image to enhance its quality.

Gray/Color Map

A method of adjusting the gray or color levels in an image. A 2-D line graph represents the incoming and outgoing brightness/color values.

Grayscale

An image that contains continuous tones from white to black. (See also **Continuous-Tone**.)

Halftone

The *screening* of a continuous-tone image into small dots of varying sizes. (See also **Screening** and **Continuous-Tone**.)

Hard Disk

Similar to a floppy disk, except that the disk itself is made with a rigid material like metal. Hard disks always spin much faster and have higher operating tolerances, so they can store much more information than *floppy disks*.

Hidden-Surface/Hidden-Line Algorithm

An algorithm used to determine which surfaces are "behind" a 3-D object from the viewer's perspective, and thus should be "hidden" when the computer creates (or *renders*) a 3-D image.

Highlight

The lightest areas of an image.

Histograms

A 2-D graphic representation of the pixel value distribution of an image. The horizontal coordinate is the pixel value, wheras the vertical coordinate represents the number of pixels at a given value.

HLS (Hue, Saturation, and Lightness)

A color model based on the hue, saturation, and lightness of a color. (See also **Color Model**, **Hue**, **Saturation**, and **Lightness**.)

HSB (Hue, Saturation, and Brightness)

A color model based on the hue, saturation, and brightness of a color. (See also **Color Model**, **Hue**, **Saturation**, and **Brightness**.)

Hue

Another term used to describe color. Hue usually represents the color without its brightness or *saturation*.

Huffman Compression

A method of compressing data developed by David Huffman in 1952. Commonly used to compress graphics files. (See also **File Format** and **Compression**.)

Icons

Small graphics symbols used to represent programs, data, or other functions within a *graphical user interface*. (See also **GUI**.)

Image Processing

The capture and manipulation of images in order to enhance or extract information.

Incidental Light

Light that is shining directly on a surface.

Inkjet

A printing technology that uses minute, high-speed streams of ink to form characters and graphics on the paper.

Input

The process of entering information into a computer.

Interpolation

The calculation of smooth transitions from one value to the next.

Interface

The connection between two *hardware* devices to allow them to exchange data.

Invert Filter

A filter that inverts the pixel values of an image, creating a negative.

Jaggies

The jagged "stair-stepping" effect often seen in images where the *resolution* is so small that the individual *pixels* are visible. (See also **Anti-Aliasing**.)

JPEG

A file format and compression method for storing images. The JPEG compression algorithm is a *Lossey* compression technique. (See also **File Format** and **Lossey Compression**.)

Kilobyte

A unit of storage that represents one thousand *bytes*. Often referred to as K, as in 640K. (See also **Byte**.)

Lightness

Lightness is a component of the HLS color space. It is determined by taking the average maximum and minimum values in each RGB channel. Sometimes called Luminance. (See also **HLS**, **Color Model**, and **Channel**.)

Lossey Compression

A method of compressing images by throwing away unneeded data. JPEG is a lossey compression method. (See also **File Format** and **JPEG**.)

LPI

Lines Per Inch. A measure of resolution, often used to describe screens. (See also **Resolution** and **Screening**.)

Luminance

See **Lightness**.

LZW

Lempel Ziv Welch. A compression algorithm based on work done by Abraham Lempel, Jacob Ziv, and Terry Welch. Commonly used for compressing graphics files. (See also **File Format** and **Compression**.)

Magic Wand

A painting tool that selects any range of similar, adjoining colors. Most magic wand tools include a similarity or tolerance setting. (See also **Painting Tool**.)

Masks

A special type of image that can be used as a stencil or mask for any painting operation you might make.

Megabyte

A unit of storage that represents one million *bytes*. Often referred to as a "Meg." (See also **Byte**.)

Memory

Electronic chips that can store patterns, which the *CPU* can decipher into letters and numbers.(See also **CPU** and **RAM**.)

Menu Bar

Used in *graphical user interfaces* to organize groups of commands in *menus* along the top of a program's window. (See also **Menus** and **GUI**.)

Menus

A group of related commands provided on a list that drops down from a *menu bar*. Used in *graphical user interfaces*. (See also **Menu Bar** and **GUI**.)

Metafile

A type of file format for graphics that stores both *raster* and *vector* graphics. (See also **File Format**.)

Morph Points

Points placed on an image, which can be moved to warp or distort the image during a morphing sequence. (See also **Morphing**.)

Morphing

A method of distorting images or sequences from one state to another. Two types of morphing exist: transition morphing and distortion morphing. Transition morphing transforms one scene into a different one. Distortion morphing manipulates a single scene by warping it. Sometimes called *warping*. (See also **Distortion Morphing** and **Transition Morphing**.)

Mosaic Filter

A special-effects *filter* that breaks up an image into a group of square blocks.

Motion Blur

A special function in most image-editing programs to simulate the blur of an object when it moves while a photograph is being taken. 3-D animation programs can also simulate motion blur by rendering multiple frames and then compositing them together.

Motion Capture

Using sensors that can detect movement in 2-D or 3-D space to record movements of actors that can later be applied to 3-D animation.

MOUSE

A common *input* device used to move a *cursor* around on the computer screen. Usually a small, hand-sized, plastic device with one or more buttons on the top and a roller ball underneath that detects movement as you push it across a desktop.

MULTISESSION CD-ROM

A new type of CD-ROM and CD-ROM drive technology that allows CD-ROMs to be recorded on during multiple sessions or at different times. A standard record could be considered single session, since it is created in one pass. If a record were multisession, you could take it back to the record store and have them add more songs to it until it was full. Photo CDs are multisession since you can continue to add images to them until they are full. (See also **CD-ROM** and **Photo CD**.)

NOISE FILTER

An image *filter* that adds random noise (pixels) to an image to simulate a grainy look.

NURBS

Non-**U**niform **R**ational **B**-**S**pline.

OUTPUT

The process of getting data out of a computer. Printing is one form of output; sending images or pictures to a computer screen is another. The opposite of *input*.

PAINTBRUSH

A *painting tool* that simulates painting with a paint brush. (See also **Painting Tool**.)

PAINTING TOOL

A command or function of an image-editing program that simulates traditional art or photographic tools. The *paintbrush tool* is an example of a painting tool that simulates paintbrush strokes.

PAINT PALETTE

An electronic version of an artist's palette. It allows the user to select from a wide variety of colors or even mix new ones.

PASTE

The final step of a cut-and-paste operation, where the data is applied to the document.

PC PAINTBRUSH FORMAT (PCX)

A graphics file format that stores *raster graphics*. Made popular by ZSoft's PC PaintBrush program. (See also **File Format**.)

PCD

The Photo CD format. This is the graphics file format that Kodak uses to store images on Photo CDs. (See also **File Format**, **Raster Graphics**, and **Photo CD**.)

PCX

The graphics file format created by ZSoft's PC PaintBrush program. This graphics file format stores *raster graphics* images. (See also **File Format** and **Raster Graphics**.)

PENCIL TOOL

A *painting tool* that simulates drawing with a sharp pencil. (See also **Painting Tool**.)

PHONG SHADING

A 3-D surface shading method developed by Phong Bui-Toung in 1974. His shading method accurately interpolates the colors over a polygonal surface, giving accurate reflective highlights and shading. The drawback to this is that Phong shading can be up to 100 times slower than Gouraud shading. Because of this, even today, when animators are creating small, flat, 3-D objects that are not central to the animation, they will use Gouraud shading on them instead of Phong. As with Gouraud shading, Phong shading cannot smooth over the outer edges of 3-D objects. (See also **Flat Shading** and **Gouraud Shading**.)

PHOTO CD

A new technology developed by Eastman Kodak to scan high-resolution 35mm or professional-quality images and write them to a *CD-ROM*. The resulting PCD (Photo CD) can be viewed with consumer players that attach to televisions. They can also be viewed on personal computers that have *multisession*-compatible *CD-ROM* drives. (See also **CD-ROM** and **Multisession CD-ROM**.)

PHOTOMULTIPLIER

A very sensitive vacuum tube that detects light and converts it to electrical signals. Commonly used in high-end *drum scanners*. (See also **Drum Scanners**.)

PHOTOSHOP

A Mac-based image-editing program. Available from Adobe Systems. (See Appendix A, "Resources.")

PHOTOSTYLER

An image-editing program for the IBM PC and compatibles, from Aldus Corporation. (See Appendix A.)

PINCH FILTER

A special-effects filter that squeezes the center of an image to make it appear pinched. The opposite of the *Punch Filter*. (See also **Punch Filter**.)

PIXEL

A picture element. The smallest element of an image that has been *digitized* into a computer. The more pixels per square inch, the higher the resolution of the image will be.

PIXELLIZATION

The effect when the *pixels* making up an image are so large that they are visible. (See also **Mosaic Filter**.)

PROCEDURAL TEXTURES

The use of shaders, or small pieces of programming code, for describing 3-D surfaces, lighting effects, and atmospheric effects. (See also **Shaders**.)

PROCESS COLOR

The four color pigments used in color printing. (See also **CMYK**.)

PUNCH FILTER

A special-effects filter that causes the image to appear as if the center has been expanded. The opposite of the *pinch filter*. (See also **Pinch Filter**.)

RADIOSITY

A rendering method developed by Cindy Goral, Don Greenberg, and others at Cornell University in 1984. It uses the same formulas that simulate the way heat is dispersed throughout a room to determine how light reflects between surfaces. By determining the exchange of radiant energy between 3-D surfaces, very realistic results are possible.

RAM (RANDOM-ACCESS MEMORY)

The working memory of a computer, into which the computer stores programs and data so that the *CPU* can access them directly. *RAM* can be written to and erased over and over again. (See also **CPU** and **Memory**.)

RASTER GRAPHICS

Computer graphics where the images are stored as groups of *pixels*, as opposed to *vector graphics*, which are stored as groups of lines. (See also **File Format** and **Vector Graphics**.)

RAY TRACING

A shading method for 3-D objects developed by Turner Whitted in 1980. It simulates highly reflective surfaces by tracing every ray of light, starting from the viewer's perspective back into the 3-D scene to the objects. If an object happens to be reflective, the computer follows that ray of light, as it bounces off the object, until it hits something else. This process continues until the ray of light hits an opaque non-reflective surface, or it goes shooting off away from the scene. As you can imagine, ray tracing is extremely computationaly intensive. So much so that some 3-D animation programmers refuse to put ray tracing into their 3-D software. On the other hand, the realism that can be achieved with ray tracing is spectacular. (See also **3-D Graphics**.)

ROM (READ-ONLY MEMORY)

Identical to *Random-Access Memory* except that *Read-Only Memory* can only be written to once. They usually store programs vital to the operation of a personal computer. (See also **Memory** and **RAM**.)

RENDER

To create a new image based on a transformation of an existing image or a three-dimensional scene. (See also **Morphing**.)

RENDERMAN

The Renderman standard describes everything the computer needs to know before rendering your 3-D scene, such as the objects, light sources, cameras, and atmospheric effects. Once a scene is converted to a Renderman file, it can be rendered on a variety of systems, from Macs to PCs to Silicon Graphics workstations.

RESIZE

To alter the resolution or the horizontal or vertical size of an image.

RESOLUTION

1. For computer displays, their height and width in pixels.

2. For images, the height and width in pixels.

3. For output devices, the dots-per-inch they can produce.

RETRACE

The return of the electron beam (inside a computer display) back to the upper-left corner, after making one pass. It can also refer to the return to the left side of the screen from the right. (See also **Vertical Retrace**.)

REVERSE CROPPING

The process of artificially extending the boundaries of an image to obtain more space. Performed by duplicating existing elements in the image.

RGB (RED, GREEN, AND BLUE)

A color model that describes color based on percentages of red, green, and blue. Commonly used by computers and television to produce or simulate color. (See also **Color Model**, **HLS**, and **HSB**.)

RIPPLE FILTER

A filter that creates fluid ripples in an image, simulating waves in water.

ROTOSCOPING

1. The frame-by-frame projection of a live action scene in order to trace the movements of objects.

2. A method of capturing live action one frame at a time.

RUN-LENGTH ENCODING (RLL)

A method of compressing data by replacing long, consecutive runs of numbers with the number and a count of how many times it repeats. (See also **File Format** and **Compression**.)

SATURATION

The degree to which color is undiluted by white light. If a color is 100-percent saturated, it contains no white light. If a color has no saturation, it will be a shade of gray.

SCANNER

A hardware device for converting light from a source picture or transparency into a digital representation.

SCANLINE

A single line of pixels displayed on a computer monitor to be scanned in by a *scanner*. (See also **Scanner**.)

SCAN RATE

1. A measurement of how many times per second a scanner samples an image.

2. A measurement for the speed that a monitor's electron beam scans from left to right and top to bottom.

SCREENING

The process of converting a grayscale image to patterns of black-and-white dots that can be printed commercially. In the case of color images, the color is split into primaries, and they in turn are individually screened. Those screens are then printed in their respective primary colors, and the original color image reappears.

SELECTION

An area of computer data that is currently chosen to perform some type of operation.

SELECTION BORDER

An option used to select only the border of the current selection. (See also **Selection**.)

SHADOW

The darkest areas of an image.

SHADERS

Small programs that algorithmically generate textures based on mathematical formulas. These algorithmic textures are sometimes called *procedural* textures or *spatial* textures. Not only is the texture generated by the computer, but it is also generated in 3-D space. Whereas most texture-mapping techniques map the texture to the outside "skin" of the object, procedural textures run completely through the object in 3-D. So if you were using a fractal-based procedural texture of wood grain on a cube and you cut out a section of the cube, you would see the wood grain running through the cube. Shaders are an integral part of Renderman.

SHAREWARE

Computer software that is copyrighted but still made available for anyone on a trial basis. If you decide to keep and use the software, you are expected to pay a registration fee to the author.

SHARPENING

A filter that increases contrast between pixels, with the end result of a sharper-looking image. (See also **Smoothing**.)

SIGGRAPH

Special **I**nterest **G**roup, **Graph**ics. A group of the ACM that puts on conferences and exhibits dealing with computer graphics. (See also **ACM**.)

SLIDER

A method of entering numeric values used in *graphical user interfaces*. By moving the slider back and forth, numeric values can be adjusted.

SMOOTHING

A filter that averages pixels with their neighbors, thus reducing contrast and simulating an out-of-focus image. (See also **Sharpening**.)

SPECULAR

The bright highlight or reflection on a 3-D surface. The color of a highlight is often called the *Specular Color*.

SPEECH RECOGNITION

The use of a computer to input and analyze the sound from a human voice. The words spoken are then detected and stored or acted upon.

SPHERE FILTER

A special-effects filter that simulates wrapping the current image around a 3-D sphere.

SPLINE

A mathematically defined curve that smoothly links a series of dots.

SOLORIZATION

The photographic effect of reducing the number of colors in an image. This effect is also simulated by many image-editing programs.

STATUS BAR

An information bar common in *graphical user interfaces*. Status bars display important information about the current status of the document, or file, you are working on. (See also **GUI**.)

STEREOSCOPIC

An image or viewing system that appears to produce a three-dimensional scene which gives the illusion of depth.

Anaglyphs are stereoscopic. (See also **Anaglyph**.)

SUBTRACTIVE COLOR MIXING

A color model that mixes colors in a way that simulates how pigments (paint) work when you mix different colored pigments together. The more pigments you mix together, the more colors of the spectrum they absorb, resulting in a darker color. This is the opposite of *additive color mixing*, as in mixing different colored lights together where the result is always lighter. (See also **Color Model** and **Additive Color Mixing**.)

SUPERCOMPUTERS

Very high-speed, high-capacity computers. The fastest in the world.

TAGGED IMAGE FILE FORMAT (TIFF)

A common file format that can store both *raster* and *vector* graphics information. (See also **File Format**, **Raster Graphics**, and **Vector Graphics**.)

TARGA FORMAT (TGA)

A file format originally designed for storing video images. Since then it has been enhanced to include *high-resolution* images in *raster* format. (See also **File Format**.)

TEXTURE MAPPING

The process of applying a 2-D image to a 3-D object defined within the computer. Similar to wrapping wallpaper around the object. This allows computer artists to simulate items like wood by scanning in an image of wood grain and having the computer texture-map the wood to a 3-D model of a board. Developed by Ed Catmull in 1974 (See also **3-D Graphics**.)

THERMAL PRINTERS

A type of printer that uses heat to transfer images onto heat-sensitive paper.

THERMAL WAX PRINTERS

Printers that use heat to transfer colored wax films onto paper.

TIME CODES

Codes written on video tapes that allow their precise editing down to the second and even to the frame level. Time codes are only found on professional-quality video recorders. (See also **VTR**.)

TITLE BAR

The top bar across any window in a *graphical user interface*. The title bar usually includes the name of the program or data file that you are currently working with. By clicking and dragging a title bar, you can move the active window. (See also **GUI**.)

TRACE CONTOUR

A filter that looks for edges, then traces them while making all the different solid colors in the image the same color. This has the effect of simulating a drawing.

TRANSITION MORPHING

Cross-fading from one image or sequence to another while warping the two images to appear as if they are transforming into one another. (See also **Distortion Morphing** and **Morphing**.)

TRUE COLOR

Color that has a color depth of 24 bits (16.7 million colors). (See also **Color Depth** and **24-Bit**.)

UNDO OPTION

A command that undoes the last operation you performed.

USER-DEFINED

See **Custom Filter**.

Vector Graphics

Graphics that are based on individual lines from point A to point B. Vector graphics represent line drawings well, but cannot represent a photograph. For photographs, you need to use *raster graphics*. Early computer graphics displays used vector graphics. (See also **File Format** and **Raster Graphics**.)

Vertical Retrace

The returning of a display screen or TV's electron gun to the upper-left corner. This step takes about a 60th of a second. (See also **Retrace**.)

VTR

Video Tape Recorder. Usually referring to professional-quality video systems.

Windows

The *graphical user interface* standard for IBM PCs and compatibles.

Wipes

A transition from one scene to another. Wipes come in many different forms; the new scene can appear top to bottom, left to right, from the center out (in the case of a circular wipe), and many other ways.

X

The common reference for the width of an image.

Y

The common reference for the height of an image.

Z

The common reference for the depth of a three-dimensional scene.

Z-buffer

An algorithm that aids the process of hidden surface removal by using *zels*, which are similar to pixels but instead of recording the luminance of a specific point in an image, they record the depth of that point. The letter Z reflects the depth (as does Y for vertical position and X for horizontal position). The z-buffer is then an area of memory devoted to holding the depth data for every pixel in an image. Today high-performance graphics workstations have a z-buffer built in.

Zels

See **Z-Buffer**.

Zoom Tool

A tool for magnifying the current image you are working on.

Index

What's On

CD-ROM

the
computer
animator
CD-ROM

CD-ROM

This CD-ROM contains a wealth of PC and Macintosh animation-related software. Whether you have a Mac or a PC, your computer will only "see" the portion of the CD-ROM that is meant for it. Here's what you'll find on the *Computer Animator* disc:

- Special working versions of professional animation, rendering, and modeling software

- Samples of commercial 3-D models

- Samples of commercial textures and graphics

- Award-winning animations

- Shareware and freeware programs

The demo versions and sample clips on the disc are intended to give you hands-on experience with the capabilities and features of the full software product. The working demos usually work the same as the complete product, with the limitations of not being able to save or print your work. You'll be able to give these products a good "test-drive."

Obviously, the companies who created these demo versions hope you'll be impressed enough with what you experience to purchase the actual products. If you want more information on any of these products, contact the manufacturer or distributor; you'll find their addresses and phone numbers in Appendix A, "Resources."

The first two sections in this appendix cover the Windows and DOS software demos, followed by a section on the Macintosh demos. After that, you'll find information on the sample 3-D models, textures, animations, and shareware tools.

PC WINDOWS SOFTWARE DEMOS

Most of the software demos that work within Windows must be installed to your hard drive before you can put them through their paces. Follow these steps to set up the Windows software on the CD-ROM:

1. Start Windows if you haven't already done so, and insert the *Computer Animator* CD-ROM in your drive.

2. Switch to Program Manager or File Manager.

3. Select **File** + **R**un from the menu bar.

4. Type **D:\SETUP** and select OK. This assumes that your CD-ROM drive is D. If it is another letter, substitute that letter for **D:**. For example, if your CD-ROM drive is F, type **F:\SETUP**.

5. Select OK to continue, and follow the instructions in the setup program.

The setup program creates icons in a new Program Manager named *Computer Animator Software*, which contains icons for installing or running the software demos,

and for reading information about the sample 3-D models and textures. A second Program Manager group named *Computer Animator Flics* contains icons for viewing the animations on the disc. The setup program also installs the Windows drivers for viewing FLI and FLC animations.

After you've installed a product demo, be sure to read the "Readme" file or the documentation before running it. These files usually contain important information, such as system requirements.

All Windows demos have at least these minimum requirements:

- 386 or better processor

- 4 MB of RAM

- Windows 3.1 or higher

- VGA graphics

Any special requirements will be noted in the listing for a product. Double-click on a product's icon in the *Computer Animator Software* group to install or run the demo.

TRUESPACE

Caligari Corporation

Location on CD-ROM:
\WINDEMOS\TRUESPAC

Caligari trueSpace for Windows is an advanced 3-D package that offers integrated organic modeling, fast rendering, and broadcast-quality animation. This demo version was created specially for this book and is used in several of the chapters to illustrate animation, modeling, and rendering techniques.

MACROMODEL

Macromedia Corporation

Location on CD-ROM:
\WINDEMOS\MACMODEL

System Requirements: 8 MB RAM

MacroModel is a three-dimensional modeling program that combines the CAD accuracy of spline-based modeling with 2-D drawing tools. It provides real-time visualization from any angle for feedback. You can import and export polygon-based objects for compatibility with other modelers like Swivel 3D.

VISUAL REALITY

Visual Software, Inc.

Location on CD-ROM:
\WINDEMOS\VREALITY

This interactive presentation shows you detailed information about the suite of programs within Visual Reality, including Visual Model, Visual Font, Renderize Live, and Visual Image. You can also view a gallery of professionally rendered images.

3D WORKSHOP

Pacific Motion

Location on CD-ROM:
\WINDEMOS\3DWKSHOP

3D Workshop is an easy-to-use 3-D modeling program that works with DXF, 3DS, Cadkey, and many other types of data files. Animated sequences can be created using unlimited lighting sources and cameras. Multi-Path technology allows for easy 3-D spline path motion control.

PC ANIMATE

Pacific Motion

Location on CD-ROM:
\WINDEMOS\PCANIMAT

PC Animate is a 2-D and 3-D animation program that is easy to use but powerful. You can transform 2-D graphics into animations by moving images on defined paths, add special effects, edit the color palette, use the built-in drawing tools, and more.

GRYPHON MORPH

Gryphon Software Corporation

Location on CD-ROM:
\WINDEMOS\GMORPH

You can use Gryphon Morph to create animations and videos that feature morphing

and warping effects. It also allows you to morph moving images and create caricature effects.

PHOTOMORPH

North Coast Software

Location on CD-ROM:
\WINDEMOS\PMORPH

PhotoMorph is a morphing special effects program. You can import photos or images and sequence them together to produce an animated "morph" movie, where one image transforms into another. It supports storyboarding and chaining of events.

WINIMAGES:MORPH

Black Belt Systems

Location on CD-ROM:
\WINDEMOS\WMORPH

You can create morphing or warping animations with WinImages:Morph software, one of the first morphing programs available for Microsoft Windows.

VISUAL IMAGE LT (LITE VERSION)

Visual Software

Location on CD-ROM:
\WINDEMOS\VISIMAGE

Visual Image LT is a subset of Visual Image, an object-independent image manipulation and paint program. The software can be used to combine and collage images of any resolution and color depth, and each element is stored in separate layers on top of the background.

World Render 3D

MAZAR Software Corporation
1801 N.E. 197 Terrace
N. Miami Beach, FL 33179
(305) 936-9290

Location on CD-ROM:
\WINDEMOS\WRENDER

This software is a rendering tool that works with 3-D models created by many popular 3-D programs, including some unusual formats.

PC DOS Software Demos

To install the DOS demo programs on the CD-ROM, insert the *Computer Animator* CD-ROM in your drive and follow these steps at the DOS prompt:

1. Switch to the drive that hold the CD-ROM. For example, if the disc is in drive D, type **D:** and press the Enter key.

2. Type **\MENU** and press Enter. This will start the DOS menu program that allows you to choose which program to install or run.

3. When you choose a program, the install routine for that software will run. You'll see how many megabytes the program will take up on your hard drive before the installation proceeds.

When one of the DOS installation programs finishes, you'll be informed where the software was installed on your hard drive and what command starts the software.

All DOS demos have at least these minimum requirements:

- 386 or better processor
- 4 MB of RAM
- VGA or SVGA graphics

The DOS menu program also allows you to read information about the sample 3-D models, sample textures, and other files. You'll also be able to select and play animations from this menu.

3D Studio (presentation)

Autodesk

Location on CD-ROM:
\DOSDEMOS\3DSTUDIO

3D Studio is a modeling, materials editing, rendering, animation, and special effects package. It models in 3-D with floating-point accuracy using techniques including spline, surface, and mesh. This presentation shows you how 3D Studio works and some of the work that can be created with it.

Envisage

Byte-by-Byte

Location on CD-ROM:
\DOSDEMOS\ENVISAGE

System Requirements: 486 or better processor

RenderStar 2

Modern Medium, Inc.

Location on CD-ROM:
\DOSDEMOS\RENDSTAR

RenderStar 2 eXtension-24 creates photorealistic images and animations from 3-D models in DXF format. Rendering features include texturing, unlimited light sources, shadows, reflection mapping, and more. Only the 8-bit features of RenderStar are available in this demo.

Vistapro 3.0

Virtual Reality Laboratories, Inc.
2341 Ganador Court
San Luis Obispo, CA 93401

Location on CD-ROM:
\DOSDEMOS\VISTAPRO

Documentation: VPDEMO.TXT

This is both an interactive tutorial and a working demo for Version 3 of Vistapro, the three-dimensional landscape simulation program. Vistapro can accurately recreate high-resolution real world landscapes in vivid detail. The complete retail version can also generate and read 3-D DXF files.

MACINTOSH SOFTWARE DEMOS

The folders on the Mac portion of the *Computer Animator* CD-ROM are color-coded according to the type of software. For instance, folders for the working demos are a different color from the folders for the sample 3-D clip models.

Be sure to read the "Readme" file for a particular demo, and the information about the demo in this section. It may contain important information about system requirements or things you need to do before running the demo.

Most of the software demos can be run directly from the CD-ROM—double-click the folder to open it, then double-click the demo program. Some of the software must be installed to your hard drive before you use it, though. If a demo must be installed to your hard drive, that product's listing in this appendix will mention it. Of course, any of these demos will run faster if you drag the product's folder to your hard drive and run it from there.

FORM•Z

Autodessys

System Requirements: 6 MB of RAM

This award-winning modeler and 3-D CAD system has an extensive set of 2-D and 3-D form manipulating and sculpting capabilities. You'll find special versions of this working demo for both Macintosh and PowerPCs.

THE ANIMATION STAND

Linker Systems

System Requirements: 68000 or better processor, Floating-Point Unit (FPU) or FPU emulator, QuickTime

The Animation Stand is a professional level program for creating cel animations and special effects for broadcast and film. It can output to nearly any film or video format in the world with full frame accuracy and high resolution. 3-D animations can be imported and manipulated in the program. QuickTime 1.6.1 is included in this folder.

TYPESTRY

Pixar

System Requirements: Macintosh II series computer with coprocessor, 8 MB of RAM, System 7 or higher, 32-bit QuickDraw

Typestry turns TrueType and Type 1 fonts into three-dimensional images and animations. The software uses RenderMan® technology to apply textures and 3-D lighting effects.

MACROMODEL

Macromedia

MacroModel is a three-dimensional modeling program that combines the CAD accuracy of spline-based modeling with 2-D drawing tools. It provides real-time visualization from any angle for feedback. You can import and export polygon-based objects for compatibility with other modelers like Swivel 3D.

LIFE FORMS

Macromedia

Life Forms is a 3-D human figure animation program. It includes tools needed for creating and designing realistic human figure movement. The software comes with animation and shape libraries containing samplings of pedestrian, dance, gymnastics, and sports movements.

MODELSHOP II

Macromedia

ModelShop II is an architectural modeling package that includes support for Bézier walls, text, unlimited layers, measurements, rendering, animation, and multiple light sources. The software allows users to draw in 3-D perspective, then move around the model or create a high-quality animation.

SWIVEL 3D PROFESSIONAL

Macromedia

Swivel 3D Professional is a 3-D graphics program for technical illustration, product design, scientific visualization, and animation. Features include 24-bit image mapping, eight independent light sources, environment mapping, and linked models with constrained motion between parts.

ZOOM

Asym Technology

Zoom is a three-dimensional CAD modeling and rendering package. It provides snap controls for creation of 3-D objects, and it automatically aligns points. Modeling features include Boolean operations, mesh surfaces, splines and 3-D tools.

INFINI-D

Specular International

Infini-D is a 3-D tool that models, renders, and animates in 32-bit color. Objects can be created using primitives or through the program's orthogonal editor. It supports flat, Gouraud, and Phong shading; reflections; refractions; and 3-D TrueType fonts. The software allows animated objects to be moved in a linear path or over spline-based motion paths.

GRYPHON MORPH

Gryphon Software Corporation

System Requirements: 68030 or higher processor with 32-bit QuickDraw, System 6.0.7 or later and QuickTime

Gryphon Morph allows you to create animations and videos that feature morphing and warping effects. It also allows you to morph moving images and create caricature effects.

WORKING MODEL

Knowledge Revolution

System Requirements: 68000 processor, 4 MB of RAM, System 7 or later

Working Model is a professional motion simulation program for animators, engineers, architects, or educators. Features include Smart Editor, which maintains associations of linked objects; 20-digit numerical accuracy; CAD file import and export; and export to MacroMind Three-D, Wavefront, and QuickTime.

3-D MODELS

A number of companies have provided sample 3-D clip models to expose you to their products. These models are just a taste of the complete collections offered by these companies. If you want more information on a company's collections, see Appendix A, "Resources," for addresses and phone numbers.

> *Windows Users:* Double-click on any product's icon to read more information about the files.
>
> *DOS Users:* You can read information about these files from the DOS menu program.
>
> *Mac Users:* You'll find a *Read Me First* TeachText documents in each product's folder.

VIEWPOINT DATASETS

ViewPoint Data Labs

Location on CD-ROM:
\MODELS\VIEWPOINT (PC)
ViewPoint (Mac)

Viewpoint Datasets come pre-grouped so that you can apply your specific materials or textures in minutes. For example, vehicles come with glass, trim, tires, and body groups. Humans come with groups such as hand, lower arm, upper arm, and so on. The datasets in 3DS format will read directly into 3D Studio as if you created the model yourself. They are fully modifiable, allowing you to customize any part of the model. You'll find some rendered images in the Renderings folder (Mac) and the RENDERED subdirectory (PC).

3D Models

Shapiro 3D Models

Location on CD-ROM:
\MODELS\SHAPIRO (PC)
Shapiro (Mac)

Shapiro 3D Models offers a number of customized models. You'll find two samples on the disc, in several data formats.

Acuris Clipmodels

Acuris

Location on CD-ROM:
\MODELS\ACURIS (PC)
Acuris (Mac)

In the subdirectories named 3DS and DXF, you'll find examples of Acuris ClipModels in 3DS and DXF formats. Read the README.TXT files in each directory for more information on the files and Acuris ClipModels. ACURISPR.TGA is a rendered collage, created using Acuris ClipModels.

Blocks and Materials

Modern Medium

Location on CD-ROM:
\MODELS\BLOCKMAT (PC)
Blocks and Materials (Mac)

The full Blocks and Materials collection contains 600 3-D Blocks—meshes in DXF, DWG, and 3DS formats, which are linked to 400 bitmap textures. All materials textures and mapping coordinates have been pre-assigned to the meshes for 3D Studio, AutoVision and ARE-24. Blocks include aircraft, automobiles, people, computers, office equipment, and furniture.

I-Works Models

Imagination Works

Location on CD-ROM:
\MODELS\IWORKS (PC)
Imagination Works (Mac)

Imagination Works offers a large selection of stock human models, as well as fantasy models, futuristic "beasts," vehicles, and landscapes. The human models in the complete version come with at least 100 keyframes of an animated walking sequence to help you get started.

Fractal Graphics models

Dick Oliver

Location on CD-ROM:
\MODELS\FRACTALS

These 3DS files are provided courtesy of Dick Oliver, author of *FractalVision* (Sams Publishing, 1993) and co-author of *Fractal Graphics for Windows* (Sams Publishing, 1993).

Author's Models

Location on CD-ROM:
\MODELS\AUTHOR (PC)
Author's Forensic Models (Mac)

The two 3-D models that are used in the forensic animation section of the book are included here.

Textures and Graphics

Several companies provided sample textures from their complete collections. If you want more information on a company's collections, see Appendix A, "Resources," for addresses and phone numbers.

Windows Users: Double-click on a product's icon to read more information about these files.

DOS Users: You can read information about these files from the DOS menu program.

Mac Users: You'll find a *Read Me First* TeachText document in each products folder.

PIXAR ONE TWENTY EIGHT

Pixar

Location on CD-ROM:
\TEXTURES\PIXAR (PC)
Pixar One Twenty Eight (Mac)

One Twenty Eight is Pixar's private collection of high-quality photographic textures. These images were created specifically for use with digital imaging, and they incorporate a patented technology that allows the textures to be tiled seamlessly. The complete collection includes plug-in applications for PhotoShop and PhotoStyler.

These images are seamlessly tiling digital textures from the product, Pixar One Twenty Eight. For additional information about the complete, high quality collection, please call Pixar at (510) 236-4000. Tiling algorithm Patent Number 5,194,969.

ART BEATS BACKGROUND SAMPLER

Artbeats

Location on CD-ROM:
\TEXTURES\ARTBEATS (PC)
Artbeats (Mac)

Artbeats offers a number of unusual graphics collections, including:

Marble & Granite—An extensive and varied library of high-resolution digitized marble and granite textures.

Marbled Paper Textures—Dramatic and unusual digitized images of marbled paper, such as that found inside antique book covers.

Full Page Images Library—EPS background images of marble and wood textures, landscapes, paint splatters, 3-D textures, and more.

Backgrounds for Multimedia, Volumes I and II—8-bit and 24-bit high quality images designed with video, animation, and texture mapping applications in mind.

You'll find sample images from each of these collections on this disc.

BLOCKS AND MATERIALS

Modern Medium

See the listing in the 3-D Models section for more information on this product.

ANIMATIONS

You'll find animations from the author, some amazing work from Cyrus Lum, animations from Autodesk, and some unusual 3-D fractals on the CD-ROM.

Windows Users: You can play back these animations from inside Windows by double-clicking on the icons in the Computer Animator Flics group.

DOS Users: You can play back these animations from within the DOS menu program.

ANIMATIONS BY CYRUS LUM

Location on CD-ROM:
\ANIMS\LUM (PC only)

Cyrus Lum is interviewed in Chapter 5, "Interactive Entertainment."

ANIMATIONS BY DICK OLIVER

Dick Oliver

Location on CD-ROM:
\ANIMS\FRACTALS (PC only)

These animations were created from the 3D Studio fractal files that are also included on this disc. They are provided courtesy of Dick Oliver, author of *FractalVision* and co-author of *Fractal Graphics for Windows*.

VIEWPOINT DATA LABS

Location on CD-ROM:
\ANIMS\VPOINT

These animations were created to show the high quality of ViewPoint Data Sets.

AUTHOR'S ANIMATIONS

Location on CD-ROM:
\ANIMS\AUTHOR (DOS only)

Several animations by the author are included here. Some were featured on the Autodesk 3D Studio R2 CD-ROM.

3D Studio Animations

Autodesk Inc.

Location on CD-ROM:
\ANIMS\AUTODESK (PC only)

These serve as examples of the power of 3D Studio™ and Animator Pro™ from Autodesk. They were created by professional animators who use these products. You'll find a presentation demo of 3D Studio on this disc—see the DOS Demos section.
Animations courtesy of Autodesk, Inc.

PC Shareware

Shareware is a software distribution method that provides users with a chance to try software before buying it. If you try a shareware program and continue to use it, you should register the program with the author.

When registering a program, you get many benefits, including updated versions, extra features available only in registered versions, a printed manual, and more. These benefits will vary, depending on the author of the software.

You should always remember that copyright laws apply to both shareware and freeware software, and the copyright holder retains all rights, except as already noted.

PoV Commander

Matthew O. Alvey
3436 Kendale Drive
Ft. Wayne, IN 46835
America On-Line: NIHIL777

Location on CD-ROM:
\UTILS\POVCOMM

Documentation: POVCOMM.DOC

PoV Commander is a DOS shell for the freeware Persistence of Vision (PoV) ray-tracing program. You can find the PoV program on CompuServe, America Online, the Internet, and other on-line services. See Appendix A for more information on graphics areas within these services. This program is shareware.

PoV Scene Builder

JFFG
418 NE 7
Ankeny, IA 50021
(303) 429-8199
(515) 964-2308

Location on CD-ROM:
\UTILS\POVSB

Documentation: POVSB.WRI

PoV Scene Builder is a Windows-based modeler for the freeware Persistence of Vision raytracer. This program is shareware.

PoV Shell

Andreas Peetz
Kuehneweg 51
23795 Bad Segeberg
Germany

Location on CD-ROM:
\UTILS\POVSHELL

Documentation: POVSHELL.DOC

PoVShell is a DOS-level Integrated Development Environment (IDE) for the PoV raytracer program. This program is freeware.

PaintShop Pro

JASC, Inc.
10901 Red Circle Drive
Suite 340
Minnetonka, MN 55343
(612) 930-9171

Location on CD-ROM:
\UTILS\PSPRO

Documentation: PSP.HLP

Paint Shop Pro is a Windows program that will display, convert, alter, and print graphics images. Altering includes resizing, trimming, applying filters, dithering, palette manipulation, and much more. This program is shareware.

AniMagician

KAVIK Software
P.O. Box 261
Huntsville, AL 35804

Location on CD-ROM:
\UTILS\ANIMAG

AniMagician is a DOS-based FLI animation development program. It contains drawing tools and special effects that can be used to create or edit FLI files. This program is shareware. Upon registration, you will receive a printed manual, a sound conversion utility, and the Sound Frame option, which allows you to add a soundtrack to animations.

ProtoCAD

Trius, Inc.
P.O. Box 249
N. Andover, MA 01845-0249
1-800-GO-TRIUS (Orders only!)
(508) 794-9377

Location on CD-ROM:
\UTILS\PROTOCAD
Documentation: PC3D.MAN

ProtoCAD is a DOS-based 3-D CAD and rendering program. Ultrafast Z-buffer technology combined with camera positioning produces amazing renderings. In combination with StarFlic, it can produce FLI animations. ProtoCAD offers DXF file import and export. This program is shareware.

StarFLIC

Trius Software
P.O. Box 249
N. Andover, MA 01845-0249
1-800-GO-TRIUS (Orders only!)
(508) 794-9377

Location on CD-ROM:
\UTILS\STARFLIC
Documentation: STFL.DOC

StarFLIC is a DOS program designed to view individual TGA files and compile sets of TGA files into an FLI animation file. This program is shareware.

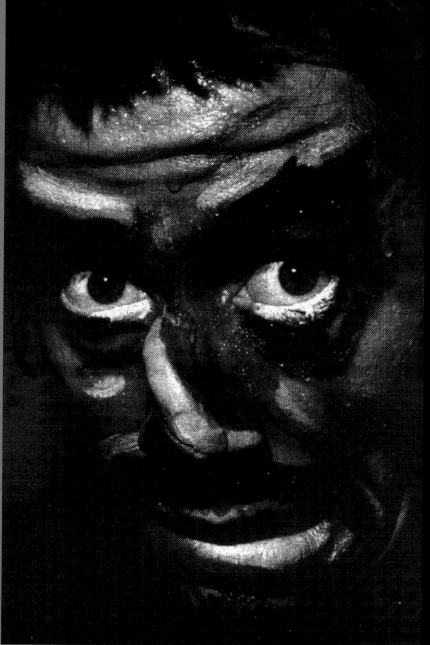

Haven't you heard?

There's a special upgrade offer to Visual Image Release 2

Included on your free CD, is Visual Image LT, the personal version of the remarkable new Image Editing Tool for Windows.

For only $49 you can upgrade to the professional version Visual Image 2.0 that includes such high end capabilities as:

- Full Alpha Channel support, letting you blend and weave photographic imagery.
- Anti-aliased Text, letting you incorporate the highest quality text for titling and advertising in the market.

Just call 1-800-669-7318 and mention promotion code SP101 to take advantage of this offer!

VISUAL
SOFTWARE INC.

Visual Software Inc.
21731 Ventura Blvd., Suite 310
Woodland Hills, CA 91364

The Computer Animator
CD-ROM
PC and Mac compatible!

This CD-ROM contains a wealth of PC and Macintosh animation-related software. Here's a sample of what you'll find:

More than 20 special working demo versions of professional animation, rendering, and modeling software

trueSpace	MacroModel	Life Forms	Envisage
3D Workshop	form*Z	Animation Stand	ModelShop II
Swivel 3D	Gryphon Morph	PhotoMorph	Typestry
...and more!			

Samples of commercial 3-D models and textures

Acuris	ViewPoint	Modern Medium	Shapiro
Artbeats	Pixar One Twenty Eight	Imagination Works	...and more!

Software, 3-D models, and textures that let you follow along with many of the book's examples.

Award-winning animations

Shareware and freeware animation tools

Getting Started

If you're itching to start exploring the CD-ROM, here's the very *least* you need to know:

Windows Users: Run the \SETUP.EXE program on the CD-ROM from within Windows. This will create Program Manager groups and install Windows animation drivers on your system.

DOS Users: From a DOS prompt, change to the drive holding the disc, type MENU and press Enter. This will start a menu program that allows you to install software and explore the disc.

Mac Users: Run the *Read Me First* file on the CD-ROM. The different types of software are organized into folders. Some of the software demos need to be installed to your hard drive.

These are bare-bones instructions, of course. The "What's on the Computer Animator CD-ROM" pages contain detailed information on the software, including descriptions, system requirements, and setup instructions.